MEMOIRS

for Jan
with love,
from Addison

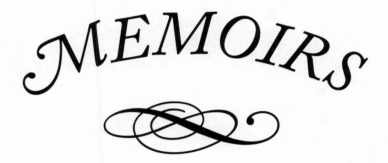

MEMOIRS

SIR GEORG SOLTI

with assistance from Harvey Sachs

a cappella

Library of Congress Cataloging-in-Publication Data

Solti, Georg, Sir, 1912-
    Memoirs / Sir Georg Solti.
        p.   cm.
    Originally published: New York : Alfred A. Knopf, 1997.
    Includes index.
    ISBN 1-55652-337-8 (alk. paper)
        1. Solti, Georg, Sir, 1912- .   2. Conductors (Music)—Biography.
I. Title.
ML422.S56A3   1998
784.2'092—dc21
[B]
                                                        98-30685
                                                          CIP
                                                          MN

This A Cappella paperback edition of Sir Georg Solti's
Memoirs is an unabridged reproduction of the edition
published in New York in 1997. It is reprinted by
arrangement with Alfred A. Knopf, Inc.

Published in 1998 by A Cappella Books, an imprint of
Chicago Review Press, Incorporated
814 N. Franklin Street
Chicago, Illinois 60610
ISBN 1-55652-337-8
Printed in the United States of America

5 4 3 2 1

For Valerie, Gabrielle, and Claudia

Contents

MEMOIRS

BUDAPEST

IN FEBRUARY 1997, when these memoirs were nearing completion, I conducted Béla Bartók's *Cantata profana* with the Berlin
Philharmonic and the Hungarian Radio Chorus. While the
performance was in progress a great realization came over me. I
understood that my whole life, the whole journey I have made, is
contained within the story of the *Cantata*.

Bartók, one of my teachers at the Liszt Academy in Budapest,
had translated the *Cantata*'s text from Rumanian into Hungarian.
It tells the story of a father who brings up his nine sons to be stag
hunters, instead of farmers or merchants—"average" men. As the
sons grow, they press their hunt into ever more remote areas of the
forest, until one day they cross a haunted bridge and are themselves
transformed into beautiful, enchanted stags. The father, worried by
his sons' prolonged absence, sets out to look for them; eventually,
he crosses the bridge, reaches a wellspring, and sees the nine stags.
He aims his rifle at the largest of them, but just as he is about to
shoot, he hears the stag speak. The stag tells him that he is the
eldest of the sons—the father's favorite—and he warns the father
that if he tries to shoot any of the stags, their antlers will tear him
to pieces.

"Come with me," the father begs his sons. "Your mother stands
waiting, lonely, loving, grieving. . . . The lanterns are lit, the table is
set, the glasses are filled. . . ."

"We shall never return," says the son, "because our antlers cannot
pass through thy doorway."

The work ends with the man's heartbreaking realization that his
sons have become alien to him and will never again be what they
were before.

I had always interpreted this story as an allegory of Bartók's life, but as I conducted the *Cantata* that day I realized that I, too, was the stag. I was born and trained to communicate music, just as the sons were born and trained to hunt, and I was lucky to have grown up in Hungary, a country that lives and breathes music—that has a passionate belief in the power of music as a celebration of life. But one day, when I was still young, I was parted from my family and left my native country. I hunted and searched for music, and destiny turned me into the object of my hunt. The circumstances of life became my "antlers" and prevented me from returning home.

I do not mean to exaggerate my importance, but, like other internationally recognized musicians, I belong to everyone and share with the whole world all I have to offer. The musical and personal rewards of the life I have led have been great, but so have the sacrifices. And there were times when I felt that the rewards would elude me forever.

HUNGARY, a flat, fertile country, is a political highway that has been trampled time and time again by dozens upon dozens of warring nations and empires. The Romans, Tartars, Turks, Austrians, French, Germans, Russians, and many others have all tried to control Hungary, and yet the country has survived, with its unusual language—unrelated to any of the major European linguistic groups—intact and its lively culture enriched.

Music is an essential part of daily life in Hungary. The folk music of the various regions, the Gypsy music that has been absorbed into the national bloodstream, the native and foreign art music, and the café music that is a combination of all these elements and others as well. All this explains why a country whose population, even today, is barely over 10 million has produced so many musicians and so much outstanding music. I am grateful for having been born and trained there.

During the first six years of my life, Hungary was one of the most important components of the Habsburg dynasty's vast Austro-Hungarian Empire, but after World War I it became an independent national entity. As a result of the consequent upsurge in Hungarian nationalism, many Hungarians with Germanic surnames were encouraged to adopt Hungarian equivalents. My parents kept the family's original surname, Stern, but my father decided that my sister and I should change it to facilitate our careers. He chose a new name at random: Solti—the name of a small Hungarian town. My first name, György, remained the same until I left Hungary, but then, as no one abroad could cope with the pronunciation of this strangely spelled name, it was changed to Georg in German-speaking countries and pronounced like George in English-speaking countries. For the same reason, the man who for many years was the distinguished conductor of the Philadelphia Orchestra began life as Jenö Blau and ended it as Eugene Ormandy.

I know only one fact about my family's distant past. In 1938, when Admiral Horthy, Hungary's dictator, began to align Hungarian policies with those of Nazi Germany, our government produced a law that compelled civil servants to trace their Hungarian roots back at least fifty years. This provision was directed mainly against the considerable numbers of Polish and Russian Jews who, after the turn of the century, had moved across the Carpathian Mountains into Hungary to escape discrimination in their homelands. As a coach at the state-subsidized National Opera in Budapest, I was a civil servant and therefore had to produce such proof. My father went to Balatonfökajár, his native village, near Lake Balaton in western Hungary, and discovered documents proving that our family had lived there for more than 250 years.

Until my father's generation, most of the Sterns had been farmers, bakers, and millers in Balatonfökajár. They had rented their land from the Tóth family, the local landowners. Aladár Tóth, one of their descendants, became a distinguished musicologist, principal music critic of the leading Budapest newspaper, director of the Budapest Opera, and husband of the pianist Annie Fischer, my good friend and former classmate. Only after he and I had known each other for some time did we discover that my grandfather had rented land from his grandfather.

Before World War I, Hungarian Jewry was assimilated and integrated into Hungarian life and had the same rights as Gentiles. The two main advisers of Franz Joseph, the Austrian emperor and king of Hungary, were Hungarian Jews: his banker, Leo Lanczy, and a commander of the army, Col. Gen. Samuel Hazai. We Sterns were able to enjoy, to some extent, the results of this relatively liberal attitude.

My memories of the Stern family are rather shadowy, but I have consulted with my cousin Elisabet, who, as I write these words, is ninety-nine years old but whose recall is exceptional. My paternal grandfather, Solomon Stern, and his wife, Fanny, had eight sons. Grandfather owned a mill and was a wealthy tenant farmer, and his sons were all hardworking and successful until the day when one of them, Miska, gambled the family into disaster. He lived beyond his means and incurred enormous debts. His brothers attempted to clear the debts, to save the family honor, and ruined themselves in the process.

My father, Móricz Stern, born in 1878, in Balatonfökajár, moved to Budapest as a young man, along with two of his brothers. He was a sweet man but utterly untalented at business, despite which, he kept trying all his life—first as a flour merchant, then as an insurance salesman, and finally as a real estate broker. He trusted everyone and was often cheated. And yet he must have had a period of relative prosperity before World War I, because I know that at the beginning of the war he patriotically invested a fair amount of money (all his savings) in war bonds, which the imperial government guaranteed at a 6 percent annual interest rate—a very high rate at the time. After the war, the old Austro-Hungarian currency became so devalued that by the time the loan could be redeemed it was worth little more than the price of a tram ticket, and my father did not even bother to collect it. Somehow, every one of his financial deals failed, but his brothers and my mother's family helped out at the worst moments.

My mother, Teréz Rosenbaum, came from Ada, a village in the Bácska region of southern Hungary (now Croatia), between the Danube and the Tisza rivers. She had a sister and three brothers, one of whom was a veterinary surgeon and had a great influence on my early life. My mother's family had several extraordinary members, the most celebrated of whom was her second cousin László Moholy-Nagy, the painter, photographer, and cofounder of the Bauhaus. I visited his studio when my mother, sister, and I went to Berlin in the mid-1920s; at that time, he was designing sets for Otto Klemperer's avant-garde Kroll Opera ensemble. He was kind but quite shy, and I remember that he wore thick-lensed glasses. Later, after having fled Nazi Germany, he established a "New Bauhaus" in Chicago and helped to establish the school of the Chicago Art Institute, but he died eight years before I arrived.

One of my first cousins—the son of Simon Rosenbaum, my mother's youngest brother—was the journalist, publisher, and art collector Emery Reeves. His original name, Imre Rosenbaum, was first changed to the Hungarian Imre Réves and later anglicized. He studied in Dresden and then worked in Berlin as secretary of the Odol mouthwash firm, but when the Nazis came to power, he moved to Paris and established a highly successful press agency. Winston Churchill and Anthony Eden granted him exclusive interviews on the European situation, and these articles circulated all over the world. When war broke out, Churchill provided him with an entry visa for Britain, and he later sponsored Emery's application to become a British subject.

Emery published Churchill's memoirs, assembled an important collection of Impressionist and Post-Impressionist paintings, of which he was a connoisseur, and bought La Pausa—Coco Chanel's beautiful villa at Rocquebrune, in the south of France—where Churchill often went to relax and paint. Wendy, Emery's wife, was a beautiful American. Emery was a strange man: highly intelligent, witty in a sardonic way, and a snob, who didn't consider me worth bothering about until I became music director of the Royal Opera in London. I shall always be grateful to him, however, for having helped my mother and sister to survive the war, in Budapest, by sending them food and money that I myself was in no position to provide.

My mother was still in her midteens when she met and married my father, and only eighteen when my sister, Lilly, was born, in 1904; my father was twenty-six. I appeared eight years later, on October 21, 1912. My birthplace was an apartment in Vérmezö Street in Buda. (Buda, on the west bank of the Danube, and Pest, on the east bank, were separate cities until 1872.) I didn't live there for long, however. When I was two, World War I broke out; although my father was already thirty-six and considerably overweight, he volunteered to work in a military office in the town of Veszprém, northwest of Lake Balaton, and he took his family with him.

My earliest memories date from our years in Veszprém. My father was a gentle, religious man who kept all the Jewish traditions, including praying every morning and attending services at the synagogue every Friday evening and Saturday morning. He used to take me with him and I would play outside with other children whose parents were attending the service. One week, a circus came to town and set up its tent not far from the synagogue. I found my way to it, got in without a ticket, and stayed until the performance ended, two hours later. It was wonderful—I had never seen anything like it. When the synagogue service finished, my father came out and was shocked to discover that I was not playing nearby. He rushed home, hoping to find me there, and when he didn't, he alerted the local policeman and a search was organized. Meanwhile, I ran home by myself, longing to tell my parents and sister what I had seen. When I came in, my mother did not scold me—although now, as a parent myself, I realize how desperate she and my father must have felt. All she said was, "Go to bed quickly, before your father gets home!"

During the war years, we sometimes visited my father's family in Balatonfökajár, which is not far from Veszprém. I clearly remember sitting beside my grandmother in a horse-drawn dray, which she herself drove; in my mind's eye, she is wearing an old-fashioned black dress and has a strange ornament stuck in her hair. She seemed to me incredibly old, but she was probably only about seventy. I also remember the delicious smell of the big loaves of bread baking in the family bakery's wood-burning oven. I have loved the smell and taste of fresh bread ever since. Normally, we visited Balatonfökajár only about once a year, but we saw my uncles, who lived in Budapest, more often.

In the autumn of 1918, in the midst of the defeat and collapse of the Austro-Hungarian Empire, we returned to Budapest, traveling in horse-drawn carriages and only at night, because by daylight the Red and White political factions were fighting each other all over the country. It was a terrible time: Reactionaries killed Communists and Communists killed reactionaries. All I remember, however, is our journey back to Budapest and the fear that something might happen to us. Since that time, I have never been able to rid myself of the fear of anyone wearing a military or police uniform, or even a customs office uniform, because in Hungary uniforms always meant persecution in one form or another.

For some time, the Reds had the upper hand, and Hungary was governed by a Communist regime led by Béla Kún, who was Jewish, like many other Hungarian leftist activists. In the long run, this proved terribly compromising for the Jews; on the other hand, it is natural for Jews to react against the extreme right, which is traditionally anti-Semitic. Béla Bartók and Zoltán Kodály, both non-Jews, held positions in the Kún regime; they simply believed in equal rights. Eventually, Admiral Horthy, the right-wing leader—and the only admiral in history with no sea to sail on—gained control of the country and entered Budapest on a white horse. Many of the Reds were executed, and Bartók, Kodály, and other Kún sympathizers were disgraced and temporarily excluded from official life.

By this time, my father was experiencing financial difficulties and was no longer able to maintain the comfortable lifestyle that he and my mother had been used to. During the chaotic postwar years, everything in Hungary was in a state of neglect, and the twenty-year-old apartment building that we moved into, on Maros Street in Buda, was no exception. The entrance hall, a few steps up from the street, also served as a place for rubbish disposal—an area that attracted rats—and my constant dread as a child was that I might step on a rat. Whenever I entered the building, I ran up the steps from the ground floor to the first floor as fast as I could; once I reached the landing, I felt safe. Our apartment consisted of a living room, kitchen, and four small bedrooms, and I remember it as being gray and malodorous. I am sure that my pathological aversion to dirt and bad smells originated during those years.

My uncle, the vet, helped our family a little financially, and somehow my mother, a marvelous woman, skillfully covered up our lack of money. We were always well turned out, and she always looked elegant and graceful. My parents were determined to give Lilly and me a good education, but there were constant arguments about the family finances. My mother would scold my father for his lack of success in business. I found this difficult to live with, but I never said anything. The fear of financial disaster still remains deep inside me, however ridiculous this may seem, and I dislike extravagance and waste.

I started attending school shortly after we had returned to Budapest from Veszprém. According to my father, as he was walking me to school the first day, I looked up at him and said, "Papa, from now on my worries will begin." In a way, I was right.

Our teachers were badly paid and the educational level certainly wasn't high, but during my first years I was a good pupil—one of the best in the class. We studied the basic subjects—mathematics, Hungarian language and literature, history—and then Latin from the age of eleven and German from the age of thirteen or fourteen. Once or twice a week, we split up for religious instruction: The Catholic majority and the Protestant and Jewish minorities each had a class. Although both sides of my family were religious, I was never forced to practice the Jewish faith. I did not really rebel against it, but then, as today, I disliked organized religion. I have a strange inhibition about praying with others. I feel that prayer is a private matter. My father would occasionally scold me for not going to the synagogue, and to make him happy, I did accompany him on the high holy days. But I was always disturbed by the chattering that went on in the background. "This is terrible!" I said to my father.

He replied, "You must understand that for a Jew the synagogue is home." I understood, but his explanation did not change my mind.

My mother seemed to me less religious than my father. She often cooked nonkosher food, such as bacon, for herself and me, and at the Passover Seder, when everyone said, "Next year in Jerusalem," she would always add, "Not me!" If only my parents had gone to Jerusalem in the 1920s or 1930s, how different our lives might have been.

I eventually came to the conclusion that the fact that Mozart lived proves the existence of a supreme being, and the older I get, the more firmly I believe that it cannot have happened by chance that Mozart came into this world, created an incredible amount of joy and beauty for humanity, and then disappeared at the age of thirty-five. There must be a higher meaning to it; there must be some force that wants to console the troubled human race. When Gabrielle, my first daughter, was born—as I held this half-hour-old human being in my hands for the first time and saw her open her eyes—I suddenly understood the miracle of life and the soul. But these feelings are as near as I come to religious belief.

At school, there was a great deal of nationalistic indoctrination. This practice was inherited from the Austro-Hungarian Empire, whose leaders had made sure that their subject nations disliked and distrusted one another, so that they would not join together to overthrow Austrian rule. The practice then became part of the post–World War I fascist-nationalist mentality—we were better people, we were stronger soldiers, we were more intelligent—which created a terrible heritage of hatred. As a schoolchild in Budapest, seventy-five years ago, I was taught that Rumanians, Czechs, and Yugoslavs were the Hungarians' enemies and that we had to be suspicious of them. The power of this form of mental corruption was brought home to me recently when I was watching a televised soccer game between Hungary's national team and Newcastle United, an English team.

The Hungarian team included Rumanians, Czechs, and Russians who had emigrated and become Hungarian citizens. It so happened that a Rumanian player was the most unpleasant member of the team—rough and aggressive—and I caught myself saying, "Ah, those horrible Rumanians!" I suddenly realized that I was reacting just as my teachers had taught me to react when I was a little boy. Even though I am antifascist, antinationalist, and antimilitarist, I sit down to watch a soccer game and all the stupid old prejudices come back.

The whole Serbian-Bosnian-Croatian disaster was created by hundreds of years of teaching hatred. It's no wonder that anti-Semitism has continued unabated in Central and Eastern Europe, although nearly all the Central and Eastern European Jews emigrated or were killed: The prejudice has become so ingrained that it can almost be described as innate. Many European Jews were themselves infected with it, and I can still remember, with shame, how pleased I was as a young man, when people would tell me that I didn't look Jewish.

FRIENDS ARE VERY important to me, and I have always had many of them. There are probably many reasons why this is so, but two seem to me more valid than any of the others: I am a naturally friendly person, and I hate to be alone. When I was a boy, soccer was the activity that cemented my friendships, and my fondest memories from my school years are connected with the joys of playing soccer. Many of my classmates were poor, and my advantage over them was that I actually owned a soccer ball. I played a great deal; I was light on my feet and a good runner. I love the game even today, though nowadays only as a spectator.

I had three or four close friends, and when we were eleven, one of them got such bad grades that he feared he would fail the course, the rest of us stole and burned the teacher's grade book. We decided to set off for France to join the Foreign Legion, but after an hour of walking we became so hungry that we went home and owned up. The next day we had to confess publicly, at school; the teacher scolded us fiercely, and we were given lower grades than we had earned. This was the sole heroic deed I have ever committed, and I did it only out of solidarity with my friends.

When I was six—the year we returned to Budapest from Veszprém, and the year I started school—my mother, who was very musical, noticed that I sang well and clearly, and she decided that I had a good ear. My cousin Elisabet remembers that when, as a young woman, she came to visit us in Veszprém, I loved to sit on top of the piano and listen to her play. From the moment my talent was remarked upon, according to Elisabet, my mother devoted all her time and energy to my musical development and made up her mind that I would take lessons. I must emphasize that the idea was hers, not mine: I might have asked for a new soccer ball, but not for piano lessons.

She made a few inquiries; someone told her that the German harpist of the Budapest Opera's orchestra was a good piano teacher, and he began to come to our house once a week. I hated him because he hit my fingers when I made mistakes or disobeyed. What was worse, the piano was near a window, and while I was having a lesson or practicing, I could see my friends playing soccer in the park below. I have a theory that there is something abnormal about children who like to practice instruments: They are either geniuses or, more often, completely untalented. I certainly did not like to practice, and the teacher who hit me, and the view of the park, did not help to improve my attitude. After about six months, I told my mother that I wanted the lessons to stop, and she was intelligent enough not to force me to continue. Besides, the lessons cost money, which was anything but abundant in our household.

So my piano playing stopped almost as soon as it had begun, and I happily went back to playing soccer. Then, during my second year at elementary school, my interest in music was revived by singing in class at school—or rather, by the boy who played the piano accompaniments. Somehow, I knew that he was terrible and that I could do the job much better. He awakened my tremendous musical ambition, which has never subsided to this day. I swallowed my pride and told my mother that I would like to start piano lessons again.

I was about eight years old at the time. Lilly, my sister, who was sixteen, had begun to study singing, and my parents thought they might save a little money if I could accompany her; I think this was a major issue for them. (Lilly eventually had a minor career as a singer. Like our father, she had a nice voice but was not very musical, and after two years of singing in provincial German theaters, she buried her operatic ambitions and got married.) On the other hand, my mother truly believed that I had the makings of a musician. She even resisted the advice of one of her brothers to make me learn a "real" profession, rather than music. In the vast majority of cases, his advice would have been correct. Only a tiny percentage of the children who take music lessons have the talent, ambition, and stamina to work ceaselessly, the toughness to survive the bad patches, and the sheer luck to succeed in a musical career. But I undoubtedly owe my life in music to my mother. Maybe she had wanted to be a pianist and had transferred her ambition to me. I don't know.

When I began lessons for the second time, my mother also took some lessons. She made good progress, and she used to practice with me. Unfortunately, she had to give up for lack of time, but she encouraged me to continue—and indeed, I have never since stopped studying music. The older I get, the more industriously and even fanatically I work.

My mother's brother, the vet, also played the piano. When I was thirteen or fourteen, I spent my summer holidays with him in the town of Nagyvárad, in Rumania, where he lived. One evening, he took me to a party so that I could accompany a friend of his—a pharmacist who was an amateur singer. The friend sang the "Piff, paff, piff" aria from Meyerbeer's *Les Huguenots,* which I had never heard before. I found the piece so funny, and the singer so awful, that I started to laugh. In fact, I laughed so hard that I could not go on playing. The singer was offended, my uncle was embarrassed, and I was sent home, to bed, in disgrace.

My mother found another teacher, Mrs. Koczy, an enchanting elderly lady married to a civil servant. She usually gave me lessons at our apartment, but I occasionally went to her pleasant home, which was in a more fashionable section of Buda than ours. The keyboard technique she taught was old-fashioned: Never spread your fingers, always keep them curved, and keep the back of your hand so flat that you could carry a pencil on it. I liked my lessons, but I never practiced more than an hour each day, instead of the two to three hours I was told to do. Mrs. Koczy made me write, in a little booklet that my mother had to sign every week, how much I practiced each day. I stretched the truth considerably. Once, Mrs. Koczy asked my mother whether it was true that I was working two or three hours a day, and my mother said, "No, he is not. I've been signing the book because he asked me to do it." I was embarrassed and immediately increased the time I practiced to one hour and fifteen minutes.

When I was ten years old, I passed an entrance examination for the Ernö Fodor School of Music, a private institution that was Hungary's most important music school after the Franz Liszt Academy. My mother or father had to take me there three times a week, because the school was on the other side of the Danube, in Pest; we went by tram across the St. Margaret Bridge. I studied with Miklós Laurisin, one of the theory professors, who also coached me at the piano. He was the first teacher who told me that sound is produced not only by the fingers but also by the palm of the hand. Although he was highly talented, he had learned to play too late to develop an outstanding technique himself, but he was fascinated by the idea of creating a method that would work well for others. He loved to teach, and he understood that the piano could make a singing, legato tone—that it did not have to sound percussive. Laurisin was very nice to me and I was grateful to him for what he taught me. Sad to say, he later became a Nazi sympathizer, and I lost all contact with him. I could not bear to see him anymore.

After two years at the Fodor School, I passed the entrance examinations for the Liszt Academy, where, for six years, I received the most significant part of my formal musical education. The Liszt

Academy is housed in a magnificent building, and its beautiful Art
Nouveau concert hall has marvelous acoustics for solo recitals and
chamber music performances. The training I received there was difficult and at times harsh, but those who survived the experience
emerged as real musicians. The academy gave me a grounding in discipline and hard work that has sustained me throughout my life, and
the lessons I learned there I now try to impress on young people.

Every morning, I would take the number 81 streetcar directly to
the Liszt Academy for classes in standard subjects—music theory,
music history, and so on—or for piano lessons. My first piano
teacher there was Arnold Székely, who, like many other important
Hungarian musicians of his generation, had been a pupil of István
Thomán; Thomán, in turn, had been a pupil of Liszt and a friend of
Brahms. Perhaps the Thomán connection got Székely his job,
because he was not much of a teacher. He favored the same sort of
old-fashioned technique that I had been taught by Mrs. Koczy and
that Laurisin had tried to correct: with the hands and arms tightened
up. I resisted much of his instruction, and this did not make our relationship a happy one.

I remember Székely as a small, elegant, indeed vain figure, but I
don't remember much about his lessons, although I studied with him
for four years. He was not aggressive, but he always repeated the
same things. The most important aspect of the lessons was the fact
that five or six highly talented young pianists met twice a week and
listened to one another play for several hours. And because we knew
that we would be playing for one another we practiced. The first
year, we learned Bach's Two-Part Inventions; the second year, the
Three-Part Inventions; the third year, parts of *The Well-Tempered
Clavier;* and every year, substantial doses of Haydn, Mozart,
Beethoven, and the other classics.

In Székely's class, I first met Annie Fischer, who, in my opinion,
was the most gifted Hungarian pianist of the century. Other friends
in my class were Edith Farnadi, an amazing child prodigy, and
György Fejér, who loved jazz and light music. He immigrated to the
United States and became the famous New York cabaret pianist
George Feyer; for years, he played at the Carlyle and Waldorf-
Astoria hotels. We have remained close friends and see each other
from time to time in New York and Europe.

When I was fifteen or sixteen, Professor Székely caught pneumonia, and we pupils were told that during his absence his lessons would be given by Professor Bartók. Although Béla Bartók was a fine pianist and needed to teach in order to earn a living, the obvious question remains: Why was he teaching piano instead of composition? The answer is he believed that composition cannot be taught. He was absolutely right. One does have to learn the elements of composition, such as harmony, counterpoint, and form, but one can't be taught how to compose anything worth hearing; one either does or does not have a talent for composing music.

Bartók presented an austere, forbidding front to the world, and even in those years, when he was still in his mid-forties, his reputation was daunting. Until Székely became ill, I had seen Bartók only in the Liszt Academy's corridors, and I had never exchanged a word with him. I can say with absolute honesty, and without leaning on hindsight, that although he had received little official recognition and was widely regarded as a raving radical, we music students knew exactly how important he was, and we revered him. We were fully aware that there was an authentic genius teaching at our academy.

When I learned that I would have to play for him, I felt terribly fearful. Bartók kept our class separate from his own; we spent several hours with him twice a week throughout the six weeks of Székely's illness. Seventy years have elapsed since then and I do not remember much about those sessions, but I do recall that at every lesson each pupil played parts of *The Well-Tempered Clavier* for Bartók. I also played some Debussy preludes for him. During one of the first lessons, I made a terrible faux pas: I sat down to play his *Allegro barbaro,* for piano solo. When he saw me set the music on the stand, he became quite upset. "No, no, not that!" he said. "I don't want to hear that!" It was stupid of me to have thought that he might have enjoyed hearing an immature pupil play one of his compositions, but my intentions had been good: I had wanted to show my love and respect for him.

After I left Bartók's class, I never again had significant personal contact with him. There was an occasional "Good morning, Professor," when I passed him in a corridor, but that was all. I attended many of his recitals, at which he played Scarlatti and Liszt (I particularly remember some of the less frequently performed pieces from the *Années de pèlerinage*), Haydn, Mozart, Schubert, Debussy, and even Schoenberg, whose music was as much disliked in Hungary as elsewhere in those years. I never heard him play Beethoven or Brahms, but I did hear him perform many of the pieces from his own *Mikrokosmos,* for which he favored a crisp, staccato articulation. Bartók was a marvelous pianist who took practicing seriously, but his playing was somewhat dry, not at all Romantic. He opted for a rather hard but extraordinarily clear sound, and he used less pedal than most pianists—very little even in Debussy.

Horthy and his supporters eventually forgave Kodály his Communist sympathies, but they never forgave Bartók, who had a much more uncompromising character. And yet, however isolated he may have been within the Hungarian musical milieu, his situation became even more difficult when he emigrated. The story of his departure at the beginning of World War II, and of his struggle for survival in the United States, where he died in 1945, is well known. Since his death, he has been recognized as one of the great composers of the century. In Hungary, he posthumously became a national hero: Most cities and towns have streets or squares named after him, and what used to be called the Franz Liszt Academy is now the Franz Liszt–Béla Bartók Academy.

I DON'T REMEMBER the name of my first teacher of musical theory at the Liszt Academy, but when, at the age of thirteen or fourteen, I won a prize in a piano competition promoted by a Budapest politician, one of the pieces I played was my own. My mother, convinced that I was a second Mozart, persuaded the politician to write a letter of recommendation on my behalf to the academy's best-known composition teacher, Zoltán Kodály.

Kodály, then in his mid-forties, was a brilliant man who went through some very bad years, on the verge of madness. There was something of the fanatic in him, and back then his youthful, ascetic face and Lenin-style beard gave him a somewhat Christ-like appearance. He believed in an almost messianic form of communism, and he became a disciple of an extremist "healthy life" cult that called for a severe form of vegetarianism, cold-water cures, and going barefoot. There was a period when he even came to the academy shoeless. His wife, Emma Sándor, the sister of a wealthy liberal member of parliament, was no beauty, but she was highly intelligent, and gifted as a composer, pianist, poet, and translator. Her wealth allowed Kodály to spend time composing and carrying out his research into folk music, which he wouldn't have been able to do so freely if he had had to teach full time.

I don't know how my mother had the courage to take me to a man of such prestige as Kodály, but there we were one day in his studio at the academy. Such was her naïveté in political matters that she didn't realize that the politican who had written the letter she handed him was right-wing; Kodály was left-wing. "My son composes and has brought along some little pieces that he has written," she said. "Would you like to listen to them?"

I am sure that the pieces were terrible, but Kodály listened patiently. "The boy certainly has talent," he told my mother, "but he must finish his education. Bring him back to me when he is eighteen, and we'll discuss the matter again." This was a fair remark, but my mother was deeply offended: How had Kodály dared to turn down her little Mozart? Instead of following his advice, she took me immediately to Albert Siklós, the other principal composition professor at the academy; he listened to my pieces and accepted me as a pupil.

Siklós represented the academy's conservative element; Kodály was the radicals' champion, although as a composer he was far more conservative than Bartók. Siklós made us study from the same composition textbooks that Liszt and Brahms had used seventy-five or a hundred years earlier, whereas Kodály invented his own method, which began with the study of sixteenth-century counterpoint and proceeded gradually through the following four centuries. To some extent, we were all influenced by his system, and I, too, learned to compose in the styles of Orlando di Lasso and Palestrina. The results must have been awful, but that didn't matter: The important thing was to understand old styles, not to compose masterpieces in them. This is how I mastered counterpoint, and this is where my special love of Bach's music was born.

After two years of writing in styles of the past, we were allowed to compose in our own styles. Most of us imitated Kodály, not only because he was the most obvious model, but also because writing pieces heavily influenced by folk music seemed new and daring. I never had much faith in my talent as a composer. I realized before long that I was unable to produce anything other than poor imitations of Kodály.

Composition exams were held twice a year; we were given blank music paper early in the morning and had to produce a certain type of composition by noon. Together, Siklós and Kodály looked at each student's work and graded it. On those occasions—and there were at least eight such tests over a four-year period—Kodály never gave the slightest indication that he recognized me. He always graded my work fairly, but he never said a word to me. I finished the course successfully and wrote a string quartet as a graduation piece, thereby ending my career as a composer. Kodály handed me my diploma, but not even then did he say a word to me.

One evening, a few years after my graduation, when I was a coach at the State Opera, I was sitting in my usual place in the opera house's restaurant before a performance of Kodály's *The Transylvanian Spinning Room*. The director came in with Kodály and asked me to show the composer the way to his box. As we walked, Kodály turned to me and said, "You see, you didn't need that letter of recommendation. You've made your way without it."

"Professor, do you remember that?"

"Oh yes," he said softly.

I didn't see him again for about thirty years. At Salzburg in 1964, after a performance of Mahler's First Symphony that I had conducted, an usher came to my dressing room and said that Professor Kodály wanted to see me. Kodály entered with his new, young wife—his first wife had died—and made the following astonishing remark: "I must apologize to you for the time I was so unfriendly to your mother," he said, "but, you see, the man who had written that letter of recommendation was my political enemy."

I saw Kodály the following year, when he attended some rehearsals and one of my performances of Schoenberg's *Moses and Aaron* at Covent Garden. Afterward, he said the nicest things to me—what a marvelous musician I had become, and so on. I was as pleased as could be, because he was a shy man and not normally generous with compliments. He died in 1967, at the age of eighty-five. His method of teaching music to children by starting with singing is logical and brilliant, because singing is the most natural form of music making. All good music making begins with the voice: This has been said many times, but it cannot be repeated often enough.

OUR PROFESSOR of music history at the Liszt Academy was the well-known musicologist Antal Molnár, a tall, strange-looking man who wore thick-lensed glasses; I remember him as a fine teacher and a very nice person. There was also a conducting class, taught by Ernö Unger, who instructed his pupils to use rigid little wrist motions. I attended the class for only two years, but I needed five years of practical conducting experience before I managed to unlearn what he had taught me. The most important class, however, for me and for hundreds of other Hungarian musicians, was the chamber music class.

Beginning at about the age of fourteen, and until graduation from the academy, all instrumentalists except the heavy-brass players (trumpets, trombones, and so on) and percussionists had to participate in this course. Presiding over it for many years was the composer Leó Weiner, who thus exercised an enormous influence on three generations of Hungarian musicians. I still remember my first class with him: Dénes Koromzay, an aspiring violinist who later played in the Hungarian String Quartet, and I had prepared Beethoven's "Spring" Sonata for Piano and Violin. We began to play, and everyone waited for Weiner to bang his fist, shout "No!" and stop us after a few bars, as was his habit. Instead, he let us play through the entire first movement.

"Very good," he said. "You are both very talented. Bring it again next week."

The class was flabbergasted, and Dénes and I were very pleased with ourselves, not so much for our playing, but for having been allowed to play the work through. But when we played the following week, the dissection began. We couldn't play more than four bars without being corrected by Weiner. Finally, he said, harshly, "Ach, neither of you has any talent." We were devastated. That sort of psychological attack is very hard to cope with, but if you're strong enough to accept it as a challenge it can prove useful. Dénes and I worked on the piece yet again and played it for Weiner a third time—and from then on he was friendlier toward us. He continued to be highly critical, but a simple "Good!" mumbled by Weiner meant more than high praise from anyone else.

In his class, I played a vast amount of repertoire, from Mozart to Brahms. I cannot emphasize enough how grateful I am to him. He was a marvelous, natural musician, but also a complete professional with a broad and profound knowledge of the art of making music. He never spoke about technique, but, rather, about musical structure, freedom of phrasing, and about probing beyond the notes. He taught us to listen to one another when we played in an ensemble, however large or small, and to develop a sense of when to lead and when to follow—and why, and how. Knowing how to listen, knowing how to assess what is going on within the ensemble, and knowing how to pinpoint and fix what is wrong—these are a chamber musician's basic skills and they are a conductor's basic skills. I am not exaggerating when I say that whatever I have achieved as a musician I owe more to Leó Weiner than to anyone else.

Like Bartók and Kodály, Weiner was interested in authentic Hungarian folk music, which influenced his own works, but as a composer he was more conservative than either of the others, and most of his works have been forgotten. I have recorded the superb post-Mendelssohnian scherzo from his ballet *Csongor and Tünde* and the Suite in F Minor. Weiner was also a highly trained pianist, but he never practiced. I don't think that any of his pupils ever heard him play more than sixteen bars in a row. He knew a great deal about the techniques of all the standard instruments, invented bowings that were appreciated by fine string players, and was proud of a conductorless forty-member chamber orchestra that he had formed and coached. They always needed an enormous amount of rehearsals in order to play and finish together. I once heard them rehearse and play a Mozart piano concerto with Annie Fischer, everyone learned a lot—especially how to listen to each other. When we students would gather in the Liszt Academy's grandiose foyer to complain about our teachers or to make fun of them, in the time-honored student tradition, no one ever spoke negatively about Weiner: He was loved and respected by all.

Weiner was a small black-haired man. Outside the classroom, he demonstrated a good sense of humor, but during lessons he was absolutely serious and seldom even smiled. His method was to be severe with the students, certainly not to treat them like spoiled children. I adored him, and I think he liked me, too. Weiner was a solitary man, and a rather sad one, I believe. The love of his life had been the pianist Ilona Kabos, a pupil of his; when she married the pianist Louis Kentner and moved with him to England, Weiner's whole world fell apart. He never married, never had a family, and seemed the classic bachelor.

Despite being Jewish, he managed to survive the war and the period of grave privation that followed; no one had enough to eat in those days. Once, shortly after the war, a friend met him on the street and was delighted to see him.

"Leó, please come over for supper!" the friend generously offered. "I've just received a gift from America: canned chicken."

Weiner's reply was typical of his perfectionism. "Canned chicken? But I don't eat canned chicken." Better to starve than to eat something below one's standards of taste. In music, he inoculated me with some of this perfectionism: Never compromise, because even the best you are capable of doing is not good enough.

When I returned to Hungary in 1947 to conduct the Budapest Symphony Orchestra at the Liszt Academy, he praised my performance of Schubert's "Great" C Major Symphony, and this made me feel wonderful. He invited me to have supper at his club, Fészek (The Nest), which was the favorite haunt of Ferenc Molnár and many other Hungarian writers, artists, and musicians. As we walked along the boulevard, he told me to stop calling him Herr Professor and to call him Leó instead. Then he stopped in his tracks and asked me abruptly, "Do you really like Bartók's music?"

"Yes, very much."

"Oh. I just don't understand it." And we promptly changed the subject. He had had to find out whether I belonged among the "modernists," because he had never been able to get beyond Strauss and Debussy. And yet he was never unjust. I learned recently that immediately after Bartók's Fifth String Quartet had been published, one of Weiner's pupils tried to provoke him by asking what he thought of the work. Everyone expected to hear a dismissive remark, but instead, Weiner gently explained why he didn't care for the piece, and then he sat down at the piano and played the tremendously difficult first movement by heart. Although he had probably known at a glance that he wouldn't like it, he had taken the trouble to learn it thoroughly, because he understood that it deserved serious attention. To me, he remains an outstanding example of what a musician should be.

During my last two years at the academy, I studied composition and piano with Ernö Dohnányi (or Ernst von Dohnányi, as he was known outside Hungary), the internationally celebrated pianist, conductor, and composer, who became the academy's director a few years after I graduated. He was a brilliant man but not a good teacher.

At first, I had a composition lesson with him once every two weeks. He would look at my work, play it through at the piano, mark it up, and discuss it with me; he was a phenomenal sight reader, and he could whip through whatever I had set down on paper, no matter how messy the scrawl. After a few months, however, he told me, "Phone me whenever you've written something." This was a fatal pedagogical error: I worked less and less, and during the second year I didn't have more than three lessons with him. His attitude toward teaching piano was the same: "Call me when you've prepared something," he would tell his disciples. And when he did give lessons, his method consisted of pushing the pupil away from the keyboard and playing the piece himself. Those who could absorb instruction by example, like Annie Fischer and Géza Anda, learned a great deal; for less talented pupils, however, studying with Dohnányi was a disaster.

Dohnányi was a remarkable pianist. His Beethoven was very free but showed a fine sense of phrasing and form. A performance he gave of Beethoven's "Pathétique" Sonata remains in my memory, not because of the wonderful interpretation, but because he got lost in the first movement's tricky development section. In an amazing display of sangfroid, he improvised his way out of the problem. Others would have stood up and left the stage, but he went on. For that matter, he was accustomed to getting lost, because he never practiced. "Don't work too hard," he used to tell his pupils. "You'll lose your freshness. If you can't learn a piece by working on it three hours a day, you'll never learn it."

There is a grain of truth in this, but the fact is that even Fritz Kreisler, Artur Rubinstein, and other famous performers who claimed not to practice much did work hard. To be an instrumentalist is a commitment; you have to work at it always. On the same subject, the pianist Eugen d'Albert is reported to have said, "If I don't practice for one day, I notice the difference. If I don't practice for two days, my wife notices the difference. If I don't practice for three days, the critics notice the difference."

Dohnányi was an elegant man and he loved women. His second wife, Elsa Galafres, a ballerina, had been married to Bronislaw Huberman, the famous Polish violinist, and there had been a scandal one day when Huberman and Dohnányi had actually come to blows over her on the street. She was not much liked, and people in Budapest's music world used to say, rather nastily, that Dohnányi had won the battle but lost the war. I met her once or twice when I went to their home for lessons, and I was surprised to discover that she had never learned a word of Hungarian.

One of Dohnányi's pupils, Sándor Kuti, was an exceptionally gifted Jewish boy two or three years older than I. He lived in the slums of Obuda (Old Buda), and I used to visit him at his family's desperately poor little catacomb of a home. I am convinced that had he lived, he would have become one of Hungary's greatest composers, but he died in a concentration camp during the war.

I don't think I realized when I was a student that most of the important teachers I worked with at the Liszt Academy—Dohnányi, Bartók, Kodály, Weiner, Siklós, and Molnár—were born between 1877 and 1890. What a crop for such a small country to produce in so few years! But the academy's director, Jenö Hubay, one of the most renowned violinists of his day, was a generation older. Hubay was married to a wealthy baroness, and we youngsters saw him as a mysterious, elusive aristocrat of the old school. He had studied with the legendary Joseph Joachim, had been enthusiastically praised by Brahms, and had produced a whole generation of accomplished young violinists, including Josef Szigeti. On the other hand, Hubay was a notoriously bad conductor. In one rehearsal, when a harp player missed his entry, Hubay asked him why he wasn't playing. The harpist replied, "I'm waiting for the cue, Professor."

"A cue?" replied Hubay. "But can't you see I'm conducting?"

Going to concerts was another important part of my education. Many wonderful pianists gave recitals in Budapest, either in the academy's small but beautiful hall, with its excellent acoustics, or in the larger Vigadó concert hall. I heard Emil von Sauer, one of Liszt's last surviving students; I also heard Rachmaninoff, whose playing impressed me enormously, but the biggest impression was made by a much younger Russian pianist, whose local debut I attended in the mid-1920s.

Hardly anyone in Budapest had heard of Vladimir Horowitz, who was still in his early twenties, and the hall was nearly empty at his first recital. We students were captivated by his precision in a Scarlatti sonata and amazed by the crescendoing double octaves in Liszt's *Funérailles*. During one crescendo, the entire audience rose to its feet. The speed and accuracy were unheard of, and equally unforgettable were the octaves in the middle of the Chopin A-flat Polonaise, whose crescendo was like a volcanic eruption. After Liszt, Horowitz must have been the most phenomenal pianistic talent in history.

I sometimes wonder how I "heard" music in those days. In my youth, I wasn't interested in musical content, and didn't really understand the composers and their intentions until I matured. My main aim was to concentrate on my technique and improve it to the very best standards. The first time in my life that a symphonic piece really touched me—I was not more than fourteen years old—was when I heard the great Erich Kleiber conduct Beethoven's Fifth. I felt as if I had been hit by lightning. The music was so powerful and all-embracing, and it was not only Kleiber's performance but also the sound of Beethoven's Fifth Symphony that really aroused in me the desire to make my life in music, whatever the consequences. I decided immediately that I wanted to be a conductor, not a pianist. When I got home, I told my mother of my decision; as a good Jewish mother, she said wisely, "Very well, but now go and practice the piano." And yet, that evening my fate was decided.

I didn't know anything about the orchestration of Beethoven's major symphonies, but I know now, seventy years later, that, as with Mozart's works, their greatness speaks equally to amateurs and professionals alike; and there is an artistic freedom within a strict form. As a boy, I didn't know any of the Mozart operas, and—apart from a single performance of *The Marriage of Figaro*—I conducted my first one, *Idomeneo*, in 1951, when I was nearly forty. I knew *The Magic Flute* from the piano and from the time I spent working as a coach in Salzburg, but I didn't grasp the incredible genius of the work until comparatively recently. It is only now that I feel I really understand its magic and the three worlds of the opera: those of the priests, the mortals, and the supernatural. For many years I conducted notes but not the philosophical content behind the notes. This is one reason why I have recorded *The Magic Flute* twice; I hope that in the second version I have come a little nearer to its truth.

WHAT I DID not understand as a boy was that the wonderfully concentrated musical education that I received at the academy had one serious drawback: the neglect of my nonmusical education. I was tutored privately in other areas, and at first this system was successful, because I learned quickly and did well on my annual exams. In the long run, however, the lack of deadlines and regular tests proved disastrous for me. My work deteriorated, and I was tolerated only because I was the piano accompanist for the school concerts.

When I was seventeen, one of the examiners told me, "We're passing you as a favor both to you and to ourselves. We don't want you to come back." So ended my formal academic education. Everything that I have learned since, I have learned on my own, by reading and through experience, and there are still tremendous gaps in my education. I love literature and all the humanities, but I have had to learn about them piecemeal. This is why I decided that my daughters should have the best possible general education.

I DO NOT REMEMBER attending many opera performances during my student years. My parents once took me to a performance of *Die Meistersinger* (I was twelve years old and I disgraced myself by falling asleep during it), and I was present when Richard Strauss came to Budapest in the late 1920s to conduct his most recent opera, *Die ägyptische Helena;* his extremely economical gestures impressed me. And yet I knew that the best way to become a conductor was to begin in the opera house, and that the best way to learn the repertoire, and the ropes, was by getting a job as a répétiteur, or coach.

Immediately after I graduated from the Liszt Academy (I received my piano diploma in 1930 and my composition diploma in 1931), when I was nineteen, I approached Miklós Radnai, the director of the Állami Operaház (National Opera House), who also taught music theory at the academy, and told him that I wanted to become a répétiteur.

"An opera house is a very immoral institution," he said, "and you are so young. Are you sure your parents will allow you to take such a job?"

"I've talked to them about it and they have nothing against it," I said, lying shamelessly.

"All right; try it for a while and see whether you like it." I was taken on as an apprentice, with no salary, for one year, and I was assigned to work with the chief répétiteur, Mr. Petö, an untalented conductor but a good musician and a kind man. Petö thoroughly understood the organization of a big opera house and knew how every type of work had to be prepared. I learned a great deal from him.

Napoleon said that one must be a good corporal before one can be a good general, and the same principle applies in the opera house. You cannot be a first-rate opera conductor if you haven't come to grips with all the elements that go into creating a production. In the opera house, where the task at hand is far more complex than in the concert hall, you learn self-discipline and organizational skills, and once you have done that, you are better able to impose discipline and orderliness on others. Of course, you can have all the self-discipline and all the organizational skills in the world, but without talent and good training as well you will never rise above mediocrity. But the fact is that hardly any outstanding conductors, past or present, mastered their art without working their way up through the ranks of an opera house. If you can deal well with the combined task of making music and making theater, you can deal with anything. And, from a purely musical point of view, working closely with singers, year after year, teaches you to make music in a way that breathes—to phrase properly, even in purely instrumental music. Anyone who watches me conducting opera will notice that I look like a fish, opening and closing my mouth; I'm breathing with the singers.

When I began to work at the National Opera, the chief conductor was Sergio Failoni, an Italian who had been Arturo Toscanini's assistant at La Scala ten years earlier. In 1928, at the age of thirty-eight, he had arrived in Budapest, where he stayed for the remaining twenty years of his life. In essence, he had the duties of music director without the title, and he was given first choice of repertoire. I would describe him as a highly talented dilettante. The English, who love brilliant amateurs, would have made him their darling had he ended up in London instead of Budapest. He had an amazing memory—he knew by heart the words of every opera he conducted, in whatever language they were written—but he mastered only the piano reduction of the score, not the details of orchestration. I remember seeing his copy of the full orchestral score of *Tristan:* Its pages had never been cut.

He imitated Toscanini's mercurial behavior and, like Toscanini, he knew what he wanted to hear. But he didn't have Toscanini's profound musical knowledge or his mastery of detail. His repertoire was extensive—especially Verdi, Wagner, and Puccini—but he wasn't interested in rehearsing the basics. This turned out to be good for me in the long run, because he wanted me to take most of his rehearsals. I would coach the singers individually and in ensemble, and then Failoni would conduct the final rehearsals and the performances.

Anton Fleischer, the second conductor, was a Jew who had converted to Christianity. Unconverted Jews were not allowed to conduct at the National Opera, but converts were tolerated there until 1939, when tougher racial legislation eliminated them, too, from the roster. Like Failoni, Fleischer was talented but undisciplined, which meant that we had two conductors who left most of the groundwork to their assistants. The third conductor was Otto Berg, who took charge of all the performances that Failoni and Fleischer did not care to do. He was untalented, unimaginative, and small-minded. Berg went to the Bayreuth Festival in 1931—the year in which Wilhelm Furtwängler conducted *Tristan* and Toscanini conducted *Tannhäuser* and *Parsifal*—and when he returned to Budapest, he talked only about some little mistakes he had heard, although, according to all expert reports, the performances had been extraordinary.

A little later, János Ferencsik, who was only five years my senior, began to take over some performances from both Fleischer and Berg. After the war, Ferencsik became Hungary's leading conductor, directing both the National Opera and the Philharmonic orchestra.

We met several times in Germany and England, when he was conducting there, and again in Budapest in 1978, when I performed there for the first time in many years. He was always generous and warm toward me, and I admired him very much for maintaining artistic standards in Hungary under difficult and restrictive political regimes, which cannot have been an easy thing to do.

I adapted easily and naturally to my work at the National Opera, and I was taken on for a second year and paid a small honorarium. By then, however, singers had begun to hire me to coach them privately. I don't know how talented I am as a conductor, but I can say without hesitation that I became the best répétiteur ever. I understood the requirements: Play rhythmically but softly, so that the singers always feel the pulse but need not tire their voices by shouting over the sound of the piano; don't play all the notes, but play all the *essential* notes; when you are coaching an individual singer in a role, take the lead, but when you are playing for a staging or ensemble rehearsal, follow—follow for dear life! I was able to follow the worst singer to hell and back. I could have followed a bird's chirping.

Before long, fifteen or twenty members of the company were engaging me on a fairly regular basis, and I was earning a reasonable living. I felt tremendously wealthy, and my parents decided to move to an apartment in Király Street, in Pest, so that I could be nearer the opera house. This is a typical example of their devotion and belief in me. The thought of living by myself never entered my head: You lived with your parents until you got married. So I lived at home until I left Hungary for good.

There were many fine singers at the Budapest Opera during the 1930s. I helped them to learn or refresh their roles, and in exchange I learned an enormous amount about good singing and good music making. I particularly remember Imre Pallo and Andreas von Rösler. Pallo, a fine baritone, was outstanding in the title role of Kodály's *Háry János*. And Rösler, a tenor, sang Florestan in Toscanini's *Fidelio* production at the Salzburg Festival in the mid-1930s. I remember him as being highly musical, but with a somewhat constricted sound. One summer, the two singers went to Milan together to study with a famous Italian singing teacher; Pallo came back singing better than ever, but Rösler returned with a totally blocked-up throat, hardly able to produce a note. This has always been a great example to me of how difficult it is to teach singing. If a singer has a natural voice, you can improve on what nature has given. But without that essential prerequisite and an instinctive sense of how to use it correctly, what nature has not endowed cannot be taught. What I learned from listening to singers during those years at the Budapest Opera has been invaluable to me throughout my career.

I knew from the start that as a Jew I would never be allowed to conduct a performance at the Budapest Opera, no matter how much experience I might build up as a répétiteur. Therefore, when Josef Krips came to Budapest to conduct Hubay's *Anna Karenina,* I seized the opportunity to ask him whether he would take me on as an assistant in Karlsruhe, Germany, where he was music director. He liked my work, and as there was a vacancy in his staff, he immediately engaged me.

I arrived in Karlsruhe at the beginning of October 1932 and took a room with a German family in an apartment near the theater. The father and the son were both unemployed. The mother rented one room, and the money from that kept them going. I quickly understood that one of the main reasons for the Nazis' rise in popularity was that Hitler promised jobs. For most Germans, this was all that mattered, and Hitler did eventually keep his promise. He ordered the building of the famous autobahns and encouraged the development of the engineering factories that later produced tanks and armaments. Retrospectively, it is easy to follow the pattern. Everything he did was the planning of a megalomaniacal madman intent on world domination; but at the time not only I, a young musician from Budapest, but also people much more experienced—indeed, many of the world's leaders—failed to appreciate the reality of a situation that would escalate into a world war.

My German was very sketchy when I arrived in Karlsruhe (in Budapest, we had performed all operas in Hungarian), but it soon improved. The first opera I coached was *Lohengrin,* followed by several others. I only worked with Krips, but I got to know the second conductor, Rudolf Schwarz, who later survived the Bergen-Belsen concentration camp and became chief conductor of the BBC Symphony in London, and the third conductor, Joseph Keilberth, a native of Karlsruhe, who was very kind to me when I met him again years later. When I think about him, I cannot help remembering that he died on the podium in 1968 while he was conducting a performance of *Tristan und Isolde* (perhaps the ideal end for a conductor), but my mind's eye pictures him back in Karlsruhe when we were all so very young. Of the four of us—Krips, Schwarz, Keilberth, and myself—Krips, age thirty, was the oldest.

Two or three months after my arrival, the *Völkische Beobachter,* a Nazi newspaper, took Krips to task for having imported an *Ostjude*—a Jew from Eastern Europe. I was the *Ostjude,* and my dismissal was demanded. Krips said to me, "I know why this has happened. One of the orchestra members is a terrible Nazi, and he is trying to get rid of me. I'll recommend you to Joseph Rosenstock, the chief conductor in Mannheim, where the Socialists are in control. Nothing like this will happen there." Fifteen years later, the same orchestra member applied for a job with me in Munich, when I was music director of the Bavarian State Opera. I recognized the name and didn't reply to his letter.

I went to Mannheim to audition for Rosenstock. He was very sympathetic and asked me to play the first scene from *Der Rosenkavalier* and a solo piano piece. I played a piano transcription of folk songs by Kodály. "All right, I'll take you," he said. "You're better than anyone I have here now. When things calm down, you can go back to Krips, but for the time being, you're welcome here."

I prepared to move to Mannheim after I had finished the productions I was working on in Karlsruhe, but I never got there. In December, Krips advised me to go home to Budapest until the German elections were over. "You'll see," he said. "This nightmare will soon be over—then you can come back and prepare the Strasbourg Festival with me." But I first went to Strasbourg forty years later. Hitler came to power on January 30, 1933, and shortly afterward Rosenstock was thrown out of Mannheim, Krips and Schwarz out of Karlsruhe, and only Keilberth, the non-Jew, stayed on. When I met him again years later, he told me that he had never seen anyone as talented, or as shy, as I had been then.

I returned to Budapest with my tail between my legs, I felt so ashamed. After all, it had been my decision to leave Budapest and go to Germany. I didn't dare venture near the opera house, in case I should meet my colleagues and have to explain why I was back home. But one day I did bump into Ferencsik on the street. "What are you doing here?" he asked. I told him what had happened and he said, "Please come back to us. We need you." I made an appointment with the director and was reengaged for the 1933–1934 season.

Many of the Jewish and other anti-Nazi conductors who had lost their jobs in Germany began to seek work elsewhere and turned up for guest appearances in Budapest, as they did in other major European cities. This gave me the opportunity to observe them all and to work with some of them. I helped Bruno Walter prepare the Verdi Requiem; I assisted Issay Dobrowen in *Khovanshchina* and *Boris Godunov;* I heard Otto Klemperer conduct Beethoven's Ninth Symphony; and I worked with Fritz Busch in a choral work. I also coached *Der Rosenkavalier* and *The Abduction from the Seraglio* for my hero, Erich Kleiber, and played the celesta in the *Rosenkavalier* performances. Kleiber, a conductor steeped in opera, had a tremendous feel for the stage. He directed the *Seraglio* production himself, placing the singers where he wanted them, acting their parts, and discussing the sets with the designer. Very seldom does one find a conductor who is so completely a theater animal as Erich Kleiber. I always wanted to be like him. He called me "Mascagni," because of my dark complexion and my, at that time, thick head of hair.

Nearly everything in my life revolved around the opera house. Theaters devour the people who work in them. You find yourself there morning, noon, and night, and colleagues become personal friends. When people ask me about café life in Budapest in the 1930s, I do not know how to answer: I did not participate in it. Although I occasionally tried to find work abroad, because I knew that my career was unlikely to go anywhere in my native country, I loved Budapest and had a good life there. But the only café I assiduously frequented was the Opera Café; as my colleagues were also habitués there, our topics of conversation during moments of relaxation inevitably revolved around our work, and we gossiped. We loved to gossip—and I still do.

Strangely, however, my two serious loves of the 1930s came from outside the opera milieu. Earlier, at sixteen, I had had a crush on a talented young pianist in Weiner's class, but I had suppressed it; many years later, I discovered that two other class members, the violinists Dénes Koromzay and Sándor Végh, had also had silent crushes on this girl. But when I was nineteen I met Ilona, a photographer, whose younger sister was a pianist and a friend of Sándor Kuti, the young composer who had been at the Liszt Academy with me. Ili's parents were Russian Jewish immigrants who owned a big photographic studio in Obuda; she ran a branch of it. Ili was my first real girlfriend, and the experience was so exciting that I decided to marry her. My mother was violently opposed to the idea, because I was so young and earning so little. "Wait a few years and see if you still want to marry her," she said. She was right: Within a year, I had changed my mind.

When I was about twenty-five, I fell in love with a writer, who became my main contact with Budapest's intelligentsia. My relationship with this lovely young woman lasted until we were separated by the war, and by the time we met again, we were both married to other people. She became active in the Communist party and eventually held a high position in the cultural bureaucracy, but she died a few years ago. I am happily still in touch with our mutual friend Zsuzsi Vermes Dancs; she and her husband, István, keep me informed about our old friends and everything that happens in Budapest's cultural life.

IN THE SUMMER of 1936, I visited the Salzburg Festival for the first time and managed to attend, unofficially, a few rehearsals and performances. Bruno Walter and several other famous musicians were taking part, but the main attraction was Toscanini, who was conducting *Fidelio, Falstaff, Die Meistersinger,* and some orchestral concerts. The experience was exhilarating—a new world of high quality opened up for me—and the following summer I made up my mind to go back. At my insistent request, the director of the Budapest Opera gave me a letter of recommendation, so that I might get into some rehearsals. I arrived in Salzburg one evening in July 1937, and the next morning I went to the Festspielhaus to present my letter to Baron Puthon, a retired Austrian general who was the festival's general manager. After a long wait, I was introduced to the baron, who read the letter and asked me, "Can you play *The Magic Flute?*"

"Yes."

"Can you come back to the Festspielhaus to play for a stage rehearsal at two o'clock? A flu epidemic has left us short of répétiteurs." Of course I said yes. Not only was it a new *Magic Flute* production but it was to be conducted by Toscanini, probably the most famous musician in the world at that time.

I arrived at the appointed hour and was introduced to Herbert Graf, the stage director—a pleasant Austrian who later immigrated to the United States and worked at the Metropolitan Opera for many years. I entered the pit, went over to the piano, and discovered that the singers were ready, onstage, but that there was no assistant conductor around. I never dreamed that the great Toscanini would attend a mere staging rehearsal, so I started in, giving cues with one hand, just as I had been accustomed to doing in Budapest. Suddenly, out of the corner of my eye, I saw a little man enter from the right side of the stage. My heart stopped. It was Toscanini. Although he had turned seventy the previous March he was at the height of his powers and prestige. He peered into the pit a little suspiciously, because he was very nearsighted and didn't know who was playing. Without stopping me, he began to conduct—very small, simple, but clear indications of tempo and dynamics. I followed him as if my life depended on it. After an hour or so, he called a break, turned to me, and said softly, "*Bene.*" I do not think that any compliment I have ever received has given me as much joy as that one word from Toscanini.

The flu epidemic continued unabated. Even Erich Leinsdorf, Toscanini's principal assistant, was knocked out for a while. I played many other *Magic Flute* rehearsals for Toscanini, several *Fidelio* rehearsals, and one or two *Falstaff* rehearsals. I know that Toscanini had a sense of humor, but I never saw it in action. When he worked, he was always totally serious, and he expected everyone to give his or her very best at all times. The level of concentration could not have been higher. I quickly became one of his assistants and ended up playing the glockenspiel for the *Magic Flute* performances.

As I recall, I wasn't paid for my work that summer, but before I went home, Baron Puthon called me to his office and engaged me as a salaried répétiteur for the following summer: Toscanini wanted me to coach four of the five operas that he had promised to conduct (the fifth was to be *Tannhäuser*), and I was thrilled with the prospect of working for him on an official basis. In October, less than two months after the festival had ended, he came to Budapest with the

Vienna Philharmonic, and—at Leinsdorf's suggestion—I went to the train station to greet him. I also saw him after the concert and dared to tell him that it had been wonderful. This was perfectly true, but I felt ridiculous saying something so obvious to my hero. It was a pleasant moment, however, and Toscanini smiled and said, "See you in Salzburg next summer." No one could have foreseen that he would never again set foot in Austria.

News of my having worked with Toscanini—and of my having been reengaged by him—was picked up by the Budapest press, and I began to be noticed as a musician. I pestered the Budapest Opera's administrators to let me conduct something, and I imagine they realized that if they didn't give me a chance, I would probably try to go elsewhere. Finally, a performance was arranged for me: *The Marriage of Figaro*, on March 11, 1938. So far as I know, it was the first time that an unconverted Jew conducted a complete opera in that house since Hungary had become an independent country.

I knew our house's *Figaro* production well—I had coached it for Failoni—but walking into the orchestra pit to conduct an opera for the first time in my life was a frightening experience, especially as I had not been allowed a single rehearsal. But after the overture, I felt absolutely comfortable and at home. The first two acts went well, and during the intermission everyone backstage seemed satisfied. But at the beginning of the third act, Mr. Lendvai, the baritone in the role of Count Almaviva—the dominant character in this scene— made all sorts of mistakes, sang incoherently, and seemed to have completely lost his confidence. I was angry with him for spoiling the duet and his aria. He eventually got a grip on himself, and when I went backstage after the performance had ended, I learned what had happened. Just as he had been about to go onstage, Lendvai had been handed a copy of an extra edition of an evening newspaper and had learned that German troops were crossing the border into Austria and marching toward Vienna; the historical event that is now referred to as the *Anschluss*, or "annexation," was taking place at that moment. And no one knew where Hitler would stop. Would he call a halt at Austria's borders, or would he send the army onward to Budapest, Bucharest, Prague? Lendvai, who was Jewish, had lost his self-control, and who could blame him? I probably would have done the same had I known what was happening.

My parents had planned a celebration to follow the performance. It was canceled, of course, and my high spirits were transformed into fear and depression. As it turned out, my conducting debut at the Budapest Opera was also my last performance of an opera there. I was only twenty-five years old, but I felt that all my hopes had been dashed. That evening left a permanent scar on my heart.

THE GERMAN ARMY did not march into Hungary in 1938, but Admiral Horthy, in order to placate Hitler, replaced the old, de facto limitations on the Jewish population with new, official restrictions. At first, I was allowed to keep my coaching position because I could prove that my family had lived in the country for more than fifty years. I remember that in 1938, when Bartók and his wife, Ditta Pásztory, gave the Hungarian premiere of his Sonata for Two Pianos and Percussion, with Ernest Ansermet conducting, at the Budapest Opera, I was called upon at the last minute to turn pages for Mrs. Bartók. As I had not seen the complicated score before, the task was not easy. I have never in my life attended any other performance that had as little success as this one. When the piece ended, most of the audience remained silent; then there were a few perfunctory claps. I felt sad and embarrassed for Bartók.

The thickening clouds over Central Europe made me decide to look for work elsewhere. My first opportunity came about thanks to my friendship with Antal Dorati, whose father was a violinist in the Budapest Opera's orchestra. Dorati had gone abroad when he was in his early twenties; since 1933, he had been conductor of the famous Ballets Russes de Monte Carlo. He must have heard good things about me from his father, because he invited me to come to London to conduct part of the Ballets Russes' 1938 summer season at Covent Garden.

I stayed in London for about a month. I knew no one apart from the Dorati family, and I felt very strange and foreign. Dorati and his wife, Clary, had arranged for me to stay in a little hotel on a side street near the British Museum; it provided bed and breakfast. The hotel was rather dirty and it had neither a good bed nor a good breakfast. I hated the English bread and I'd never eaten porridge or bacon and eggs before; my Hungarian palate didn't much enjoy the experience. Worst of all, though, most of the time I felt unbearably lonely because I couldn't communicate with anybody: I couldn't really speak either English or Russian.

The Doratis couldn't have been nicer to me, and I spent many hours at the flat they had rented for themselves and Tonina, their little daughter. I used to walk to work—it was only about five minutes from the bed-and-breakfast to Covent Garden. I always ate lunch at Lyons Corner House in the Strand, where I could order only by pointing to whatever caught my eye on the menu. Most of the time, when I wasn't working, I walked around the streets on my own, looking at this extraordinary and very foreign city.

I don't know how I managed to communicate with the orchestra, the London Philharmonic, but I suppose I must have conducted well enough, because if a conductor is clear in his gestures he doesn't really need words. However, a few more words than I had in those days would have been useful.

I was overwhelmed by the British. I went through my time there in a sort of trance, and my memories are very hazy. One thing I do remember, though, is that I went to Montague Burtons, the tailors, in the Strand and bought myself a blue Harris tweed suit, which turned out to be a good investment, as it was the only suit I owned through the war years and beyond.

The Ballets Russes de Monte Carlo was not as exciting an ensemble as the great Ballets Russes had been before World War I, under the leadership of its founder, Serge Diaghilev, when Picasso and Stravinsky, respectively, designed and composed for it. *The Firebird, Petrushka,* and *The Rite of Spring* had world premieres with the company, and so had Ravel's *Daphnis et Chloé* and Debussy's *Jeux.* Nevertheless, in 1938 it was still a very impressive company under the artistic leadership of Michel Fokine and his wife. I was asked to conduct *Les Sylphides,* the Polovtsian Dances from Borodin's *Prince Igor,* and Glazunov's arrangement of Schumann's *Carnaval.*

I was determined to do my best, and I studied hard in the library of the opera house. The Fokines, who were particularly kind and supportive, as was the entire company, took me to the dancers' rehearsal room somewhere in London during the time of the piano rehearsals, so that I could judge the tempi of the pieces I was to conduct. I was terribly upset, however, when I discovered that I would have to push and pull the tempi about in a most unmusical way in order to accommodate the dancers' movements. But I thought I had better do as I was asked, and everyone seemed pleased with my work.

A few days before the season ended, Colonel de Basil, the ensemble's director, called me to his office and offered me a contract to tour Australia with the company. This would have meant a guaranteed job for several months outside Hungary, and it would have been a wonderful opportunity for me to get out of Europe. I thanked him and said I would give serious thought to the proposal. I suppose I didn't jump at the offer, which, given my circumstances at the time, I should have done, because I didn't see the European situation as being very serious and, also, I'd realized at the first rehearsal that I didn't like conducting ballet because of the necessity of changing tempi.

At my last performance, I decided to conduct *Carnaval* in accordance with Schumann's tempo instructions; the poor dancers had to adjust as best they could, because most of the tempi were far too fast for them. They were not happy, and the stage manager said to me after the curtain call, "Get out before they lynch you." It was a moment of sweet revenge for both Schumann and myself.

Dorati and his wife, whose perspective was much more cosmopolitan than mine, understood how urgent it was for me to get out of Hungary before Germany swallowed up the rest of Europe, and they urged me to join them on the Ballets Russes' Australian tour. But I didn't listen to them. I was more concerned with escaping from London's endless, depressing rain and mysterious inhabitants. The Doratis spent the war years in the United States, where Antal eventually became music director of several important orchestras, including those of Dallas, Detroit, Minneapolis, and Washington, D.C.; later, he directed such major European ensembles as the BBC Symphony and the Stockholm Philharmonic.

Before I returned home, however, I went to Oslo, where Issay Dobrowen had engaged me to coach a new production of *The Marriage of Figaro* that he was conducting at the opera house there. Today, I would be frightened out of my wits if I had to travel on my own across the North Sea in such a small ship as the ferry from Harwich to Esbjerg, but in 1938 it was an adventure. The train to Oslo seemed to me exceptionally clean and spacious, and opposite me sat a ravishingly beautiful blond girl. We struck up a conversation in rudimentary English and German, but regrettably she was not staying on in Oslo, only changing trains.

Dobrowen, a Russian Jew, had conducted a great deal in Berlin and Dresden before 1933, when he had begun to wander around Europe. I had worked with him in Budapest, where he had conducted and directed *Boris Godunov* and *Khovanshchina,* and he was a frequent guest in Norway. He was a kind man and an intuitive, great, and natural musician, as well as a good, well-organized director. I think of him as a precursor of Mstislav Rostropovich and Gennady Rozhdestvensky. He was not a natural Mozart conductor; he needed a strong musical assistant for *Figaro* and had remembered my work in Budapest.

I don't remember the Oslo Opera orchestra's playing, which probably means that it wasn't very good. Dobrowen didn't do the production; the director was Karl Aagaard Oestvig, a tenor married to the soprano who was singing the part of Susanna. Oestvig had been an outstanding Wagner tenor with an international career; he had sung major roles at the Vienna State Opera and the Berlin Municipal Opera, and he had sung the part of the Emperor in the world premiere of Strauss's *Die Frau ohne Schatten.* But he had lost his voice in his early forties and had turned to directing.

He did some incredibly stupid things. In preparing the scene in the Countess's boudoir, he had forgotten to tell the set designer to put in a window for Cherubino to jump out of. At the last moment, to my great amusement, they had to put a hole in the set for the famous window.

Every night, Oestvig and the designer would go to a famous Oslo pub and get drunk. Rehearsals were held in the evenings, by which time the director had sobered up; but after each rehearsal the pub routine would start again.

Dobrowen had found me a room in a little pension, a short walk from the theater, on Karl Johan, the main street. Once, when I was visiting Dobrowen at his home, a lady to whom he introduced me said, to my surprise, that she already knew me quite well. "My window overlooks Karl Johan," she explained, "and every morning I see you walking down the street, with your head swiveling around in every direction at once so that you can look at all the blond girls." I enjoyed my stay in Oslo, thanks to the long, happy northern summer evenings, the Norwegian people, who were very warm, and especially the beautiful blond girls.

AFTER THE Munich conference, at the end of September 1938, we all naïvely believed in the statement of British Prime Minister Neville Chamberlain: "Peace in our time." I felt very safe; I was at home, and I had a job. I thought over Colonel de Basil's offer for the Australian tour, but as the prospect of being a ballet conductor didn't fill me with enthusiasm, I sent him a polite refusal. The Doratis went to Australia; I stayed in Hungary, where, six months later, I lost my job. In 1939, a new anti-Semitic law stated that Jews could no longer occupy government-paid positions, no matter how long their forebears had lived in Hungary. Employees of the Budapest Opera, a state-subsidized institution, were civil servants. Therefore, from one day to the next, I was unemployed.

I was able to earn money by giving private coaching to singers, but the overall prospects were bleak. Despite this, I never regretted turning down Colonel de Basil's offer, and in the long run my decision proved to have been the right one. I might have spent the rest of my days as an unwilling ballet conductor, or I might have remained in Australia and never returned to Europe. This was the first of many times in my life when, looking back, I feel that my actions were guided by what can best be described as a "guardian angel."

I tried to think of ways of finding an occupation for myself. I began to consider forming an all-Jewish opera ensemble, with two pianos for accompaniment, along the lines of the Jewish Opera Company that had been founded in Berlin. In January 1939, I returned to Scandinavia as a pianist, to play Leó Weiner's Piano Concerto in two performances—one with the Norwegian Radio Orchestra in Oslo and one with the Swedish Radio Orchestra in Stockholm—thanks to a recommendation from Dobrowen.

The train I took crossed Germany, and as I had promised friends in Budapest that I would bring presents to a woman they knew in Berlin, I stayed overnight at a hotel near the station. There was a Nazi congress, and in the morning, when I got up, I found the corridor lined with storm troopers' jackboots. I was appalled to see that the woman I had to visit was wearing a yellow Star of David sewn onto her sleeve, to indicate she was Jewish—a law enforced by the Nazis. Before I boarded the train, which was leaving in the early afternoon, I stopped at a little restaurant and saw for the first time the sign: JUDEN VERBOTEN (Jews forbidden). I was shocked, but as I was also very hungry and did not look particularly Jewish, I went in anyway. I am renowned in my family for eating very fast, but I consumed this meal in record time.

On the boat train, I shared a compartment with a Norwegian couple. Until we got out of Germany, I was tremendously afraid that some Nazis might board, check identification papers, and force me to leave the train. All Hungarian identification papers stated the religion of the bearer. When we boarded the North Sea ferry, which headed for Sweden via Denmark, the Norwegians gave me some whiskey. It was the first time I had ever tasted it. I thought it was some terrible antiseasickness medicine. In the intervening years, I have changed my mind: My companion every evening is a glass of malt whiskey.

The Radio Orchestra was Stockholm's second orchestra, in terms of quality; the first was the Stockholm Philharmonic, and during my stay it was being conducted by Fritz Busch. He was staunchly anti-Nazi—like his brothers, the celebrated violinist Adolf and the noted cellist Hermann—and he had voluntarily exiled himself from Nazi Germany, just as Toscanini had voluntarily exiled himself from fascist Italy.

I called on Fritz Busch in Stockholm, hoping that he might help me to find a job somewhere in Scandinavia. He remembered me from Budapest and invited me to lunch at a restaurant. Although I was in awe of him, he was very friendly, but as the meal progressed, I realized what an unhappy man he was. He drank champagne in large quantities, his face became redder and redder, and his conversation more and more animated. He told me that the Berlin Philharmonic had recently performed there and that he had gone secretly to their rehearsal; the conductor was Wilhelm Furtwängler. Furtwängler had stopped the orchestra to correct something, and had told the musicians to play especially well because a great German conductor was living in Stockholm. I could see that Busch had been deeply touched by what Furtwängler had said: Busch was, after all, one of the leading contemporary exponents of Germany's great musical tradition, but because of his principles, he had left the Dresden Opera, where he had been general music director for eleven years. I believe this departure from his home and country, which he loved so much, may have contributed to his premature death at the age of sixty-one, only a few years after the war.

Kind and well-disposed though he was, Busch couldn't help me find work in Scandinavia, which was overrun with refugee musicians, many of them much better known than I, a relative beginner. I went back to Budapest and tried to scrape by with my private coaching. In June 1939, Alfréd Fellner, chairman of the Friends of the Opera and head of one of the most prominent Budapest industrial families, invited me to his home to have lunch.

Fellner was a sincere music lover and a genuine friend. He had always followed my career and had attended one of the *Magic Flute* performances in Salzburg, where he was an habitué. He asked me what I intended to do in the future. I told him about the plans I had for forming a Jewish opera company, but he, understanding the hopelessness of the situation, told me to get out of Hungary as quickly as possible, warning that my entire future and, indeed, my life could be at stake. He suggested that I go to Switzerland, where Toscanini was conducting at the Lucerne Festival. "Ask the Maestro to help you find work in America," he said. I didn't want to do this, as I felt embarrassed to ask someone as important as Toscanini for a favor. But Fellner insisted. When I invented the excuse that I didn't have enough money for the trip, he said, "I'll give you the money." I went home and told my parents that I was going to Lucerne for a few days.

On August 15, 1939, at the age of twenty-six, I said good-bye to my mother and sister, picked up a little suitcase containing a pair of shoes, some clean shirts and underpants, and my Harris tweed suit from London, and with my father took a tram to Budapest's Western Railroad Station. My father was the mildest, sweetest man imaginable. He had never scolded me or denied me anything. I was the light of his life, and he cared more about me than about anything else in the world, just as I now feel about my own daughters. I loved him, too, but was not as devoted to him as he was to me. (I now understand, as a parent, that children can never love their parents as much as their parents love them.)

When we got to the station, we stood on the platform, chatting, as the train arrived. Just as I was about to climb aboard, my father began to cry. I was very embarrassed. "Why are you crying?" I asked him. "Look, can't you see I'm only taking this one little suitcase? I'm coming back in ten days' time!" But it was as if he knew with certainty we would be parted forever.

The sight of his tears and the harsh tone of my voice have haunted me ever since. I have never forgiven myself for my abruptness. I was never to see him again.

ZURICH

O N MY WAY to Lucerne from Budapest I felt relatively tranquil about the political situation, and strangely, I had none of the fears I had experienced earlier in the year on the boat train to Oslo, although by this time, in the summer of 1939, Vienna was occupied by the Nazis. Europe had seemed on the brink of war in 1938, when Hitler had claimed the Sudetenland, part of Czechoslovakia, as German territory. I still remember the broadcast from the Nuremberg rally and the great shouts of the crowd when Hitler denounced Eduard Beneš, the president of Czechoslovakia, for withholding their rightful territory from the German people.

The situation had been defused by Neville Chamberlain and French statesman Edouard Daladier, who met with Hitler and Mussolini in Munich and agreed to the German annexation of the Sudetenland. Chamberlain's policy of appeasement, so shameful in retrospect, seemed to have won the day. The only possible excuse is that Chamberlain may have been playing for time, in order to rearm Britain. What right have we to make judgments, when we have only recently proved over the Bosnian situation that we still have many of the defects and weaknesses that we criticize in the actions of others almost sixty years ago? Despite the threat of Nazi domination, many people, including myself, felt that the situation was under control. In the spring of 1939, Hitler began to turn his attention to Poland and the city of Danzig. When the situation escalated in the summer, the general view was that there would be another conference, similar to Munich's, and that everything would calm down again.

Those were my feelings as I looked out of the train window at the Austrian and Swiss summer landscape: I was going to enjoy a short summer holiday. When I arrived in Lucerne, I found a small hotel on the edge of the River Reuss, not very far from the station, near the famous covered wooden bridge. The hotel Adler was family-run and the meals were delicious. It was the first time I had eaten Swiss food; I loved it then and still do to this day. The order and cleanliness of the hotel and town made a great impression on me. I spent my first day walking around Lucerne, sitting beside the lake and looking at the mountains, entirely on my own, as I didn't know anybody there. It was exciting to be in Switzerland, in this beautiful little town with its festival atmosphere, and it would be correct to say that I was enjoying myself very much.

I immediately began to plan how to contact Toscanini. In Lucerne, just as in Salzburg, he was surrounded by people who wanted to protect him from intruders, and I didn't know quite how to approach him. I attended a wonderful performance he gave of the Verdi Requiem in the Jesuit church, but most of the time I would wait outside the Kunsthaus after rehearsals, trying to summon up enough courage to talk to him. The Kunsthaus was a modest establishment with mediocre acoustics and a cramped podium. The orchestra was the Swiss Festival Orchestra, which was made up of musicians from different Swiss orchestras.

It took me four or five days before I had a chance to speak to the Maestro, as rehearsals were strictly closed, although I did manage to hear one or two of the all-Beethoven concerts that he conducted a few days later with his great friend, the violinist Adolf Busch, as soloist. Toscanini would arrive each morning with his driver, a tall Italian who acted as chauffeur and a sort of bodyguard. Toscanini never came out on his own; he always had the driver or somebody from his family with him. Several times I had the opportunity to approach him, but I was too timid and in awe; frankly, speaking to him was, for me, like speaking to a god. Finally, one morning, I summoned up enough courage to walk up to him as he was about to leave the Kunsthaus. He was very nearsighted, so I asked him whether he recognized me. *"Maestro, mi riconosce? Solti? Salisburgo?"*

"Oh sì, sì, sì, sì!" He was very friendly, very nice. In fact, he was always good to musicians—always.

I said, "Maestro, I must go to America." I described the situation in Budapest, and he listened to me quietly and seriously.

"All right," he said, when I had finished. "I live in New York. When you come over, contact me, and I'll try to help."

I was as happy as a little bird, because I thought that this was all I needed. I wanted to go right back to Budapest and prepare to leave for America from there, but the next day my mother sent me a telegram: DON'T COME HOME. Her warning was instinctively intelligent: World events were rushing toward a catastrophe. I, on the other hand, wasn't unduly worried. I still thought there would be a last-minute solution, as there had been in Munich.

I didn't know what to do. My first instinct was to go home, despite my mother's warning. I didn't think I knew anybody in Switzerland, but fortuitously I remembered Max Hirzel, a Wagnerian tenor from Zurich who had been a member of the Dresden Opera and had sung a few times in Budapest, where I had met—and coached—him. Hirzel, a kind and decent fellow, was someone I felt I could ask for help and advice. I searched for his name in the telephone book, found it, and dialed the number. He answered the phone. I explained to him my situation, and he spontaneously invited me to stay at his home until my American visa came through, which I thought would be a simple formality. He said to me, "Solti, you're just the man I need. I'm learning *Tristan*. You can come and coach me."

These were the words I needed to hear, because the money that Alfréd Fellner had given me for the trip was quickly disappearing. Toscanini's last Lucerne concert, in which his son-in-law, Vladimir Horowitz, played Brahms's Second Piano Concerto, took place on August 29, and on September 1, the day Germany invaded Poland, I boarded the train for the one-hour journey to Zurich. It was filled with Swiss soldiers: There was a general mobilization. Although Switzerland planned to remain neutral if war broke out, it had a very well trained army, prepared to defend the country if necessary. Seeing the troops finally brought home to me the gravity of the situation. Two days later, Britain and France declared war on Germany.

I took myself and my little suitcase to Hirzel's home in Mühlebachstrasse, and a few days later I visited the United States consulate to apply for a visa. What I didn't know, until I was told by an official, was that the quota for Hungarian immigrants to the United States was full for the following fifty years. There was absolutely no hope of obtaining a visa unless I could present a document showing that I had an official invitation for a professional engagement in America.

I knew several Hungarian musicians who had immigrated to the United States a year or two earlier, and I quickly wrote to Sándor Salgo, a professor of violin at Stanford University, in California, to ask if he could help me. He replied immediately, saying that he knew a manager who could sell me a contract to work as a répétiteur in the 1940 summer opera season in Cincinnati. I would be engaged for the job, but first I would have to send five hundred dollars to the manager, who was an Italian of dubious reputation. I agreed and arranged to send the money, which represented my total savings from my previous summer's engagement; I had left it in a bank in Oslo. A few weeks later the contract arrived, and armed with this document, I went to see a Mr. Altaffer at the U.S. consulate general in Zurich.

I have had plenty of unpleasant conversations, but the five minutes I spent with Altaffer was one of the most painful experiences of my life. He read the precious contract that I had received from the United States, tore it to bits, and threw the scraps in the wastebasket, saying, "This is a fake. Not only am I not giving you a visa; I'm putting your name on a blacklist. You will never be allowed into America." Fortunately, in the long term, he was quite wrong, but at the time I was totally devastated. I was trapped. I had no money, no documents, no family, and no home, apart from the little room I occupied at the Hirzels'.

As it transpired, it was a good thing that I did not go to the United States in 1939 or 1940. I am sure that Toscanini would have helped me, but as America was already saturated with European musicians—many of them accomplished—I might have spent the rest of my life as a coach with a provincial opera company, and I am glad, in retrospect, that I did not reach the United States until I was already an established conductor. In that dreadful autumn of 1939, however, I felt terribly bitter about the way in which I had been treated by Altaffer. More than thirty years later, a Zurich-based photographer came to my home in Italy to take photographs of me. One evening, after dinner, we were chatting and I complimented him on his English; he spoke American English without any trace of a Swiss accent. He explained to me that he was American, saying that his father, a Mr. Altaffer, had been the U.S. consulate general in Zurich.

Young Altaffer was a good photographer, and fortunately, despite the efforts of his father thirty years before, I had survived and was now able to employ his son to take my publicity photographs.

Back in 1939, when I told Hirzel what had happened, he generously invited me to stay on at his place. In the end, what was to have been a short stopover in Mühlebachstrasse lasted a year and a half. For him, this presented no problem, but his wife was less pleased. Until I came along, Mrs. Hirzel had been her husband's coach, but when I moved into the house, he stopped working with her, which made her feel neglected by her husband and jealous of me.

Max Hirzel came from a prominent Zurich family—in the center of town, there is a statue of one of his ancestors, a famous mayor—and he himself was quite a character. He was bald and rather fat, and his wife, who believed that tenors should look young and handsome, was always trying to improve his appearance. She made him wear a toupee, but when he perspired, he took it off, even at social gatherings. "Max! Max!" Mrs. Hirzel would exclaim desperately, until he replaced it. She tried to keep strict control of his diet by giving him salads and low-calorie meals; she never understood why he didn't lose weight. The reason was quite simple: Every day at about noon, after he and I had worked together for a couple of hours, he would say, "Come, Solti, let's take a walk now." The walk always ended very quickly—at the nearest pub, about two hundred yards from his house. He would sit down and order a huge hunk of Gruyère cheese with lots of bread, and a big beer. Then he would go home and happily eat the lettuce leaves that his wife offered him for lunch.

Among the many good deeds that Hirzel did for me, one of the most important was to introduce me to his friend Mr. Düby, a music lover and amateur baritone who headed the Fremdenpolizei—the police department in Bern, in charge of foreign residents. As a result, I was never interned in one of the work camps where many able-bodied refugees, including musicians, were required to do hard physical labor, and which could have ruined my hands for the piano.

At first, I had to renew my residence permit every week, but later only once a month and eventually once every six months. As I could not obtain a work permit, the musical jobs open to me were few, badly paid, and illegal. At the very beginning, however—late in 1939—I had a short but memorable engagement at the Palace Hotel in St. Moritz, where I accompanied the tenor Richard Tauber in a recital. Tauber knew Hirzel from Dresden, where they had sung together many years earlier, and he turned to his former colleague for advice about a pianist for St. Moritz. Hirzel said, "I have the best possible accompanist, and I'll lend him to you—for a short time."

I found the whole excursion tremendously exciting. To begin with, traveling with me on the train up to St. Moritz was the beautiful young Austrian soprano Hilde Gueden, who had fled to Switzerland, where she sang with the Zurich Opera. Then there was the experience of staying at the Palace Hotel—at Tauber's expense, of course. I had never known such luxury, or anything even remotely similar. But my spirits were somewhat dampened by an encounter, at the hotel, with a correspondent for an important American newspaper. When I asked him what Americans thought about the war, he said, "There's nothing to be done about it: This time, the United States will *never* enter the war." This was *vox populi*. What a genius Roosevelt was, to turn public opinion around so dramatically in only two years.

Tauber, an Austrian Jew who had married an Englishwoman and become a British subject, was an international celebrity not only in the opera and operetta repertoires but also in the movies. He wore a monocle and was always well dressed, although he had become bald and his film-star look of former years was beginning to wane. If I am not mistaken, our program at St. Moritz consisted mostly of popular Schubert and Schumann songs. We rehearsed one day—morning and afternoon—and performed on the evening of the following day. I do not have a clear recollection of how he sang on that occasion, but he was a fine singer, and I remember his musicality as being similar to that of Dietrich Fischer-Dieskau. He was very nice to me and even gave me some money. I never saw him again: He went back to England via France, which had not yet been conquered by Germany, and he died in London in 1948, at the age of only fifty-six.

At that time, it was possible to hear both refugee and prominent German artists performing in Switzerland. I took advantage of every opportunity to hear the best German artists. Some of my friends said, "What? You're going to listen to those Nazis?" But my musical curiosity was stronger than my personal feelings and political convictions. I remember, for instance, a beautiful piano recital by Walter Gieseking; I can still hear the cantabile of the right hand as he played the great Schubert B-flat Major Sonata, Opus Posthumous; more than fifty years later, I still have the sound of his playing in my ears. I also remember some concerts conducted by Furtwängler, and a magnificent performance of *Die Walküre* given by the Munich State Opera under Clemens Krauss, with Hans Hotter as Wotan and Helena Braun as Brünnhilde. When the young Hotter made his entrance in the third act of *Walküre* singing "Where is Brünnhilde?" the audience almost shook with fright, such were the fury and physical impact of his delivery. Nobody has ever sung a better Wotan than Hotter.

Despite occasional musical events of this sort, however, I felt desperately miserable and lonely during my first months in Switzerland. In June 1940, I decided to return to Hungary via Italy and Yugoslavia, but on that very day Italy invaded France and thus became one of the belligerent nations. I had no choice but to stay in Switzerland. It was fortunate, because this almost certainly saved my life, and yet I cannot say that I feel only gratitude toward the country that gave me shelter; the shelter was given most grudgingly. I still have a copy of the questionnaire that I had to fill out for the Fremdenpolizei in December 1940, when I had been in the country for well over a year; its accusatory tone jars, even now. The questionnaire asked people to state their religion, so that the police would know who was Jewish and therefore especially desperate to stay in the country. I lied when I wrote on the document that I had been offered a teaching position in Palestine. My friend Lorand Fenyves, a Hungarian-born violinist who had become one of the concertmasters of the Palestine Symphony Orchestra— which is now the Israel Philharmonic—had indeed sent me a visa for Palestine, but I invented the story of the teaching position to make the police believe that I would leave Switzerland as soon as I could safely do so.

I also lied when I wrote that I possessed three thousand Swiss francs in cash, and that my parents in Hungary and friends in the United States sent me a few hundred francs once in a while. But, on the other hand, I was furious at the impertinence of the question regarding how much I was paying for room, board, and other expenses. Why did the police need to know this? On the questionnaire, I admitted that visa problems had prevented me from taking a job with the Cincinnati Opera, but I lied when I wrote that the U.S.

consul had told me that he would give me a visa if I secured a teaching position in the United States, and I made the lie worse when I said that Otto Herz, an accompanist friend of mine who had moved to New York, had written to say that a contract for a teaching position was being sent to me. No such contract had even been discussed. Finally, the question as to how soon I would be able to leave Switzerland was outrageous. The Swiss authorities knew perfectly well that crossing the border into Germany, Austria, Italy, or occupied France would almost certainly have meant deportation to a concentration camp for a Jew, but their only interest was in finding some technicality whereby they could make me leave. I did not answer this question. So I patiently continued with Hirzel, who was a good friend and protected me as much as he could. Without the help of his friend Düby, my Swiss existence could have ended any day.

HIRZEL NEVER did master *Tristan* completely: There was too much text for him to remember. Eventually, however, he sang the role in Bern, under the baton of Otto Ackermann, a very talented Rumanian Jew who had been working in Switzerland since well before the war. At Hirzel's insistence, I sat in the prompter's box. Parts of the opera went well, but Hirzel often got lost and began to stumble, no matter how many musical and verbal cues I fed him. Luckily, he always managed to regain his balance, and somehow he got to the end. Tristan died safely—a miracle! The performance was much more nerve-racking for me than for Hirzel.

Early in 1941, I moved out of the Hirzels' place—at Mrs. Hirzel's insistence—and into a tiny basement flat that I had rented in a steep side street, not far away. I was even lonelier than before, and yet happy to be living on my own. I had an upright piano, and as I had heard about the Geneva piano competition and knew I would be allowed to enter it, I practiced three to five hours a day. One morning, at about 8:30, the police arrived. "You must stop playing," one of the officers said. "You are disturbing Swiss citizens." He intimated that if I didn't stop, they would expel me. I do understand that being a pianist's or violinist's neighbor can be a trying, even maddening, experience. But instead of coming to me and discussing the matter, my neighbors had turned to the police. Their behavior seemed to me

almost Nazi-like, but I apologized and agreed not to play before
10:00 a.m. or after 8:00 p.m., and to play softly. But I really wished I
could leave.

I never felt quite safe in Switzerland until June 1944, when the
Allies took Rome and landed in Normandy. The Nazi troops could
have marched into Switzerland at any time, and we were only too
well aware of what the consequences would be. We refugees, and
many of the Swiss, too, listened to the BBC; we knew about the concentration camps, and I was always aware of the terrible fate hanging
over my head. Churchill's broadcasts on the BBC were a great sus-
tainer and gave me enormous courage. As late as the Ardennes
offensive, at the end of 1944, when the Germans temporarily stopped
the Allied advance, people feared that Switzerland might be occupied. Fortunately, the Swiss army was so well trained that an invasion
would probably have cost the Germans more than they were willing
to risk, but even a three-month occupation could have had perilous
consequences. There was, however, little need for a German invasion
of Switzerland, as the authorities allowed German troops and
ammunition to move through the country and across the Saint
Gotthard Pass at night.

Had I returned to Hungary early in the war, when repatriation was
still possible, the chances are that I, like most other Hungarian Jews,
would have died before the war ended. My own family was relatively
lucky: My mother remained in Budapest and paid the porter of the
block of flats where she was living to keep her hidden in a cellar; my
sister survived by pretending to be a peasant and working in the fields
near Novi Sad, in what is now Serbia. From time to time, I would
receive an unsigned postcard in Lilly's handwriting, with the message
"Your friends are alive and well," or "Your mother is well." My father
died in 1943, but not because of the war. He had been severely diabetic
for most of his life, and he died in a Budapest hospital before the war
hit Hungary in the worst way. His profound religious beliefs helped
him to pass away peacefully. He told my mother that he was not afraid
to die. I was terribly upset by his death—I felt so far away and obviously there was no possibility of going to his funeral. I tried to help my
mother and Lilly as best I could, and I even managed to obtain for
them in Switzerland citizenship papers for San Salvador, in an unsuc-
cessful attempt to protect them from persecution in Hungary.

During the last fourteen months of the war, I lost all contact with my family. The Hungarian Nazis came to power under Ferenc Szálasi and committed the most terrible atrocities. My sister's husband was pressed into a Hungarian auxiliary unit to assist the Germans on the Russian front; when the going got rough and the Germans retreated, they stripped the auxiliaries of their clothing and left them to perish of exposure in the winter cold. This was what the German propaganda machine described as the "*Siegreiche Rückzug*"—the "victorious retreat."

The conditions under which my mother spent the last year of the war were grim. She was entirely on her own, concealed in a basement, her husband dead, her daughter hidden far away, her son in exile. I saw her only once after the war, when I returned to Budapest in 1947; she was emotionally broken and suffering from a severe heart condition. By then, I was married, and I think that by bringing my wife along, I hurt my mother very much. She did not want to share her beloved son with his wife; she wanted him to herself. It was not a happy visit. I could see signs of approaching death on her face, and unfortunately I was right: She died only a few months later. My parents and Lilly are buried together under a rosebush in the Budapest cemetery, which I visit every time I'm in the city.

In 1995, on a German television program, I said that Hungarians are more talented than Germans, even at killing, and I added that the Hungarians were so talented that they had managed to kill about 2 million Jews in little over a year. After the broadcast, I received a letter from an unrepentant Hungarian fascist living in Austria, who criticized me for denouncing my fatherland by highly exaggerating the number of Jewish deaths. I checked and found that I was indeed wrong: The official figure of murdered Hungarian Jews during the last year of the war was 600,000. I wrote back to the man, apologizing for the numerical error but pointing out that since one murder is a terrible crime, 600,000 murders must constitute a crime of unbelievable magnitude. I never heard from him again.

WHEN YOUNG MUSICIANS ask me how to gain conducting experience, I tell them, "There is only one way: Pester people until somebody gives you a chance. If you do well, very likely you will make

The Stern family in Budapest, 1913. From left: Lilly, Teréz, György, and Mórícz

Dressed as a soldier, 1916

With my mother and Lilly at Lake Balaton, 1916

At the piano with Lilly

At the Ernö Fodor School
of Music, 1923

With Lilly and our mother
in 1925, during my student
days at the Liszt Academy

My parents on holiday
in Yugoslavia, 1936

Béla Bartók, piano: We students
already knew he was a genius.

LEFT: Ernö Dohnányi, piano
and composition, photographed
in 1913

Leó Weiner, chamber music:
"Whatever I have acheived as
a musician I owe more to Leó
Weiner than to anyone else."

Zoltán Kodály, composition:
He invented his own teaching
method, beginning with
sixteenth-century counterpoint.

The earliest picture of me conducting: Budapest during the 1936–1937 season

Arturo Toscanini, with whom I worked at the Salzburg Festival in 1937

With Issay Dobrowen (second from left) in Norway, 1938. Dobrowen had engaged me to coach a new production of *The Marriage of Figaro* at the Oslo Opera.

In Zurich, 1941, at my
lifelong habit of reading
books and newspapers

Outside a chalet in the
Swiss Alps

At the time of the Geneva
piano competition, 1942

With friends at the
sanatorium at Leysin,
where I gave a recital
in 1943

Conducting the Tonhalle
Orchestra in Zurich during
World War II

With Hedi outside the
Prince Regent's Theatre in
Munich at the time of my
conducting *Fidelio* in 1946.
As a result of its success,
I became music director of
the Bavarian State Opera

Rehearsing in Munich in front of the safety curtain of the bombed-out State Opera, 1947

RIGHT AND BELOW: With Richard Strauss, at the dress rehearsal of *Der Rosenkavalier* at the State Opera, 1949

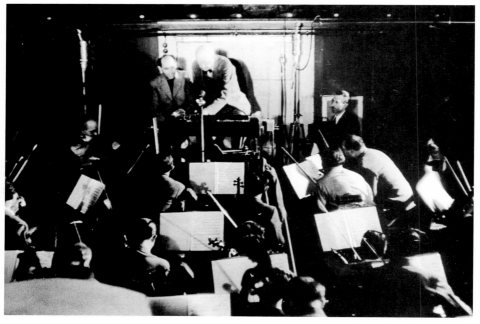

rapid progress. However, if you don't do well, there will be no second chance, and you should immediately consider a second profession." I pestered many people in Switzerland, and in February 1942, I was allowed to conduct two performances of Massenet's *Werther* at Geneva's Grand Théâtre. The orchestra was Switzerland's finest, the Orchestre de la Suisse Romande, founded by Ernest Ansermet, and the part of Charlotte was sung by the young Belgian soprano Suzanne Danco, who had recently made her house debut. I had never even heard *Werther*, and I did not have much time to study the score. Rehearsals were few, I had trouble communicating with the orchestra because I spoke no French, and I imagine that the performances were very bad. On the first night, at the end of the interlude, a member of the stage crew must have fallen asleep, because the curtain didn't open. The orchestra played on and the invisible singers began to sing, but the curtain remained closed. We eventually stopped and went back to the beginning of the interlude—and this time the curtain opened at the right moment. I have never wanted to touch *Werther* again, and for many years I managed to forget completely that I had ever conducted it.

The Geneva experience depressed me, but my spirits were lifted a month later, when I conducted a concert with the Winterthur Stadtorchester in the little hall of Zurich's Tonhalle. This engagement was organized by the Bär family who have remained my closest friends, particularly Hans and Ilse Bär, and Hans's sister Marianne Olsen and her husband, Jørgen. I don't think the performance can have been very good, as I had had so little conducting experience, but Willi Schuh, the famous music critic (and a friend of Richard Strauss), who was at that time on the staff of the *Neue Zürcher Zeitung*, wrote, "Keep your eyes on this young man; he will really become something."

I tried to get a position as a répétiteur at the Zurich Opera, but as a refugee without a work permit, I was not eligible. I got a temporary job there once, for about a month, probably as a substitute for someone on leave; I recall that the set designer, Teo Otto—a German who later became very well known—used to exclaim during rehearsals, "Look at this man! He is the only one in the theater who knows how to coach an opera!" In my opinion, the practice of not giving jobs to foreign musicians has been a restrictive factor in the development of Swiss orchestral life. The recent decision to admit several American

and other foreign musicians into the Tonhalle Orchestra has completely changed the standard of the ensemble playing.

I made an important breakthrough in Geneva early in October
1942—three years after my arrival in Switzerland—when I won first
prize in the piano division of the Swiss Music Competition. The
competition had been created in 1939, and that year the first prize for
piano was won by the illustrious Arturo Benedetti Michelangeli.
The jury in 1942 included the German pianist Wilhelm Backhaus,
who was living in Lugano, the Swiss composer Frank Martin, and
the Swiss pianist Emil Frey.

During the time of the competition, I stayed at the beautiful
home of a Geneva banker, Mr. Hentsch, who was married to a Russian pianist. She allowed me to practice on her piano. These arrangements had been made for me by my guardian angel in Zurich, Irma
Schaichet, a Hungarian piano teacher who was married to the violin
teacher Alexander Schaichet. Irma took me under her wing and
introduced me to many people who were able to help me, including
the Bärs and the Hentsches.

The competition took place at the Conservatoire. There was an
obligatory repertoire: Bach's Partita in C Minor, one of the last three
Beethoven sonatas (I chose the A-flat Major, op. 110), a well-written
toccata by the Swiss composer Othmar Schoeck, an important work
by Schumann (I played *Kreisleriana*), and a Debussy piece (my
choice was *L'Isle joyeuse*). After a general audition, sixteen semifinal-
ists were chosen; a second round narrowed the selection to four finalists—two men and two women; and at a public concert, the ranking
of the finalists was determined.

I got through the first two stages and then worked feverishly for the
final recital. We were to play in alphabetical order, and as I was the
last one on the program, I didn't arrive at the Conservatoire until
the third pianist was already performing. I sat down at a piano in the
artists' room and began to warm up by launching into the fugue in
the last movement of the Beethoven sonata. Suddenly, after the third
entry of the subject, I couldn't remember how to proceed. I was so
confident it was all in my head, I hadn't bothered to bring the
printed music with me. The classic nightmare of every pianist had
come true. I started again, faster, but I still couldn't remember. The
problem was that I hadn't really memorized the piece in my head,

but only in my fingers—purely physical, "muscle" memory—the worst possible method. All my life, I had memorized that way. Once, when a pupil of Liszt's boasted to the master that he knew a certain piece by heart, Liszt said, "Sit down and write it out for me." This is the real criterion. If you can write a piece out correctly by memory, then you really do know every detail of it.

Absolute panic overtook me. I went upstairs to the competition's office to say that I couldn't play because I wasn't feeling well. But the office was empty: Everyone was in the auditorium, listening to the recital. Downstairs, I found an official looking for me. "It's your turn now," he told me. Before I could say anything, I was pushed onstage. I began to play, got safely past the terrible place in the fugue . . . and won first prize. It should have been a jubilant moment for me, but I was still in shock and I felt sad not having any of my family with me to share in my success. In any event, there wasn't much time for celebrating, as I had to prepare for the concert the following day, but Mrs. Hentsch took me out and gave me a fondue supper. I had never eaten cheese fondue before, and in my nervous state, I ate too much and had an unsettled night.

My memory lapse was not the only incident that marred the Geneva competition: I nearly missed it altogether because of an injury to my hand. Throughout my life, even to this day, I have a tendency to get very hungry, and when I'm hungry, I have to eat immediately. One day, after practicing the piano, I was terribly hungry, so I went back to the friend's house where I normally ate. There was nobody in, so I went into the kitchen, took a knife, and sliced off a piece of bread—and a piece of my finger, as well. Fortunately, my hostess returned and bandaged the finger, and I managed to continue practicing, but I have never touched a kitchen knife since then; in fact, I make it a point never to go near a kitchen if I can help it.

During those years, my circle of friends naturally increased; many of them were refugees living in Zurich. It was from them that I learned to play bridge. The flow of money from Hungary had stopped, and therefore many Hungarian refugees had no funds other than what they could make playing cards. My card-playing friends soon co-opted me into their group. The experienced ones were very fast and always seemed to win, and I can remember now hesitating over a card and being shouted at. "Just play *something*, you idiot, but play it fast!" It was a hard school but a good one, and I have never lost my love of bridge, and play it whenever I can.

One of my friends contracted tuberculosis and was sent to a sanitorium in Leysin. He kindly arranged for me to give a recital to entertain the other patients. These were the days before penicillin was in use, and the only cure for TB was mountain air, which doctors believed would kill off the virus. I stayed overnight up there, finding it dreadfully gray and depressing. Everybody slept on the balconies, covered up with blankets.

My other mountain excursion was to Arosa, with my Hungarian bridge-playing friends. They decided to go skiing. I had never been on skis before, but it looked very easy, so I had a go on the nursery slopes, in German, *Idiotenwieser*—"idiots' fields." I fell a few times and picked myself up, but then I lost total control, couldn't stop, and shot down the hill, across a main road, and straight in through the open door of a ski shop. On another occasion, unbowed by my previous experience, I went up on a ski lift, which then broke; I was left hanging for over an hour in the mountain sunshine and came down with sunstroke.

One weekend, in Zurich, the same group decided to go rowing. We had reached the middle of Lake Zurich when the boat capsized. We had to hang on to the hull in the icy water for more than forty-five minutes, until help came. I was so cold, I thought I was dying. I went home to bed, retreated under a pile of blankets, and woke up the next morning with no aftereffects at all, not even a sniffle. Looking back, I realize that these adventures were equally as threatening to my career and existence as were the outside political forces, but the circle of friends helped me to overcome my feeling of loneliness.

The Geneva prize and the concert were a turning point in my Swiss life. The prize money provided me with an income for a year, and I was immediately engaged for concerts in small places; they didn't pay much, but each small fee kept me going for another month. In November 1942, I played the Mozart E-flat Major Concerto, K. 271, with the Zurich Chamber Orchestra under Alexander Schaichet, and later that season, with the same orchestra, I played the Mozart C Major Concerto, K. 467, and Bartók's Sonata for Two Pianos and Percussion, with Irma Schaichet as my partner.

The most valuable asset I received as a result of the prize was a degree of recognition from the Swiss government: I was granted a partial work permit that allowed me to teach up to five pupils. I still have that permit. For me, it is a historic document, but also an example of meanness and small-spiritedness.

As soon as I was able to do some coaching, my life in Switzerland became much easier. One of the singers I coached was the daughter of a wealthy industrialist. She had a voice like a castrated frog's, but she was a lovely girl and I was grateful for the eighty francs she paid me each week for her two lessons. There was also the secretary of a leading Swiss banker—a passionate soprano, who unfortunately had little talent but was very musical and also played the piano well. Max Lichtegg, another of my singers, was a good lyric tenor, whom I accompanied in lieder recitals and who, a few years later, gave me what proved to be an exceptionally important recommendation to Moritz Rosengarten, the director of the fledgling Decca Record Company. I also advised some aspiring pianists and gave them suggestions about technique and interpretation, but I never actually gave piano lessons.

During the latter half of my seven-year stay in Zurich, I performed there and in several smaller cities, as both pianist and conductor. As a pianist, I gave recitals in the Tonhalle's Kleine Saal in January 1944, December 1945, and January 1946, and I played in a Bartók memorial concert in 1945, a few weeks after the composer's death. I recently came across a letter of thanks from the Émigrés' Cultural Society in Winterthur for having participated in a concert in memory of Stefan Zweig, the Austrian writer who had fled to Brazil in 1940; he and his wife were convinced that Germany was going to win the war, and they both committed suicide early in 1942. Eight months later came the turning point in the war, at Stalingrad.

As a conductor, I gave a few concerts in the Tonhalle's small auditorium with the Winterthur Stadtorchester and, later, with members of the Tonhalle Orchestra. In one concert, my friend and compatriot Géza Anda was the soloist in Mozart's G Major Piano Concerto, K. 453. I had a tremendous hunger to conduct. I think the musicians must have hated me because I was very ambitious but had neither rehearsal experience, nor any of the technique one acquires with practice. My work must have been very primitive. I wanted too much too soon and probably stopped the orchestra every ten seconds during the rehearsals. A young conductor doesn't always know how to organize rehearsals, and I certainly didn't.

An indirect result of the Geneva competition was that in 1945 the pianist Nikita Magaloff, who had been a judge in the 1941 competition and who was married to the daughter of the great Hungarian violinist Joseph Szigeti, invited me to his home at Clarens, on Lake Geneva, to meet his father-in-law. I accompanied Szigeti in Beethoven's "Kreutzer" Sonata, one or two Brahms sonatas, and one or two other pieces. He liked my playing very much and, as he needed an accompanist, he asked me to come to the United States with him. I was very pleased, but a wise young friend of mine advised me not to accept his offer, pointing out that it might divert me from a conducting career.

SHORTLY AFTER I first arrived in Switzerland I had become desperately lonely and depressed. I had been accustomed to the warm, emotional life of Budapest, and the switch to discreet, bourgeois, wartime Zurich was hard. I had no family, no career, no money—only Mr. and Mrs. Hirzel, to whom I was slowly becoming little more than a parasite. I also had a terrible feeling that my youth was slipping away and that I would never have a chance to start my career. Things changed for me when, in 1940, I fell in love with a young Swiss pianist who came to me for coaching and gave me helpful criticisms of my own playing. She was about my age, and this closeness with another young person was enormously important to me. She warned me from the start that our relationship would go nowhere, because she was already engaged to be married, but our love kept me alive, intellectually and psychologically. I was devastated when she married, but we remained friends and still see each other now and again.

At about the time this love affair ended, Irma Schaichet introduced me to a comfortably placed Zurich lady whose modern apartment was within walking distance of my tiny basement flat. The apartment contained a grand piano, and Mrs. Schaichet, who knew that I needed a good instrument to practice on as well as a home and some care, arranged for me to become a sort of paying guest with the family, taking my meals with them, using their piano, and actually living at the apartment on weekends. But what began as a very nice friendship soon became painfully complicated. I am afraid I exploited the situation shamelessly, because it allowed me to study and eat regularly.

The "wise young friend" who had advised me against becoming Szigeti's accompanist was Hedwig (Hedi) Oechsli, whom I met in 1943 and who, within two days of our meeting, put an end to my complicated domestic arrangement. She was later to become my wife. Hedi was also introduced to me by Mrs. Schaichet, who was quite consciously playing the role of matchmaker: She knew Hedi was unhappy in her marriage and knew too how desperate I felt about my relationship with the other lady. The beginning of our life together was extremely difficult. Hedi was married to Professor Gitermann, an historian and member of parliament, and was the mother of a young boy. When we met, she was two or three months' pregnant with a second child. But she was determined to get away from her husband and even, sadly enough, from her children.

Hedi, whose father taught chemistry at the University of Zurich, was well placed among Zurich's intelligentsia. She was very smart and sophisticated, and I owe her a great deal. Although I was her senior by two years, she seemed much older than I in many ways. I was a late developer, really quite backward, and in some respects neither intelligent nor well educated. I fear that when I was thirty-one, my mental level was more like that of a twelve-year-old. Because of my music, I had never had a proper high school education. Music was really all I knew. My only outside interests were sports and politics. From the beginning of my stay in Switzerland, I read the *Neue Zürcher Zeitung* every day because I wanted to know what was going on in the world; I was a great admirer of Churchill and Roosevelt and remain so to this day. Hedi gave me a little grace and taught me how to behave—although she never *completely* succeeded in this. She was good to me and for me—it was she who encouraged my self-education through reading, a process which I still continue today.

IN 1945, when the war ended, my craving to conduct became stronger than ever. I was nearly thirty-three, and my opera-conducting experience consisted of the one performance of *The Marriage of Figaro* in Budapest on March 11, 1938, and two performances of *Werther* in Geneva. Without connections, I just didn't know how to proceed.

Somehow or other, I learned that Edward Kilényi, a pianist who had been a classmate of mine under Dohnányi, was helping to run Munich's musical life for the U. S. Army; he was an American of Hungarian extraction. The German postal system was nonexistent at the time, but a politician friend of Hedi's, Dr. Obrecht, a member of the Swiss parliament, was going to Munich to advise the Allied military government on the rewriting and republishing of German school textbooks, which during the war had been full of Nazi propaganda. I wrote a letter to Kilényi, and Hedi gave it to Dr. Obrecht, who agreed to deliver it. In the letter, I asked if I could be of any use as a conductor somewhere in Germany. To my great surprise, Dr. Obrecht brought back a reply from Kilényi, which said, "Be at the German border crossing at Kreuzlingen at eight o'clock on March 20. An American jeep will bring you to Munich, and the next morning I'll take you to the Bavarian State Opera. They desperately need a conductor."

On the appointed day, I took a train to Kreuzlingen, and there I waited. Eight o'clock passed, eight-thirty, nine o'clock . . . but nothing happened. There was no jeep. The last train back to Zurich left at nine-thirty, and I decided that if the jeep hadn't appeared by then I would return to Zurich. The jeep was the only means of transport to Germany. There were no civilian trains. In a way, I was relieved when the jeep didn't arrive, because I had heard terrifying stories about die-hard Nazi snipers shooting haphazardly among the ruins. The stories were false, but I didn't know that. Shortly before nine-thirty, an open jeep with three soldiers in it appeared. Someone asked me whether I was Mr. Solti; I got into the backseat, and off we went.

I cannot remember ever having felt as cold as I did that night, driving through the darkness in an open jeep. The soldiers had thick fur-lined jackets; I had only a thin coat. Worse even than the cold was my first view of a bombed city as we approached Munich at dawn. The closer we got to the center, the more acutely aware I became of the degree of the destruction. There were piles of rubble, tottering facades with blown-out windows, open craters, no streetlights. It was a shattering experience after the protection of Switzerland, where we hadn't seen as much as a bombed-out house. If I could have turned back, I would have.

I was put up at what had been the Bavarian Film Studios, where the Americans had made their headquarters. There was only a sofa to sleep on, but the room was wonderfully well heated, for which, in my frozen state, I was very grateful. Kilényi came to collect me the next morning and we went to see Dr. Bauckner, the general manager of the Bavarian State Opera; he was the only person from the old administration who had not been a Nazi party member. The opera building was totally ruined, reduced to a water-filled bomb crater. Therefore, the company performed in the Prinzregenten-Theater (Prince Regent's Theater). Kilényi introduced me to the great Dr. Bauckner, who looked up from his desk and said to Kilényi, "Why did you bring him here? We don't need him."

"You told me to find someone with no political affiliations," Kilényi replied.

"Oh no, we don't need him."

"But he made an overnight trip in an army jeep to come here." Kilényi was furious. He phoned a colleague in Stuttgart and explained the situation, and almost before I knew what was happening, I found myself bound for Stuttgart aboard a windowless train in the March cold.

The cultural officer in Stuttgart, a nice man, met me at the station and took me to the theater to meet Mr. Wetzelsberger, the general manager. He was not a very good conductor, but he was knowledgeable about opera. He asked me whether I knew *Fidelio,* and when I replied that I did, he said, "We have a *Fidelio* performance scheduled for next week. Will you conduct it?" I knew only the piano score of the opera; I had coached many rehearsals of the work, but I had never set eyes on the orchestral score.

For about five days, I studied feverishly—not only the opera but also a concert program that I was asked to conduct a few days before the opera: Mendelssohn's Overture to *A Midsummer Night's Dream,* Mozart's "Haffner" Symphony, and Brahms's Fourth Symphony. There were only two rehearsals for *Fidelio,* and at the first of them I made a classic blunder. After the big recitative—"*Abscheulicher! wo eilst du hin?*"—which precedes Leonore's aria in the first act, the horns have a beautiful introduction to the aria, "*Komm, Hoffnung.*" I noticed that only three horns were playing, and I thought, This is terrible! I stopped abruptly and asked, "Where is the fourth horn?"

One of the horn players said, "Maestro, we never play it with four; we always play it with three." I looked carefully at the score and saw that in fact the passage is written for three horns. Every other horn passage in the opera is for two or four, but that part is for three. It was a difficult situation: The players thought I was trying to find fault with them, and I thought that by proving beyond a doubt that I did not know the piece, I had made a total fool of myself.

Nevertheless, the performance, which occurred on April 21, was a big success. I don't remember the names of most of the singers, but the Florestan was the young tenor Wolfgang Windgassen, who soon became very famous. Afterward, the general manager told me that the company wanted to engage me as music director. "Could you come to the Ministry of Culture tomorrow morning so that we can draw up a contract?" As the German mark was worth nothing in those days, the most important part of the contract involved decent housing. I worked out the details with the minister, Theodor Heuss, and I returned to Switzerland to tell Hedi our new life was about to begin.

Word of my success in Stuttgart reached Bauckner, who asked Kilényi to invite me back to Munich to conduct a performance of *Fidelio* there. *Fidelio* was performed a great deal in Germany immediately after the war, not only because of its theme of liberation from oppression and dictatorship but also for the practical reason that it doesn't require elaborate sets or costumes, most of which had been destroyed in the bombing. I returned to Munich because I hoped to get the position there, which was much more important than the one in Stuttgart. The remarkable cast for my second *Fidelio* included three of the people I had heard in *Die Walküre* with the Munich State Opera in Zurich a few years earlier: Helena Braun (Leonore), Franz Völker (Florestan), and Hans Hotter (Pizarro).

While I was working on this memoir, Professor David Monod, a Canadian historian, was kind enough to send me copies of documents he had uncovered in researching the role of American music officers in occupied Germany and Austria. Some of the information that he turned up I had either forgotten or never known. In an official report dated June 29, 1946, John Evarts, the U.S. music officer in Munich—the successor to Kilényi, and also a friend—wrote that following my *Fidelio* performance Bauckner had told him, "This is our man." Evarts himself declared that "the improvement in playing of the orchestra was little short of miraculous. Mr. Solti himself said that with only two rehearsals it was practically improvised, implying he could have made a much better job of it." I was glad to have read this document, half a century later, because it helps to explain why Bauckner offered me, an inexperienced, totally unknown conductor, the music directorship of the Bavarian State Opera. I said yes, signed the contract, and wrote an apologetic letter to Stuttgart.

There is a postscript to this story. A few years later, in Cologne, I conducted a concert that was attended by Indonesia's President Sukarno. Wilhelm Backhaus, who had been one of the judges at the Geneva competition in 1942, was my soloist in Beethoven's "Emperor" Concerto. At the postconcert reception, I met Chancellor Adenauer, who seemed brusque, in contrast to Theodor Heuss, first president of the German Federal Republic (West Germany), who greeted me warmly. To my great surprise, Heuss said to me, "Well, I suppose you don't regret not having taken the job in Stuttgart, do you?"

"Do you still remember that episode, Mr. President?"

"Yes, I do. I was very angry with you. In fact, I've never forgiven you."

THREE

MUNICH

I HAVE OFTEN been asked how I, as a Jew, could justify going to work in Germany after the unspeakable crimes perpetrated by the Nazi regime. For more than eight years, with the few exceptions I have already mentioned, my music making had been confined to the piano. The prime of my life, when, in normal circumstances, a young conductor would have been forming his career, had been wasted. The desire to conduct was an irresistible force in me: It was far stronger than anything else. (Sometimes, I think, like Faust, I would have been prepared to make a pact with the Devil and go to hell with him in order to conduct.) This does not mean that I had chosen to ignore the atrocities of the Holocaust, or what had happened to my fellow Jews and indeed to members of my own family. But in terms of my career I was effectively in a hopeless situation. I couldn't stay indefinitely in Switzerland, but where was I to go? The United States was overflowing with European conductors, so there was little point for me, with neither experience nor reputation, to make an attempt there, apart from which there was also the visa problem. Other countries were either not open to me or not worth considering. My home, Hungary, was in a desperate state, both politically and economically. Budapest had been literally blasted apart by the opposing Russian and German forces during the last months of the war. I had written to the director of the Budapest Opera, asking him if I could have my old job back. Understandably, he replied with a very abrupt note that said, "We don't need you. Stay where you are."

I was strongly influenced by the words of Winston Churchill, who came to Zurich and made the famous Rathausplatz speech, in which he said that Germany and France should forget the past and work as partners to build a new Europe. I firmly believed in the concept of a new Europe. Despite the horrors that had been perpetrated, reflection could alter nothing; we had to look forward. I still believe today, fifty years later, that our only way forward is through a united Europe.

I was incredibly lucky to have arrived in Munich when I did. Because of the de-Nazification process, the great conductors Wilhelm Furtwängler, Herbert von Karajan, Hans Knappertsbusch, and Clemens Krauss were banned from performing in Germany. A year or two later, when the position was relaxed and they were allowed to work again, a person with as little experience as I had could never have become music director of the Bavarian State Opera, one of the most important conducting positions in Europe. It was also fortunate that, from the Allied military government's point of view, there were no politically acceptable German conductors available at the time to fill the post.

Looking back, I believe subsequent events have proved that I did the right thing, once again reinforcing my belief in a guiding force in my life, my guardian angel. The timid fellow I was by nature had the courage to go to Germany, through the ruins by night in an open jeep, on the strength of a message. When I think about it now, it seems like a mad dream.

The entire repertoire of the State Opera had to be reconstructed from the bottom up. The bombings and fires that had destroyed the opera house had also wiped out all of the company's sets and costumes, as they had elsewhere. Every production had to be created anew, which meant that only three to six new productions could be put on each year. I was young enough, strong enough, ambitious enough, and talented enough to be able to learn one score while rehearsing another opera and conducting performances of yet another, but if I had had to deal with a full repertoire—ten or fifteen operas in a season—I wouldn't have survived. My career would have ended virtually before it had begun.

After the Munich *Fidelio,* the jeep took me back again to Switzerland, where I stayed until October, when John Evarts, the U.S. music officer, arrived with an open military truck to take Hedi and myself with all our belongings back to Munich. We had fourteen large suitcases filled with clothes, chocolate, tinned food, salami, and, most important of all, cigarettes. There was very little food for civilians, no heating, and no proper housing, and cigarettes were the only real currency at the time that could buy anything. Most people were living in the cellars of bombed-out buildings, without heat and running water. Evarts had found us accommodations—one small room on the first floor of a partially bombed-out building in the Maximilianstrasse, which was occupied by one or two other people and a milliner's shop that belonged to Frau Dathe. The city was cold, gray, and depressing. I believed it would take fifty years to rebuild Munich from its ruined state. How wrong I was! By the time I left, six years later, it had been transformed into a full-fledged city; today, barely more than fifty years after it was reduced to a pile of rubble, it is one of the most luxurious cities in Europe.

The Munich years were the happiest time of Hedi's and my life together. Her energy and intelligence were of enormous help to me. She gave me artistic advice and looked after the day-to-day running of our lives, exchanging cigarettes and theater tickets for fresh vegetables and other foods, which were in very short supply. The first winter was bitterly cold. During one rehearsal of the *Carmen* production, in the icy foyer of the Prinzregenten-Theater, one of the musicians noticed that when I worked, beads of sweat froze immediately into icicles on my head.

Everyone was hungry for music, and every performance was greeted by the most wonderfully enthusiastic public. One evening, as we were sitting in our little room in Maximilianstrasse, someone knocked on the door, saying, "I thought you might need this." He handed over a sack of coal, as precious to us as if it had been a sack of gold. Our benefactor was a Mr. Faltermeyer, a coal merchant from the outskirts of Munich, whose family were great opera fans and friends of one of the leading sopranos. Not only did we have gifts of food and fuel from time to time but I was given an official car, which had been confiscated from a black marketer by the German police. It was a green Opel, virtually without brakes. The Prinzregenten-Theater is on top of a hill; going up was no problem, but coming down was always an alarming experience. However, the situation didn't last for very long, as the original owner, the black marketer, stole the car back.

It was a heroic time, both for Germany and for me. Within a day or two of my arrival, in 1946, I had begun a series of discussions about the forthcoming season. There were serious disagreements between the conductor Ferdinand Leitner—who had been made a sort of codirector—and me, and these confrontations continued throughout the season. We met again much later in our careers, in Chicago in the 1970s, when he was conducting the Lyric Opera and I the Chicago Symphony. All the confrontations of the past had been put aside, and we spent many pleasant evenings together talking about the old days.

My debut as director of the Bavarian State Opera took place on November 1, 1946, with a performance of the Verdi Requiem. This was followed by three more performances of the Requiem, two lieder recitals in which I accompanied the soprano Helena Braun and the bass-baritone Ferdinand Frantz in works of Wolf, Brahms, and Richard Strauss, and two symphony concerts in which I conducted pieces by Haydn, Mozart, and Beethoven; in the Mozart work—the Piano Concerto in E-flat Major, K. 271—I was soloist as well as conductor.

The opera season proper opened with a performance of *Carmen* that almost did not take place, as Evarts's report of December 22, 1946, makes clear: "The premiere of Bizet's 'Carmen,' conducted by Georg Solti, is scheduled at present for January 3rd, but the lack of fuel may make it necessary to close the State Opera for the month of January. Steps are being taken to make adjustments for the emergency, but nothing definite can be said at this time." In the end, the fuel was made available, and the premiere took place two days earlier than originally planned, on New Year's Day, 1947. Helena Braun gave a wonderful portrayal of Carmen and it was an enormous pleasure to conduct her in the part; I couldn't help remembering the time I'd seen her in *Die Walküre* in Zurich. I would never have dared to think then that five years later I would be music director of the opera house where she was performing.

Besides *Carmen* and *Fidelio, Die Walküre* was the only opera I conducted during the 1946–1947 season, but I also presented further performances of the Verdi Requiem and three more concert programs—one of them to commemorate the fiftieth anniversary of Brahms's death. My complete opera repertoire during my directorship in Munich and elsewhere, later in my career, is listed in the appendix of this book; I shall mention here only the productions that remain most important in my memory.

During my second Munich season, we gave the German premiere of Hindemith's *Mathis der Maler,* which had been banned by the Nazis; Hindemith attended the rehearsals and the first performance. He was rather short and bourgeois-looking; he seemed more like a Swiss banker than a composer. I remember that when I was a coach in Budapest, we had performed his *Hin und Zurück* (*There and Back*), which began with a canary singing and climaxed with somebody dying; then the dead person stood up and the opera went all the way back again and ended with the canary singing. It was regarded as highly revolutionary at the time; certainly, Hindemith had had very revolutionary views in his youth, but by the time I met him, he was calmer, and he looked more like a Swiss banker. I remember him as a sweet, gentle person. Together with Arnold Schoenberg, Alban Berg, and Kurt Weill, he had been one of the main musical targets of the Nazis' attacks on what they called *entartete Kunst*—"degenerate art"—but after his immigration to the United States, he became a professor at Yale University and something of a Catholic religious mystic, and he had lost his revolutionary spirit. When he revisited Europe after the war, he toured several cities giving a lecture about the ethos of music. It was quite dry and academic in content, to say the least. I was told that after he had delivered the lecture in Zurich he asked if there were any questions, and Otto Klemperer, the conductor, who was in the audience, stood up—a tall, imposing figure—and said, *"Herr Hindemith, wo sind hier die Toiletten?"* ("Mr. Hindemith, where are the toilets?"), which sadly reflected his opinion of Hindemith's lecture. But his music was very interesting, and *Mathis der Maler* is a fundamentally fine and intense opera. While in Munich, I also conducted his wonderful *Der Schwanendreher,* for solo viola and chamber orchestra. The soloist was my fellow refugee Georg Kertész; we recently remet and enjoyed reminiscing.

The concerts I gave in Munich helped me to form a symphonic repertoire. The series of concerts given by the opera orchestra is one of the oldest in the world; it is called the Musikalische Akademie, and still continues to this day. In the series, I had the opportunity to work with some well-known soloists, including Adolf Busch, who played the Beethoven Violin Concerto. He was a fine, warm man, but his playing had declined by then and he was a shadow of the great player he had been. It is a sad thing for many violinists that with advancing years their muscle control and flexibility deteriorate, and they are no longer able to produce the technical brilliance for which they were once renowned. Age treats conductors more kindly. Strauss was the great example: He moved with difficulty and could not see or hear well, but his small gestures and brilliant conducting technique communicated everything he wanted to the orchestra.

I had the same experience with Joseph Szigeti as I had had with Busch; he played the same concerto with me but could no longer cope with the piece. In Szigeti's case, it was particularly sad, because I had heard him ten years before, when he was at the height of his powers. The wonderful pianist Alfred Cortot, who also appeared in one of the Academy Concerts, kept getting separated from the orchestra in the Schumann Piano Concerto, but with the outstanding skill of a great musician, he managed to find his way back before anyone noticed.

I also gave my first performance of Bach's *St. Matthew Passion* in these concerts. Nearly fifty years later, at a party at the German embassy in London, the ambassador revealed that he had been in the children's chorus in these performances, which had taken place in the Deutsches Museum. On one occasion at the museum, where both performers and members of the audience had to enter the auditorium through the main doors, I was prevented by the usher from going in as I did not have a ticket. (Concert tickets were in great demand at that time, as they were one of the few things that you could buy in those postwar days of austerity.) I said to the Cerberus, "I am the conductor!"

He replied, "Anyone can say that."

While I was standing arguing, my factotum, the orchestra porter, six-foot-three-inch-tall Herr Klinger, arrived and greeted me, saying, "Ah, there you are, Herr General," and so saved me from the usher, who, thinking I was a military general in civvies, bowed me through.

As money became more available in Germany and the situation improved, so did the performances at the opera. We even went on tour and performed Purcell's *Dido and Aeneas* and a concert at the Franconian Festival Weeks in Bayreuth, at the old Margrave Theater.

Thanks to my years at the Budapest Opera, I was already thoroughly familiar with the organizational side of a big opera company.

I knew how to set up rehearsal schedules, what preparations staging rehearsals require, how much time the conductor needs for working with each type of vocal ensemble, and how many orchestra rehearsals are necessary for certain works. This knowledge was a great help.

The orchestra musicians didn't realize that their new conductor was a beginner, and they accepted me graciously and generously. In those days, the State Opera orchestra was not as good, overall, as the Munich Philharmonic, but it had some extraordinarily fine players. There were an exceptionally good principal cellist, Mr. Uhl, principal horn, and trumpet players. The woodwinds were weaker, but the first flute was excellent. The chorus was good, even with respect to intonation. We had to use a great deal of initiative when it came to dressing them, as there was such a costume shortage. For example, the monks' costumes for the second act of *La forza del destino* became choir robes for performances of the Verdi Requiem.

I had three conductors working with me, including one who was really not good at all. As he conducted, turning the pages with one hand he would wait on the beat with the other. Ratjen, a very nice man from a banker's family, was another. I remember him as being tall and slim, with glasses; he knew his scores well but conducted without any emotion. The third was Eichhorn, a good musician who, however, never really learned anything properly.

My luck in getting the Munich job was equaled by my good fortune in having at my disposal what was probably the best vocal ensemble in Germany in those years. Basically, the company had been created during the war by Clemens Krauss, a musical disciple of Richard Strauss but a political protégé of Goebbels. For the Nazis, Krauss was a god. His opera house had every possible luxury; it was said that even the door handles in his production of *Rosenkavalier* had been gold-plated. Unfortunately, I can't confirm this rumor, as those sets, like most of the others, had been destroyed during the war. I never met Krauss. Once, when he was visiting Munich, a friend invited him to attend a performance of *Tristan* that I was to conduct, but he declined. A little later, a flute player in the orchestra told me that when Krauss had heard I was conducting *Tristan* for the first time, he said to him, "No one who is conducting their first *Tristan* can do it well"—and he was right to a point. But there are some amazing talents who are exceptions to the rule. Furtwängler, on the other hand, did attend one of my *Tristan* performances and told his secretary that I showed real promise.

But my attitude toward Furtwängler the musician is complicated. When I worked for Toscanini at Salzburg, I was so profoundly under his spell that I automatically considered Furtwängler wrong on every interpretive point. Later, I learned that there are many ways of making music, and I became more interested in Furtwängler's ideas. During the war, I heard him rehearse a Bruckner symphony with the Winterthur Orchestra, and I was amazed that he let this not very good ensemble play straight through each movement before he began to work on the details. I did not yet understand that this was the only intelligent method to use, *especially* with a second-class ensemble: Let the musicians get their bearings, or you will waste a tremendous amount of time. Later, I heard Furtwängler in Munich and Salzburg. After one of his Salzburg concerts, his face lit up with pleasure when I told him that the Vienna Philharmonic had played much better for him that evening than for Karajan the night before. As my opinion counted for very little, the joyousness of his reaction made me realize that his dislike of Karajan must have been intense.

I have since changed my mind again about Furtwängler. When I was recently restudying Beethoven's Ninth, I listened to his recording of the first movement and found it incredibly slow. There is enormous conviction and great power, but I now feel that the concept is wrong and that the work should be performed much more dramatically. Obviously, it is all a question of taste, and my disagreement over interpretation in no way diminishes my respect for this great conductor. I agree with Klemperer's statement to the effect that Furtwängler was not a natural opera conductor. He was a superb musician and he thought profoundly about music, but he didn't really "breathe" with singers. When he was in the orchestra pit, I always had the strange impression that he didn't quite belong there. But I learned a great deal from him about how to mold a phrase freely, which I hadn't yet learned from Toscanini. My aim has always been to combine strength with Furtwängler's freedom.

Furtwängler did not like the United States. When I told him once that I was going to be a guest conductor with the Lyric Opera in Chicago, he said, "Why? You should stay in Europe. Don't go!" I believe he was anti-American because he had been rejected by the board of the Chicago Symphony after the war. They felt that he had been a Nazi sympathizer, while he felt he had been unfairly treated and was a sacrificial lamb of the de-Nazification process.

When I arrived in Munich, there were many young German singers between twenty-five and thirty-five who faced the major career problem of not being able to travel abroad without the permission of the Allied military government. There was also virtually no public transport—no buses, no trains. By the time they were able to travel, many were no longer at their vocal peak. This meant that in the German opera houses, particularly in Munich, we had stable ensembles that worked and developed together. Nowadays, at so-called repertory theaters, performances of any given work are spread out over the course of a season, with various singers coming and going. Often, they don't know the production, or the conductor; they just sing and leave, and two days later other singers take their places. If a well-known singer is prepared to spend a whole month at a major house, everybody is delighted; it is the most one can hope for. But in those days, we had a permanent company of wonderful singers, and when I cast a production, I had the very best to choose from.

Hans Hotter must be singled out for special mention. Even now, in his eighties, Hotter is amazing. He is still able to sing—he sang at my eightieth birthday party, when he was eighty-three—and he is also a highly gifted teacher. But the young Hotter, with his full vocal power and striking appearance, was phenomenal. I am a quick learner, and if a singer has made an interpretive decision that seems to me better than my own I adopt it right away. In this respect, I learned a great deal from Hotter, especially when he was my Wotan in *Die Walküre*. Years later, when we recorded the opera together in Vienna, I asked him to sing a certain phrase in a legato style.

"I can't do it that way," he said.

"Hans, I learned it this way from you."

But his voice had matured and, great artist that he was, he had altered his phrasing and technique in order to accommodate the changes that had naturally occurred in his voice. Hotter is one of the most musical singers I know. He was enormously handsome, with a charisma and fascination that were irresistible. He had many fans, especially devoted ladies.

When Helena Braun sang the title role in *Carmen*—my first production as music director and one of the greatest musical pleasures I had in Munich—she was in her early forties; she had been a member of the State Opera since 1940, and she remained with the ensemble until her retirement in 1959. Her husband, Ferdinand Frantz, was one of the best-known Wotans after Hotter and also stayed with the company for a long time. Young Benno Kusche made his Staatsoper debut as Escamillo in the same *Carmen* production and went on to sing with the company for thirty years, although he also performed at other major theaters. Micaëla was sung by Elisabeth Lindermeier; a young Hotter pupil and a remarkable talent, she married the conductor Rudolf Kempe. When she stopped singing, she became a music critic in Munich. The Don José was sung by Lorenz Fehenberger, a Bavarian farmer's son and one of the most extraordinary tenor talents I have ever worked with. He had the musical instinct of a Domingo and an Italianate voice similar to Beniamino Gigli's. (We performed *Carmen* in German. It was only in the 1950s that the principal German houses somewhat hesitantly began to perform French operas in French and Italian operas in Italian.) Fehenberger, a deeply religious man, was an enchanting person—one of the first people I met in Munich who made me understand that many Germans had not been Nazi sympathizers. He gave a profoundly moving performance as the Evangelist the first time I conducted the *St. Matthew Passion,* and yet he had the ability to produce Don José's ferocious jealousy in the last act of *Carmen.*

Another production I remember with particular affection was *Salome,* which opened in September 1948. Annelies Kupper, an amazingly fine soprano who was just beginning to get into some of the heavier parts, sang the title role, and the Jokanaan was Hans Reinmar, a very good baritone. Later, our *Elektra* production featured the young Swiss soprano Inge Borkh in the title role. She was a Teutonic Callas—hysterical, a wild beast in every sense, but a brilliant singer. Maud Cunitz, another highly gifted soprano, joined the State Opera at about the same time Kupper and I did, and the two performed many roles with me, and remained with the ensemble long after I had left. All in all, in Munich I was able not only to learn my profession but to learn it with the best possible singers, and to develop an instinct for distinguishing good singing from bad.

I profited greatly from my work with the director Georg Hartmann, who succeeded Bauckner as the Munich Opera's general manager. He came from a family of theater managers and directors. Our first production together was *Mathis der Maler*. It was a naturalistic production, and we had enough materials available for our workshops to produce good-looking sets and costumes depicting seventeenth-century Germany. We worked very well together; he was a true professional and very musical. Our good collaboration continued on productions of *La forza del destino*, *Der Rosenkavalier*, *Don Giovanni*, *Boris Godunov*, and *Tannhäuser*. When I moved to Frankfurt, I invited him to produce another Hindemith opera, *Cardillac*. He taught me that one can produce an opera without distorting it or setting oneself above the composer.

MUNICH'S FAVORITE SON was Richard Strauss. I met him only three times, but he had a great influence on my professional life. Strauss had spent the immediate postwar years in Switzerland, where he composed his *Four Last Songs*, but he returned to his home in Garmisch, in the Bavarian Alps, shortly before his eighty-fifth birthday, on June 11, 1949. In honor of his birthday and homecoming, the Staatsoper put on a new production of *Der Rosenkavalier*. Strauss, whose health was frail, declined to attend any of the public performances, but he let us know that he would attend the dress rehearsal.

As a conductor first diving into this vast score, you feel lost, absolutely lost, in the mass of sound and action, and you are not sure how to deal with the problems of balance—balance within the orchestra and balance between orchestra and stage. If I had to do my first *Rosenkavalier* today with the composer in the audience, I would die of fear. At that dress rehearsal in Munich during the intermission between the second and third acts, a short news documentary was filmed, showing Strauss conducting for a few minutes. I have a copy of the film; today it amazes me to see myself—a young man, with hair—standing behind the elderly composer, who was born more than 130 years ago. As I brought him into the pit, he said to the orchestra, "Good morning, gentlemen." He then sat down, and I stood behind him, on his right. He asked me, "Where are the horns sitting?"

"The horns are on the left, the trumpets on the right, Dr. Strauss."

"I can no longer see or hear very well," he said. Then an astonishing thing happened: As soon as he began to conduct with his small beat, the feebleness of old age was replaced with power and control. He began with the waltz at the end of the second act, and just before Ochs's musical entrance Strauss, though nearly blind, automatically looked up at the stage and gave a cue with the instinctive assurance of a seasoned *Kapellmeister.*

Shortly afterward, I went to Garmisch to accompany a violinist in a performance of Strauss's Violin and Piano Sonata, in a small concert that was being given in honor of Strauss's eighty-fifth birthday. When we had finished, Strauss said to me, "I didn't know that you play the piano so well. Come and visit me. I would like to talk to you." My joy at that invitation was only comparable to the "*Bene*" I had received from Toscanini almost twelve years earlier in Salzburg.

Two or three weeks later I visited him at his home, and I brought along three scores: *Der Rosenkavalier, Elektra,* and *Salome.* When I rang the bell, the door was opened not by a servant but by Strauss himself. This was the first of two occasions in my life when I found myself reduced to utter silence. He took me into the room where he worked, overlooking the well-kept garden of his villa and the distant mountains. His worktable was in front of the window and it was very hard to imagine that these tranquil, orderly, bourgeois surroundings had been the birthplace of two of his most violent operas, *Salome* and *Elektra.* I stood there completely tongue-tied, clutching my scores. He sensed my nervousness, and, to put me at my ease, he asked me to sit down and tell him the latest gossip at the opera. His tactic worked, because once we were trading gossip, I lost my fear of him. In short, he treated me like a colleague, and I quickly overcame my shyness.

I asked Strauss how certain tempi in *Rosenkavalier* ought to be performed; he gave me an all-purpose answer. "It's very easy," he said. "I set Hofmannsthal's text at the pace at which I would speak it, with a natural speed and in a natural rhythm. Just recite the text and you will find the right tempi." I have followed his recommendation ever since and I have always found it correct that the natural recitation speed of the words in *Rosenkavalier* is always the right tempo; if you go a little too slowly here or a little too quickly there, everything becomes distorted. Strauss had a unique talent for setting words. He told me to conduct the waltz in one beat to the bar, not in three. "Don't do what Clemens Krauss so often does," he said. "He beats the waltz in three. Try to stay in one. This makes the phrasing more natural." This is, of course, much more difficult, but I've always tried to follow his advice.

Apart from these comments on the tempi in *Rosenkavalier*, he did not want to discuss his own music. He asked me, "Do you know *Tristan*?"

"Yes, I've conducted it," I said.

"Then tell me why it is that in the last chord of the opera all the instruments play except the English horn." This is true: Even the harp plays the last chord, but the English horn drops out for the last three bars, in B major. I couldn't tell him why. "The English horn represents the love potion," he said, "and by the last chord, when both Tristan and Isolde are dead, the effects of the potion have ended." I later reported the story to my dear friend Willi Schuh, the musicologist and critic who had "discovered" me in Zurich a few years earlier, and who was Strauss's friend and biographer.

"Oh, don't take it badly," Schuh told me. "He likes to trick everyone by asking that question."

Strauss was surprised when I told him that I loved Verdi's *Falstaff*; he was mainly a Mozart and Wagner man himself. I understand that when he was younger he said that *Falstaff* was a great masterpiece, but he must have had second thoughts in later years. At a more practical level, Strauss said something that I have found very useful ever since. "When you were rehearsing *Rosenkavalier*, did you ever leave the pit so that you could listen from the auditorium?" he asked. I said that I hadn't. "You really should have," he said, "because what you hear from your place in the pit is totally different from what the audience hears." From that day on, I have always done this, even in Bayreuth. I usually ask someone else to conduct the orchestra while I go out into the auditorium to listen and judge the balance. It is a worthwhile practice, not only for opera but also for choral and symphonic music, and I highly recommend it for my younger colleagues.

Strauss's second piece of advice was not to get too involved with the music, but to stay somewhere outside it—not to lack passion, but to be dispassionate in the execution. (This is good advice, although it's not always easy for me to remain "outside" the music.)

I spent about two and a half hours with Strauss, including lunch, for which his wife joined us. The daughter of a general, in her youth she had been the famous soprano Pauline de Ahna. Strauss had dedicated many of his songs to her, both before and after their marriage. She was famous for being strict and difficult, and to the end of her husband's life, she used to say, "I have made a mésalliance. I should have married an officer, not a composer."

While we were at table, Strauss asked me, "*Warum fuchteln Sie so, wenn Sie dirigieren?*" ("Why do you wave your arms around so much when you conduct?") "You beat too much and your gestures are far too big."

Frau Strauss immediately said, "Richard, you know perfectly well that you gesticulated terribly when you were young. The doctor even said you might damage your heart."

"Yes, it's absolutely true," he admitted, laughing. Everyone knows that the mature Strauss was a model of economy in his conducting gestures. He must have been quite wild as a young man.

Immediately after lunch, Frau Strauss said abruptly, "Young man, you must go now. Richard must take a nap."

He courageously protested. "Oh, don't send him away yet. Just a bit more time," he said. "I want to put some little drops of wisdom into him." I remember those words precisely. But she was insistent, and so I said good-bye. "Do come back in September," Strauss said. "We can talk some more." In particular, he wanted to talk about Mozart, and I would have loved to hear what he had to say about *Figaro,* which was his favorite opera, and *Così fan tutte,* which he was known to have conducted brilliantly. But he had a heart attack a few weeks later and died on September 8.

I conducted at his funeral. As he had requested in his will, the music was the final trio from *Der Rosenkavalier.* Marianne Schech sang the part of the Marschallin, Maud Cunitz was Oktavian, and Gerda Sommerschuh was Sophie. One after the other, each singer broke down in tears and dropped out of the ensemble, but they recovered themselves and we all ended together. I also conducted the Funeral March from Beethoven's "Eroica" Symphony; it can't have been very good, as I'd never performed it before. Afterward, Frau Strauss came over to thank me. She was heavily veiled, and the proud general's daughter had turned into a totally broken, weeping old woman. She died not long after, unable to live without her beloved Richard.

A few years ago, when I was conducting Strauss's *Die Frau ohne Schatten* at the Salzburg Festival, I spoke with his grandson. As we sat talking in a friend's garden, he told me that after the war his grandfather had despaired for the future of German opera houses, most of which were in ruins and the rest of which were an artistic and administrative shambles. Strauss thought this was the end—and in a sense it was, because the old German lyric-theater tradition died out within the following decade. But after my visit to Garmisch, he told his family, "This young man gives me a little hope." I hadn't known this and I was of course delighted to hear it forty-five years later. I think Strauss must have sensed my enthusiasm and determination to do as much as I could, as well as I could. But I regret very much that my time with him was so short, because his advice has been a guide for me throughout my entire career.

During the half century that has passed since my encounters with Strauss, I have conducted a great many of his orchestral works and operas. I never performed his early tone poem *Aus Italien,* but I did once do another early orchestral piece, *Macbeth,* and liked it very much at the time. Only with *Don Juan,* a brilliant Mozartian splash of orchestral verve, written when Strauss was in his early twenties, did he reveal himself as one of the great talents of his day. Equally brilliant are *Death and Transfiguration* and *Till Eulenspiegel,* which were followed by the larger-scale tone poems *Also sprach Zarathustra, Ein Heldenleben,* and *Don Quixote.* I haven't conducted *Don Quixote* for quite some time and mean to look at it again, but as for *Zarathustra* and *Heldenleben,* although I still admire them, I confess I sometimes tire of them, perhaps because I have conducted them so often. The *Sinfonia Domestica* is brilliant but a little bit old-fashioned, and too long. The *Alpensinfonie* is surprisingly uneven, considering that Strauss was at the height of his maturity when he wrote it, but I enjoyed recording it. I have conducted with great pleasure both of his horn concerti, the Oboe Concerto, and the *Four Last Songs,* which I think are miraculous. I have never performed the *Metamorphosen,* which is scored for solo strings. I may have misjudged it when I first heard it many years ago, when it seemed to me drawn out and boring.

I feel Strauss was at his greatest as an opera composer, and my favorite Strauss opera is *Salome,* whose originality and inventiveness fascinate me endlessly. I think of it as an exotic, perverse *Così fan tutte,* and I am always happy to conduct it. *Elektra* is also a masterpiece, but I go through phases with it: I love it for a while, and then I find it too heavy, musically and dramatically. If I have been conducting Wagner, I love *Elektra* as much as *Salome.* As with *Elektra,* so with *Der Rosenkavalier*—I have an up-and-down relationship: Sometimes I love it, but at other times it seems to me too sweet. I would like to do *Ariadne auf Naxos* again; I haven't conducted it for a very long time and I think it is one of Strauss's best operas. *Die Frau ohne Schatten* is one of his most massive works; some of it is incredibly beautiful and communicates a deep sense of inner peace, but other parts are too heavily orchestrated. At its premiere in Vienna in 1919, Strauss had at his disposal some of the great voices of the age, including the sopranos Maria Jeritza and Lotte Lehmann, and the baritone Richard Mayr, but today *Die Frau* is hard to cast: Such big voices are very hard to find. Even in the case of *Salome,* for that matter, finding a proper soprano for the title role has become a problem. Years ago, I did some concert performances of it in Chicago, with Birgit Nilsson. As we were walking off the stage after the first performance—which was a triumph for her—Birgit began to sing one of the Queen of the Night's coloratura passages from *The Magic Flute.* I laughed and asked her how she could bring off such a feat after having just sung so enormously demanding a role as Salome, and she answered, "Oh, I'm just testing my vocal cords." Despite all the heavy-duty singing she had just done, her vocal cords remained remarkably loose.

Salome, Elektra, Rosenkavalier, Ariadne, Die Frau, and probably *Arabella*: these are six Strauss operas that will remain in the repertoire forever, in my opinion. I have never conducted *Daphne, Die Liebe der Danaë, Die ägyptische Helena, Die schweigsame Frau, Intermezzo,* or *Capriccio.* To be truthful, the reason is that I have never really appreciated them enough. Strauss's two earliest operas, *Guntram* and *Feuer-snot,* I don't know at all.

ANOTHER COMPOSER I got to know in Munich was Werner Egk, a clever and elegant man whose work was controversial. His ballet *Abraxas* contained orgy scenes with simulated copulations onstage—unheard-of doings in the late 1940s. This gave it a considerable suc-cès de scandale in much of Germany but also earned Egk the hatred of Bavaria's archconservative burghers. His works have largely disap-peared from the repertoire, and I lost contact with him after I left Munich.

I also knew the Munich-born Carl Orff, who is remembered today almost solely for his *Carmina Burana.* He was a charming Bavarian and was nice to me because he sensed I had talent, and he hoped that I would become the great Orff conductor. Unfortunately, I didn't like his music, although some of his works are brilliant from a purely theatrical point of view. Early in 1951, I conducted the first Munich performances of his opera *Antigonae;* a recording of one of these performances exists, and it has recently been issued by the Munich Opera in association with Bavarian Radio. The work is written in a dreadfully repetitive style: Everything is stated fifteen times, so that eventually even the most idiotic member of the audi-ence says, "I get the point!" At one of the rehearsals, Orff asked me to do a certain detail differently. As he had stolen the passage in question from Stravinsky's *Oedipus Rex,* I said, exasperatedly and with infinite impertinence: "Oh yes, I know that bit, but in *Oedipus* it is much faster."

He laughed and said, "Bravo, bravo, very funny," but of course he was deeply insulted and never forgave me. I still feel badly about having been so rude to someone who, after all, was a skilled and pop-ular composer.

Karl Amadeus Hartmann, another German composer, was head of Musica Viva, an ancillary organization to the opera. He selected pro-grams of music that had not been performed in Germany since 1933, such as the work of Schoenberg, Berg, Anton von Webern, and Bartók—in other words, the composers of *entartete Kunst.* He was a Schoenberg pupil and wrote twelve-tone symphonic pieces that were not often performed in Germany. He didn't have much self-discipline, but he was jovial and loved both music and food. He and his brother Adolf, a successful painter, had both managed to survive the Nazi years, but unfortunately Karl Amadeus Hartmann died quite young, in 1963. He was a lovely fellow who had great joie de vivre.

I have always had difficulties performing experimental pieces and any music that falls outside my learning abilities, and for that reason I have never performed electronic music. I have made it a rule only to perform music for which I have the necessary technical expertise and understanding. I don't feel I am lacking in vision or initiative; after all, in my youth my colleagues and I were the protagonists of the then new music—that of Bartók and Stravinsky. Nowadays, as a member of the older generation of musicians, I prefer to leave the avant-garde to my younger colleagues.

After all, Bartók and his contemporaries were regarded as revolutionaries when I was young. There was confusion among the public then as there has always been for something new and outstanding. Mozart astonished the public with *Figaro,* after the performance of which, the emperor, his patron, made his famous remark, "Too many notes, dear Mozart." The first performance of *The Rite of Spring,* at the Théâtre des Champs-Elysées in Paris, in 1913, must have been an extraordinary event. Sybil, the Marchioness of Cholmondeley, whom I met in London when she was in her eighties, told me that she had attended that Paris performance, which had caused a near revolution. There was such a riot in the theater that it was impossible to hear the music over the shouts of the audience. She said to me, "It was such fun! Many of us jumped onto the stage and attacked the dancers with our umbrellas." Even in the 1940s and 1950s, when I first conducted Bartók and Stravinsky in Munich and Frankfurt, people could not understand the harmonic and rhythmic brilliance. For them, it was still revolutionary music, and they reacted in a hostile manner: There was very little applause and much booing. I don't think any composer today has had the same cataclysmic and revolutionary effect as Stravinsky with his *Rite of Spring.*

EARLY IN MY Munich years, I made my first recordings—though not in Munich. The story of my career as a recording artist begins in about 1945, when Max Lichtegg, a singer I had worked with in Zurich, introduced me to his friend Moritz Rosengarten, the head of Decca Records in Switzerland. A brief meeting took place at Rosengarten's modest office in Badenerstrasse; I said that I would very much like to make some recordings, but at first nothing happened. Then, on January 29, 1947, during a visit to Zurich in the middle of my first Munich season, I signed a Decca contract that called for me to record Beethoven's *Leonore* Overture No. 3, and, as a pianist, three Brahms sonatas, the Mozart sonata in B Flat, as well as Beethoven's "Kreutzer" Sonata with the splendid violinist Georg Kulenkampff— a German who had fled to Switzerland late in the war. I was to be paid thirty pounds, or five hundred Swiss francs, for each of the three sessions, and the contract was valid until the end of 1948.

The "Kreutzer" Sonata, my first recording, was made at Radio Beromünster's Zurich studio, and the producer was Radio Beromünster's music director, Rolf Liebermann, the future head of the Hamburg Staatsoper and Paris Opéra. I still played the piano well then, and I took naturally to the recording process; I was not nervous and the recordings were successful. With Zurich's Tonhalle Orchestra, I recorded Beethoven's *Egmont* Overture, instead of the *Leonore* Overture. In 1949, I went to London to record Haydn's "Drum Roll" Symphony and some overtures by Franz von Suppé with the London Philharmonic, and at that point my recording career really started.

Another important event in my career during my Munich years was my debut with the Vienna Philharmonic, when I conducted at the 1951 Salzburg Festival. The engagement came about through Bernhard Paumgartner, the musicologist and director of the Salzburg Mozarteum, who came to Munich and asked me to conduct a version he had prepared of Mozart's then rarely performed *Idomeneo*. We had a fine cast; I particularly remember that the Ilia was Hilde Gueden, whom I had met in 1939 on my way to Tauber's recital at St. Moritz. And the director, Josef Gielen—father of the conductor Michael Gielen—did a nice, sober production. He was a product of the theater, but he was very musical.

Unfortunately, I had my first run-in with the Vienna Philharmonic that summer. At the dress rehearsal, a handsome double-bass player arrived for the first time; I had never seen him before. I protested and said that he could not play the performances because he had not attended any of the rehearsals. When the dress rehearsal ended, he said to me, "I am the solo bassist of the Vienna Philharmonic, and you can't do anything about it. I am in any case much better than you are."

I liked *Idomeneo* very much but have never had the opportunity to conduct it since—though by chance, not design. That summer, Furtwängler conducted *The Magic Flute* and *Otello* at Salzburg, and he heard me conduct *Idomeneo*. Thanks to his recommendation, I was invited back to Salzburg a few years later.

LIKE EVERYONE ELSE, I suffered the privations of early postwar Munich. I was somewhat undernourished, as we all were, and I recall that once, after I had conducted an exhausting performance of *Tristan*, Herr Klinger, the orchestra's gigantic porter, had to push me up the five flights of stairs to my apartment. But this deprivation soon ended, as the overall economic situation changed.

In 1948, currency reform took effect, and every German citizen was issued the sum of fifty marks of the new currency. Consumer goods began to appear in shops that had previously been bare. Suddenly there was food, clothing, and furniture, and Munich began to emerge from its ruins. Hedi and I moved out of our single room in Maximilianstrasse and into a very pleasant apartment opposite the Prinzregenten-Theater, which meant that I was able to stroll to work every morning. By this time, we had a large circle of friends, who met either in our apartment or at a large one that overlooked the river and was rented by the American officers. Most of the opera people met there because there was always plenty of food and drink. I was in a very positive mood, as I felt I could really make my mark on the rebuilding of musical and operatic life in Munich. However, my optimism was short-lived.

At first, I was received warmly and with tremendous enthusiasm. I was a great favorite with public and press. Yet, despite all my luck, those years were extraordinarily difficult, mostly because I had to work so hard. I studied in the office all morning and rehearsed in the afternoon and evening. I was trying to make up in a rush for the missing years in my career, and this required a terrific struggle. I sometimes felt I was drowning, and it was only a perpetual will to work that got me through.

From the very beginning, I faced a certain amount of opposition from German musicians and music lovers, who objected to the presence of the American army's cultural organization and of a non-German at the helm of the Bavarian State Opera. The U.S. government documents clearly reflect the atmosphere. John Evarts's weekly report of April 10, 1947, to the Information Control Division of the Office of Military Government for Bavaria, said:

> On Easter Sunday, Monday and Tuesday, Hans Knappertsbusch conducted the Munich Philharmonic. . . . The concerts . . . were thronged with music lovers and Knappertsbusch admirers. It was an occasion, because it marked the conductor's first appearance publicly in Munich since he was cleared [of alleged pro-Nazi sympathies]. Music lovers were more than a little disappointed at the outrageous liberties that the conductor took with the symphonies [nos. 2 and 3 of Brahms] . . . but Knappertsbusch admirers were wildly enthusiastic about the full eye-and-ear-full [*sic*] which they received. An apparently well-organized clique raised their concerted voices at the end with cries of "We want Knappertsbusch back at the opera." A few Americans, ignorant of K.'s position in the hearts of his countrymen, wanted to know what all the shouting was about. "Is that guy really supposed to be good?" they asked.
>
> Internal events within the Bavarian State Opera organization have taken turns for the better and worse during the last weeks. The position of Generalintendant [general manager of both the opera and drama theaters] ceased to exist as of April 1st, and Dr. Bauckner withdrew from the general picture entirely—for the time being. It was announced that Opera Director Leitner would "take over the Intendanz [of the Bavarian State Opera]." Under "normal" circumstances this change would have seemed to make the situation ideal. But the circumstances were not quite normal or peaceful. The Ministry had not informed Mr. Solti of the proposed changes or of the probability that Dr. Bauckner would not take over [again] as Intendant of the opera. Concentrating on his music work, he was not au courant with political and administrative changes. During the past weeks, there had also been a growing disaffection and misunderstanding between the Messrs. Leitner and Solti. These have been caused by an accumulation of small things, misunderstandings and disagreements, aided and

abetted by the love which most theater people have for intrigue and gossip. Under the new set-up Mr. Leitner will have the power to alter Mr. Solti's musical plans if he wishes to do so. This, obviously, causes Mr. Solti much concern. Mr. Leitner, on the other hand, has had a tempting offer to take over the position of music director of the Stuttgart opera. He is at present weighing the advantages to be had in both positions. Then, there is a certain influential group which is very interested in getting Eugen Jochum into the position now held by Mr. Solti.

Leitner decided to go to Stuttgart—to take over the position that I had turned down the previous year—and that problem was resolved. The new intendant was Georg Hartmann. But how well I remember the hysterical screams of approval that greeted Knappertsbusch whenever he got near the podium. Coexisting with him was terribly difficult for me. Maybe I should not have taken his success as a negative criticism of my work: After all, he was my senior by nearly a quarter of a century, and an established figure, whereas I was a young newcomer with no reputation. I, too, was fascinated by him. In a way, he was a German version of Sir Thomas Beecham, with a personality so strong that it swept everything before it. He had tremendous control over an orchestra—his crescendos, for instance, were so powerful that they nearly knocked the house down—but I don't think he ever thoroughly mastered a score's details. He was notorious for not wanting to rehearse. Once, when he was rehearsing a Mozart symphony with the Vienna Philharmonic, someone in the orchestra begged him, "Dr. Knappertsbusch, please, at least let us play it through once before the concert." His reply was, "You know it; I know it. Why bother?" At the concert that evening, half the orchestra made the repeat in the first movement and the other half didn't; chaos ensued. Afterward, his comment was, "That's what comes of all your damned rehearsing." He had an exceptional musical personality and was a charming grand seigneur.

Eventually, I lost the struggle to keep my position in Munich. Hundhammer, the newly appointed Bavarian Minister of Culture, did have a certain sympathy for me, probably because he had taught German in Hungary, but because he was an arch-Catholic his natural affinity was with Germans of his own faith. Eugen Jochum, who was mentioned in Evarts's report, was a German Protestant who had converted to Catholicism, and these qualifications combined to make him Hundhammer's great favorite. There was an unwritten understanding that Jochum would succeed me in Munich, but, as I had acquired a tremendous following, the process of eliminating me had to be carried out gradually and subtly. Orff once said to me, "Solti, you must be tough if you want to survive. You must learn to survive. Nothing else is important. Don't go under." But I wasn't tough enough, and in the end the people who didn't like me managed to undermine my confidence.

In the spring of 1951, I was called into Hundhammer's office; sitting with him was Hartmann, the intendant, and Sattler, the undersecretary from the Ministry of Culture. (Sattler later became Germany's ambassador to the Vatican, during which time I saw him quite frequently, as his sister was a neighbor of mine when I bought a home in Italy.) The three men offered me a contract for three more years, but with drastically reduced powers. I had no alternative but to accept. From then on, I kept hoping that some other job would turn up, and it did—on the corner of the Prinzregentenstrasse.

One day, late in 1951, I was walking from the theater to my flat when I bumped into Harry Buckwitz, the director of the Munich Kammerspiele, a first-class drama theater. "I'm so glad to see you," he said. "I've been appointed general manager of the Frankfurt Opera starting next season, and I need a new music director. Can you recommend someone?"

"Yes, I can," I said. "Take me."

"Are you serious?"

"Yes, I am." And so it was decided, right there on the street. I resigned from my position as music director of the Bavarian State Opera. I knew new arrangements were well in hand when the new secretary of state for Culture, visiting me on some matter, said before he left, "You have a lovely apartment. I'm going to try to get hold of it for myself after you've gone."

In the late summer of 1952, before moving to Frankfurt, I had my first non-European engagement, with the Buenos Aires Philharmonic Orchestra. The invitation had come from a Mr. Schramm, a Bavarian who was head of the Buenos Aires concert bureau. I was tremendously excited: I had never flown before, and at Frankfurt airport I was received like a king by the Pan American Airways representative, Erich Bleich, who was later to become a friend. I was traveling alone—Hedi had stayed behind to organize our move to Frankfurt—and I thought the trip was sheer magic. It was a great adventure for me; today, I would be horrified by the distance, but then, in those prejet days, the endless journey, with stops in Lisbon, Dakar, Recife, and Rio de Janeiro, wasn't long enough for me. I sat in my first-class compartment, enjoying service and luxury for the first time in my life, and catching a glimpse of other countries. The figure of Christ on top of Sugar Loaf Mountain in Rio, viewed from the plane, was one of the most beautiful things I had ever seen.

The Philharmonic Orchestra played in a cinema, and in the middle of one of the first rehearsals the orchestra manager rushed in, shouting, "Stop! Stop! Revolution!" An anti-Perón revolt, complete with shooting, was taking place in the streets, and we were ordered to go home. Never much of a hero, I clung to each building along the route to my hotel. As always, I was hungry, so on arrival I telephoned Schramm and asked him where the nearest restaurant was. I didn't want to have to walk far, given the circumstances.

"No problem," he said. "When you come out of the hotel, turn left, and you'll see a restaurant almost in front of you, below ground level. I guarantee that you can eat well there, and I'll join you a little later." I did eat well, especially after the postwar restrictions of Europe. Food, particularly meat, was abundant in Argentina. When you ordered a small steak, something the size of a dinner plate arrived. I did, however, have some difficulty trying to communicate with the waiter in my nonexistent Spanish. When Schramm arrived, he said, "You could have spoken to him in German. He speaks it well. In fact, you could have spoken to him in Hungarian: He's from Budapest." And so my first revolution ended happily.

The rehearsals continued and the concerts took place as planned. The audiences were sophisticated—mostly European émigrés—and I found the Argentinians extremely friendly. One evening, accompanied by a beautiful young woman, a secretary in Schramm's office, I went to an opera performance at the Teatro Colón. It was unforgettable. As we walked into the beautiful auditorium, which looked like a larger version of La Scala, with tiers of boxes, I could almost feel the acoustics. I regret never having been back, because it is surely one of the greatest opera houses in the world. All in all, I felt very satisfied with my stay in Buenos Aires, but I must admit that throughout my time there I continued to hope that the Bavarian authorities would contact me urgently and ask me to stay in Munich.

On my way back to Europe, disaster nearly struck when the plane landed in Dakar. It was very hot and I went to the washroom in the airport, then sat in the restaurant and ordered a coffee. I suddenly realized that I had left my jacket and passport in the men's room. Because I was stateless, my passport was the most important document I possessed; without it, I might not have been able to get out of Dakar, let alone return to Germany. I rushed back, and by some miracle my jacket and the precious passport were still there. Ever since that day, I have appreciated what a privilege it is to have a passport, and I will always be grateful to both the German and British governments for granting me official status. I think anyone who has grown up in their native country and is issued a passport, automatically on request, can never fully appreciate the hopelessness of being without one.

With a heavy heart, I flew back directly to Frankfurt to start my new job. I was terribly unhappy about the move from Munich, where Rudolf Kempe, not Eugen Jochum, had succeeded me. I thought of Frankfurt as a demotion or punishment. I could not have imagined that I was about to begin one of the happiest and most productive periods of my life.

FOUR

FRANKFURT

F RANKFURT, better known today as an international financial and industrial capital, was, historically, a major artistic and intellectual center. Indeed, it was the birthplace of Goethe.

Frankfurt's opera house was destroyed during World War II and only reopened, as a concert hall, as recently as the 1980s. After the war, the first opera performances were given in the Stock Exchange, until a new, modern opera house was built in 1951, the year before I arrived. The new house had some acoustical problems, because the auditorium was high but not broad enough to allow the sound to develop. The company I inherited, despite the presence of a few good singers, lacked musical and real vocal quality. In Munich, I had learned a great deal, although I had been surrounded by the intrigues of musical politics. Now, at the age of forty, I could begin to shape an ensemble to my own taste, with no outside interference. The organizational skills that I had learned in Budapest and in Munich were soon put to good use.

The architect of my happy years in Frankfurt was Harry Buckwitz, the general manager, a clever, charming man who had started life as an actor and had subsequently run hotels in Africa and Poland. Immediately after the war, he had returned to his native Bavaria, where he became codirector of the best drama theater in Munich, the Kammerspiele, where I had met him. We became close friends during my stay in Frankfurt, and he directed one of the productions I conducted, a new *Fidelio* in 1959. He protected me from intrigue, never refused anything I asked of him, and helped me to develop as a music director. He was an ideal partner.

Much of Frankfurt still lay in ruins in 1952. Reconstruction was well under way, but conditions in the middle of town were still dire.

At first, Hedi and I rented a small apartment in the center, but in 1953 we moved into a house provided for me by the city. I paid a very low rent for a villa with a big garden, on the edge of the Schwannheim forest on the outskirts of the city. It was the first time in my life that I had lived in a house rather than an apartment. I loved the garden, the terrace, and the forest, which was laced with delightful tracks, and we would often walk deep into it with our two dogs, whom we both adored—a black cocker spaniel named Mixie and, later on, a beautiful English sheepdog, Ajax. We had another dog, a young boxer, who made a short *Gastspiel* ("guest appearance"): He was so unhappy that during the first night he ran around the house banging his head on the wall, so we had to take him back to the breeder the next morning. In the Schwannheim house— Löwenweg 4—I really felt at home for the first time since I had left Budapest, and our household affairs were enormously helped by the arrival of Frau Zador.

Emilie Zador was the widow of a Hungarian army officer who had died after the war, after returning from the Russian front. She had worked as a bookkeeper for a coal mine until, with her three young sons, she had escaped from Hungary immediately after the 1956 revolution. They lived in an Austrian camp for displaced persons, where she worked as a cook. She answered a newspaper advertisement that Hedi had placed when we were looking for a housekeeper. Initially, I wasn't at all keen on engaging her, because I didn't want to have anything to do with Hungary. I knew that I could never return, and the only way I could live with this knowledge was to block it out of my mind. Frau Zador, as we always called her (we always spoke German together, out of consideration for Hedi), arrived with her sons and remained part of the Solti family until her death in Hungary in 1997. She was buried in a country graveyard outside Budapest. Frau Zador was an exceptional person, totally devoted to her children and to my family; she was a modern Mother Courage. In Frankfurt, and later in London and Italy, she was a pivotal figure in my daily life, a woman of innate good taste in everything she did, a legendary cook whose goulash, strudels, and homemade chocolates will long be remembered. She was a true Hungarian patriot who, until the Communist regime ended, preferred to remain stateless rather than to adopt a new nationality. To change citizenship would have facilitated her life, but she felt it would also have demonstrated disloyalty to her beloved native country. The recording that I made in 1997 of compositions by my Hungarian teachers Bartók, Kodály, and Weiner is dedicated to her memory.

Hedi, assisted by Frau Zador, was an enormous help to me. She was a wonderful hostess, she loved people, and she invited both friends and acquaintances who would be useful to my career to our home, where she provided lunches and dinners with Frau Zador's delicious food. I was immensely proud of our home, which was beautiful. Every detail was impeccably planned for my comfort when I was working and for enjoyment in recreation, such as the volleyball matches and bridge games I played with my friends.

The only bad thing that happened at the villa was an attempted attack on me. In the opera company, there was a singer whose boyfriend was a member of the orchestra. She was very ambitious, but her voice was good enough only for supporting roles, and this neither she nor her friend would accept. One night I came home and found two men waiting in the shadows. Fortunately, a man with a dog came out of the next house, and the two men ran away. We reported the event to the police and I was given police protection for a few months. I always felt that the would-be attackers were hit men engaged by the orchestra player on behalf of his lady, because he was later heard to brag that he had given Solti a real beating.

My sister, Lilly, who was by now living on her own in Budapest, under difficult circumstances, came to stay with us. But it wasn't a happy solution. Lilly spoke little German, so she conversed with Frau Zador in Hungarian, which upset Hedi, who could not understand what they were saying. The two never got on well. Hedi had a different life: She was sophisticated and had a brilliant intellect. Lilly had a simpler view of the world, had lost all her family, including her parents, husband and, to a certain extent, me, and was living in the dark and restrictive atmosphere of Communist Hungary. I now know I should have intervened and tried to make a life for her with us in Frankfurt, but I was too preoccupied with my career and was afraid of scenes. Lilly didn't fit into our life as it was then; she felt unhappy and decided to return home. I have never forgiven myself for my lack of care for her.

MY FRANKFURT DEBUT took place on March 7, 1952, before my Munich contract actually ran out. We performed *Carmen,* an opera I've always loved. I believe it belongs in the group of great operatic masterpieces. I consider Bizet a major opera composer; an authentic genius of melodic, harmonic, and instrumental invention, he died at the age of thirty-seven, after having produced only one real masterpiece. His orchestration is so magnificent—he could paint a scene brilliantly with only a few masterly strokes—that it could be called Mozartian. The Prelude to Act I begins with a tremendous cymbal stroke, followed by the excitement of the crowd scene, the toreador's motif, the colorful crowd scene again, and the fatal ending passage. When the act opens, even before the chorus begins to sing the orchestra communicates the heat, the dust, the lazy atmosphere of a summer afternoon in Andalusia. There is such a difference in character between the Habanera and the Seguidilla, the nostalgic beauty of the Micaëla-José duet, employing the simplest, most concise means to combine lightness with such tragic fatalism. The entire *Carmen* takes less time to perform than the first act of *Parsifal.* I understand now why Nietzsche wrote that *Carmen* "approaches lightly, lively, politely. It is amiable, it does not sweat. . . . The good is easy, everything godlike runs on light feet. . . . First proposition of my aesthetics. This music is wicked, cunning, fatalistic: it remains at the same time popular. . . . It is rich. It is precise. It constructs, organizes, finishes, it is therewith the antithesis of the polyp of music, 'endless melody.' . . . *Carmen* dispenses with the lie of the grand style. . . . *Il faut méditerraniser la musique,*" Nietzsche concludes.

After *Carmen,* in early September 1952, I got to work on my first new production for Frankfurt: Verdi's *Otello.* The producer was Hans Hartleb, who created a simple production that gave the singers a situation. I found it favorable to produce the style, the dramatic impact, and the incredible variety, but I had to work hard to learn the music and to achieve at rehearsals the balance between stage and orchestra.

The orchestration of *Otello* is so heavy in certain parts that you must take great care not to allow the sound of the orchestra to overpower the singers' voices.

My Frankfurt company included many young singers. They did not have the experience and reputation of the singers I had worked with in Munich, but they had vitality. One of a music director's responsibilities is to foster the careers of young singers, while also helping them to develop technically and artistically. But there were also some singers whose voices were past their prime; in fact, some of these people sang quite badly and had to be handled with great diplomacy. During my first season, a fading prima donna came to me and said, "I would like to sing Aida next year." I knew that she could not manage the part, but instead of saying no right away, I foolishly told her that I would give the proposal some thought. Within a minute of having left my study, she went to Dr. Hallasch, the artistic planner, who had been Clemens Krauss's musical assistant and who worked successfully with me throughout my Frankfurt years. "Solti has promised me Aida. Give me the dates," the soprano told him. This incident taught me a lesson: A conductor must never tell singers anything but the truth. If you have to say no, say it outright. Some singers will hate you for this; it is of course hard for them, particularly when they are confronted with something they already know in their heart, but cannot face up to. One of the unfortunate elements of being a singer is that the voice does not last forever, and wise singers will retire at the right moment. The two great singers Renata Tebaldi and Dame Janet Baker both had the wisdom to do this, leaving the public with memories of them in their full vocal bloom.

Ernst Kozub, a splendid Wagner tenor from East Germany, was a member of the company, and I had problems with him similar to those I had faced with dear old Max Hirzel in Zurich and that I was later to face with Reiner Goldberg at Bayreuth. Kozub had a first-class voice, but he was unable to remember both music and text at the same time; he could manage either the music or the words, but never the two. Working on a role caused both of us great suffering, and yet he sang in many of my productions with great success; his voice was so beautiful, one of the best heroic tenors I have ever heard. Alas, he died when he was very young, before his international career truly blossomed. I remember him with great warmth.

Early in my Frankfurt days, I realized that many of the best young singers were coming out of the United States. A number of the previous generation's best singers and voice teachers had relocated there to escape the war, and they helped nurture the vocal talent in the many fine conservatories of their new country. I engaged so many young American singers that people made a joke about it. The opera in Düsseldorf was called Deutsche Oper am Rhein, while that in Frankfurt, because of the large number of Americans in the company, was known as the Amerikanische Oper am Main—(after the river in Frankfurt).

One of the finest of my American discoveries was Claire Watson, a lyric soprano. She had studied with the great Elisabeth Schumann but had then married a wealthy businessman and had had four children. She wanted to continue her singing and bravely decided to resume her voice training, coming to Europe to study in Amsterdam. She auditioned for me in Salzburg and I recommended her to Buckwitz. When I brought her to Frankfurt, in 1955, her whole family moved there with her. She was still only twenty-eight. Her husband hated Frankfurt and left, taking the children with him. Although the children often visited their mother, the family was destroyed. I have always felt guilty about this, because I was the music director who gave Claire her first major contract. But since she went on to sing at most of the big European opera houses as well as at the Met, I imagine that if I hadn't engaged her, someone else would have. Following her divorce from her first husband, Claire married David Thaw, a lyric tenor who was another of "my" Americans. They met in a performance of Haydn's *Creation*. Alas, she died early, at the age of fifty-nine. I remember her as an exceptionally fine singer, a lovely person, and a friend. I loved her dearly.

Another young American singer was a lovely light lyric soprano from Florida, Sylvia Stahlman, who sang in my first recording of Mahler's Fourth Symphony. She was an enchanting person with a wonderful sense of humor; we became close friends and she, together with Claire Watson and David Thaw, was a regular visitor at our home in Schwannheim.

The other outstanding young soprano I worked with in Frankfurt was Anny Schlemm. I engaged her for *Cardillac* when she was only eighteen. She was a delightful Pamina in *The Magic Flute* and

Zdenka in *Arabella*. Thirty years later, she sang the part of the Witch for my recording of *Hänsel und Gretel*, and I understand that she is still singing professionally, nearly forty-five years after I first engaged her.

One day in the late 1950s, an aspiring eighteen-year-old soprano came to audition for me. I asked the usual question: "What would you like to sing?"

She answered, "I can do three things: the *Liebestod* from *Tristan* and Pamina's aria and either of the Queen of the Night's arias from *The Magic Flute*."

These three roles require three different soprano voices: Isolde, a dramatic soprano; the Queen of the Night, the highest coloratura soprano in the repertoire; and Pamina, the most beautiful light lyrical voice. I was so amazed that I said, "All right, let me hear all of them." She sang all three with great confidence and distinction: She had the top notes, the bottom notes, and the middle notes, and she was a brilliant actress, too. It was the most astonishing audition I have ever heard, and I asked Buckwitz to engage her immediately. Her name was Anja Silja.

Anja did not stay long in Frankfurt, however, because she soon fell in love with Wieland Wagner, the composer's grandson and a brilliant régisseur (stage manager), who was producing his celebrated "New Bayreuth" stagings of his grandfather's works. He gave her all the major Wagnerian roles—Senta, Kundry, Isolde—and worked with her in other theaters, as well. She achieved the remarkable feat of singing the roles of both Venus and Elisabeth in the same *Tannhäuser* performance. She had a highly successful international career, and we have worked together several times over the years. After Wieland Wagner's death, she married Christoph von Dohnányi, whom she had first met in Frankfurt.

Among the many interesting acquaintances I made during my Frankfurt years, I particularly enjoyed meeting Thomas Mann, then, and now, one of my favorite writers; there was a time when I reread *Joseph and His Brothers* every summer. He came to Frankfurt and gave a lecture on Gerhart Hauptmann. Before and after the lecture, I conducted two short pieces by Mozart. Afterward, the city gave a lunch in his honor at the Frankfurter Hof, and I sat beside him. He was a great music lover, and I was flattered when he said to me, "I didn't know there was such good music making in Frankfurt. I must come here more often."

One year, while Hedi and I were on holiday in Switzerland, I met the writer Hermann Hesse, who was also staying in the Waldhaus Hotel in Sils-Maria. The Soviet Union had just launched its first orbiting satellite, and the hotel manager invited us up to the roof to watch it. As we looked up at the tiny starlike speck moving across the sky, Hesse said, "A new epoch has begun this evening." How right he was.

The most fascinating of my Frankfurt acquaintances was probably Theodor Adorno. Although he is remembered primarily as a social philosopher, Adorno had studied music with Alban Berg and the pianist Eduard Steuermann, and he wrote a great deal about twelve-tone music. In his mid-twenties, he had joined the Institute for Social Research in Frankfurt, his hometown, but he had been forced to flee Germany when the Nazis came to power. After a fifteen-year stay in the United States, he returned to Frankfurt and to the reorganized institute, where he remained until his death. He was nearly ten years my senior, highly educated, and brilliant. I loved his company and enjoyed listening to him talk.

As a writer on music, Adorno is remembered, above all, for championing Schoenberg's and Berg's music, but his musical tastes were broad: His knowledge of Mozart's operas was profound, and he came to the Frankfurt Opera's performances of Verdi, Wagner, Strauss— whatever we put on the program. I owe him a great deal. One day, he said to me, "You must conduct Mahler. It's perfect for you." I was not at all convinced at that time that Mahler was a major figure. Adorno persisted and gave me some extremely rash but probably excellent advice: "Why don't you start with the Ninth Symphony?" he said. In a way, it was foolish of me to start with Mahler's most difficult work, but its complexity fascinated me immediately. The Ninth's structure eluded me at first, but I quickly came to like it; and after having done one Mahler symphony, I was impatient to do all the others. When I told Adorno that Bruckner's symphonies always put me to sleep, he insisted that we play the Seventh on the piano, in a four-hand arrangement. He was an excellent pianist and I enjoyed the experience. I began to study the Seventh seriously, and soon I was adding not only Mahler but also Bruckner symphonies to my repertoire.

Adorno also helped me understand the greatness of Schoenberg's

Moses and Aaron. I was unable to schedule it in Frankfurt, but I later conducted its London premiere. He persuaded me to perform Berg's *Lulu* in Frankfurt, and we brought off the difficult task with great success. I asked Adorno, who had known Berg well, to say a few words about the opera and its composer before the first performance, but, to my great dismay, I forgot to ask him to speak for less than five minutes: People go to the opera to hear music, not to listen to speeches. He went on lecturing in a professorial manner for fifteen or twenty minutes. I was already in the pit with the orchestra, the singers were onstage, ready to begin, and the public became more and more restless. Finally, when people began to shout "*Aufhören!*" ("Stop!"), he brought his talk abruptly to a close. As he left the stage, he had tears in his eyes.

IN 1953, I made my first visits to the United States. Interestingly enough, given the turn my career eventually took, my North American debut was originally scheduled to take place at the Ravinia Festival, in the summer of 1952, with the Chicago Symphony Orchestra. But my U.S. visa application was turned down. The American consul in Frankfurt kindly explained that my visa had been denied because I was listed as belonging to the Soviet Friendship Association, a Communist organization. I couldn't understand how this could be, as I had never belonged to any political group.

Fortunately, I knew a Dr. Müller, the Minister of Internal Affairs, and he telephoned the police in Munich to authorize them to show me the document. This document turned out to be a list, prepared by this Communist organization, of prominent non-Communists in cultural life who were to have propaganda material sent to them. With that information in hand, I went back to Frankfurt and explained to the American consul that the list they had seized was not a list of members of the Communist party, but merely a mailing list of people in cultural life.

Joseph McCarthy, the notorious United States senator, was carrying out his anti-Communist witch-hunt during those years; the slightest whiff of interest in communism was enough to wreck the lives of American citizens, let alone the visa applications of those born in Eastern Bloc countries.

Indeed, in the late 1940s, representatives of the U.S. military government in Bavaria had informed me that if I wanted to maintain my position in Munich, I would have to give up my Hungarian citizenship; by then, Hungary had become a Soviet satellite state. I was not sad about renouncing my original nationality, but being stateless for the next few years presented endless bureaucratic complications. In the end, the West German government kindly offered me German citizenship, which I gratefully accepted, and I remained a German national for nearly twenty years.

Eventually, I got my U.S. visa, but it came so late that I had had to cancel my Ravinia engagement. However, my American debut took place the following summer, in 1953, when I conducted the San Francisco Opera. At that time, the opera orchestra drew on players from the San Francisco Symphony, which from 1936 until 1952 had been directed by Pierre Monteux, one of the most brilliant conductors of the first half of the twentieth century. I met him later in Frankfurt, when he conducted one of the museum's concerts.

I always love to tell the following story about him, so typical of a professional musician. He conducted the love scene from Berlioz's *Romeo and Juliet,* and after the performance, his wife, Doris, kissed him and said, "Darling, it was so wonderful. Were you thinking of me?" To which he replied, "No, I was thinking of Eleanor Roosevelt."

In San Francisco, I was delighted to work with an orchestra that played at a much higher standard than that of Munich or Frankfurt. My repertoire consisted of *Elektra, Die Walküre,* and *Tristan.* The bass who sang the role of King Marke in *Tristan* had a beautiful voice but was a boring interpreter. During a guest performance in Los Angeles, in the middle of one of Marke's long pianissimo passages, accompanied by the bass clarinet, a man sitting directly behind me in the audience said loudly, "That's enough!" The orchestra and I began to laugh until we nearly lost control of ourselves. It was one of the funniest things that has happened to me in all my years as an opera conductor, all the more because the man was absolutely right.

Apart from this incident, the San Francisco performances went well, and so did the performances that I gave with the orchestra when we went on tour to Los Angeles.

I returned to California in January 1954, to conduct three pairs of concerts with the San Francisco Symphony Orchestra. At a reception after one of the concerts, a good-looking woman came up to me and said, "I hear that the concert went well."

"Weren't you there?" I asked.

"Oh, no, I only go to the cocktail parties," she replied. At least she was honest.

In San Francisco, I first met Kurt Herbert Adler, the opera's Vienna-born artistic director, who was supportive and encouraging, and later on, in the 1970s, I had a close friendship with him and his young wife, Nancy. Other good friends in San Francisco were the Schwabachers, a prominent local family, and their friend John Scott Trotter, a protagonist of the popular music field in the United States during the forties, fifties, and sixties and a close collaborator of Bing Crosby. John was such a celebrity that I became well known as John Scott Trotter's friend, and only secondly as a conductor.

I conducted another pair of San Francisco Symphony concerts in 1960, but after that, I did not work with the orchestra again until 1995, when I was enchanted with its freshness and vitality. Herbert Blomstedt, the Swedish conductor who had been in charge for several years before that, must be a remarkable orchestra trainer, because the San Francisco Symphony is now virtually on a par with the so-called Big Five American orchestras: Chicago, Cleveland, Boston, Philadelphia, and New York. I know that it will continue to do well with its new music director, Michael Tilson-Thomas.

My long-delayed debut with the Chicago Symphony took place at Ravinia in August 1954, two years later than originally planned. In one of the concerts, the violinist Ruggiero Ricci and the cellist Paul Tortelier played the Brahms Double Concerto, but as a result of the intense humidity in the park, Tortelier's bow slipped during the cello's opening cadenza. He stopped, shook his head, and kept on repeating, "No good, no good," until we started again.

These performances with the Chicago Symphony Orchestra in Ravinia were an absolute joy. I still remember the performance of Beethoven's "Eroica" Symphony during our first concert—the most wonderful musical experience of my professional life up to that time. The orchestra's music director was another Hungarian, Fritz Reiner, who, along with George Szell in Cleveland, Antal Dorati in Dallas, and Eugene Ormandy in Philadelphia, was one of the Hungarian conductors who helped build the excellence of today's modern American orchestras. Even more than the much-feared Szell, Reiner was infamous among orchestra musicians for his dictatorial behavior. But he did marvelous things for the Chicago Symphony. Despite the imperfect acoustical environment of Ravinia at that time, I had no doubt that this was the finest ensemble I had ever conducted.

The poor acoustical situation was made worse by Ravinia's proximity to the local train station. The train would invariably arrive on the hour, blowing its whistle during the most delicate pianissimo. This happened to me during the slow movement of the "Eroica" in a pianissimo we had diligently worked to perfect. The train arrived, joyfully blew its whistle, and departed, taking my pianissimo with it. Sir Thomas Beecham used to describe Ravinia as the only railway station in the world with its own symphony orchestra. But that's where my love affair with the Chicago Symphony Orchestra began.

I asked my American agent, Siegfried Hearst, to do everything possible to have me reengaged in Chicago, and I returned to Ravinia in the summers of 1956, 1957, and 1958. During one of those seasons, a young woman, Margaret Hillis, arrived to prepare the chorus for Haydn's *The Seasons*. She was destined to become one of the world's great chorus masters, and we had a very close and successful collaboration in my future years with the Chicago Symphony. We also made many choral recordings together.

As a result of my first Ravinia appearance, I was invited to conduct the Lyric Opera of Chicago during their 1956 and 1957 seasons. The performances took place in the Civic Opera House on Wacker Drive. The acoustics were bad. Rather than coming from the stage, the sound always seemed to come from behind me in the auditorium. That is now a thing of the past. The auditorium has been refurbished, resulting in a great improvement to the acoustics. And, with the passage of time, it has come to be regarded as a fine example of Chicago architecture of the 1930s.

What struck me most about those engagements in the 1950s was the roster of singers: Inge Borkh and Ramón Vinay in *Salome;* Renata Tebaldi, Giulietta Simionato, Richard Tucker, and Ettore Bastianini in *La forza del destino;* Tito Gobbi, Walter Berry, Anna Moffo, Eleanor Steber, and Simionato in *The Marriage of Figaro;*

Jussi Bjoerling in *A Masked Ball;* and Gobbi, along with his brother-in-law, Boris Christoff, in *Don Carlo.* There was also the young Birgit Nilsson making her debut in *Die Walküre.*

One young member of the chorus was destined for stardom, but not on the stage. Ardis Krainik became general manager of the Lyric Opera and brought it back from near bankruptcy to become a leading player in the international opera world. She hired first-class artists, raised millions of dollars, was loved and respected by all her colleagues and staff, and improved those dreadful acoustics beyond all recognition.

In the 1950s, Carol Fox was the Lyric's general manager. She wanted me to become the company's music director, and I gave the proposal serious consideration. But after my first *Figaro* performance, in 1957, Claudia Cassidy, the *Chicago Tribune*'s chief music critic, wrote that I had conducted the finale of Act II with a smile on my face, whereas I would have done better to cut my throat. Had she written a generally fair-minded appreciation of my conducting, no lasting harm would have been done. But her viciousness wrecked my chances with the Lyric Opera, because Fox needed Cassidy's endorsement. In my experience, Cassidy was one of the worst examples of a music critic who kept her position not because she knew anything about music but because she stirred up controversy, which sells newspapers. She was an untouchable institution in Chicago, and people eagerly awaited her columns, anxious to find out who her next victim would be; musicians were her cannon fodder.

When Rafael Kubelik, a brilliantly gifted conductor and a sincere musician, took over the Chicago Symphony in 1950, he became one of her victims and was forced to leave after only three seasons. Kubelik's experience was only one among many examples of the way in which Cassidy's warped influence affected the city's musical life. Kubelik was young, unappreciated, and unable to deal with her negative influence on unthinking public opinion. She could well have ruined my chances with the orchestra in 1969 had she not been out of the picture by then.

In March 1957, I made my debut in New York with the Philharmonic, conducting seven concerts at Carnegie Hall and working with three gifted soloists: the pianists Clifford Curzon and Rudolf

Serkin, and the violinist Erica Morini. Curzon was an outstanding musician but a nervous man, and I made a terrible psychological error with him. When he asked me why I had decided not to pursue my career as a pianist, I told him about the memory problem I had had at the Geneva competition. The story of my memory lapse made such an impression on him that by the time of the concert that evening he was a nervous wreck—despite which, he played well. For me, this was an early lesson in diplomacy when dealing with artists, whose nerves can significantly affect a performance.

My relations with the Philharmonic left a great deal to be desired. I have a specific talent: I can make any orchestra play to the limit of its capacity, but only if the players are willing to make an effort. In those days, the Philharmonic musicians were rather unwilling, and I was unhappy working with them. I did not return until five years later. My first concert then took place on January 4, 1962, and I began the first rehearsal by saying, "What a good omen it is for me to be starting the New Year with you."

The principal violist stood up and said, "You say that sort of thing to every orchestra."

I always had a close friendship with the Philharmonic's manager, Carlos Moseley, who wooed me to take over the music directorship in the mid-1970s. I flirted with the idea for a few weeks, but I couldn't leave Chicago. New York had a higher international profile at that time, but I knew Chicago was my orchestra and that with patience it would gain the international recognition it deserved as a leading player in the world symphonic league. For many years, I didn't conduct the New York Philharmonic, but in recent years, my appearances have been most agreeable experiences, which I hope to repeat.

For better or for worse, symphony orchestras cannot function as democracies. In this respect, Leonard Bernstein, despite his musical brilliance and charisma, made some mistakes as a musical director, in my opinion. He was of course an exceptional musician and conductor as a guest artist, but as the boss of an orchestra, his particular style didn't always work. He encouraged the orchestra members at the New York Philharmonic to call him Lenny. Conductors may and should have friends in an orchestra, but onstage, there must be distance between the orchestra and the conductor; otherwise, the rehearsals and performances simply don't work. It's really the same sort of situation as one would find on board a ship: There has to be a captain, one person clearly in charge.

In 1957, the year of my New York Philharmonic debut, I began to strengthen what was to be a long and fruitful relationship with the Vienna Philharmonic. We had first worked together in 1951, when I had conducted *Idomeneo* at the Salzburg Festival, and in 1955 and 1956, I had returned to conduct *The Magic Flute* with them. But my first major task with the orchestra was to record the *Todesverkündigung* and Act III of *Die Walküre*, with Kirsten Flagstad, Set Svanholm, and Otto Edelmann, and Strauss's *Arabella*, with Lisa Della Casa, Hilde Gueden, Anton Dermota, and George London. Unfortunately, the orchestra and I did not get along.

I freely admit that part of my difficulties in Vienna were of my own making. Although I was forty-five years old, I had only eleven years of solid conducting experience behind me, and I had worked mainly with second-rate orchestras. Conductors who are unaccustomed to working with first-rate orchestras are often so intent on proving themselves that they do not hear the good things an orchestra can produce without being asked. I had not yet learned that as a conductor, one's first task is not to stamp one's own personality on everything, at whatever cost, but to listen. Today, if an orchestra gives me something that is better than what I had in mind, I recognize it and gratefully adopt it, but forty years ago, I did not understand such things.

Another problem was the result of scheduling necessities. Many of the Vienna Philharmonic's members rehearsed at the State Opera in the morning and performed there in the evening. The only time available for our recording sessions was from two to five or from three to six in the afternoon. Most Viennese eat a heavy lunch; thus, the musicians were feeling anything but lively and ambitious when I was jumping up and down, ready to conquer the world.

The difficulties began immediately, with the famous "Ride of the Valkyries," which opens the third act of the Wagner opera. The brass played the main motif sloppily, making the dotted eighth note too short and the sixteenth note too long. Their attitude was: When it comes, it comes. I insisted that they play the rhythm correctly—and they hated me for it. They hated me because I knew what I wanted and made specific demands of them. Whenever we differed on a point of interpretation, they automatically assumed that I was wrong. Among other things, I demanded that opening chords be played precisely together, whereas they felt that a chord that isn't precisely together sounds "warmer." To me, it is slovenly.

For a long time, the Vienna Philharmonic treated me with a "we know better" attitude. Our relations bottomed out while we were rehearsing *The Magic Flute* for the recording we made together in 1972. One of the first violins stood up in the middle of a certain passage, said, "I can't take this any longer!" and walked out. I proceeded with the rehearsal as if nothing had happened, but inwardly I was shattered. I know that some conductors abuse their power or behave with unwarranted arrogance, but orchestra members can be just as cruel and cause just as much hurt. For many years, I used to say that my favorite street in Vienna was the road to the airport. I was always so glad to leave.

Despite our past temperamental and philosophical differences, the Vienna Philharmonic and I made many superior recordings together, especially in the years before I went to Chicago. The first complete studio-recorded version of Wagner's *Der Ring des Nibelungen* is often mentioned as a milestone in the history of the recording industry. The story of the making of the recording was well told by John Culshaw, who produced the recordings, in his book *Ring Resounding,* and also by Humphrey Burton in his 1965 television documentary *The Golden Ring.* Strangely enough, the whole enterprise was the result of chance rather than of careful planning.

Culshaw had heard me conduct *Die Walküre* during a visit to Munich in 1950 and had decided then that he wanted to record the entire *Ring* with me. Given the fact that we were both at the beginning of our careers, his determination was remarkable. Nothing happened until I recorded the *Todesverkündigung* from Act II and the third act of *Die Walküre* in Vienna in 1957. The recording was well received, and I went to Zurich to discuss future plans with Moritz Rosengarten, Decca's Swiss director. "We are so pleased with the *Walküre* results," he said, "that we have decided to record the whole opera—with Knappertsbusch." I was shattered when I heard this news. Of course Knappertsbusch was a star and I wasn't, and stars were needed to sell records. The recording didn't get far, however. After the first session, Culshaw asked Knappertsbusch to come to the control room and listen to what had been recorded.

"Listen to it? But I've just heard it!" It was immediately clear from this remark that his and Culshaw's working methods were not compatible. The sessions stopped after the first act had been recorded. Knappertsbusch withdrew. Culshaw quickly persuaded Rosengarten to record *Das Rheingold* instead, with me conducting. Culshaw and I engaged a first-rate cast, including Kirsten Flagstad.

The recording was made in Vienna in 1958. On the eve of the first session, Culshaw and I met in the bar of the Hotel Imperial to discuss the following day's work; and while we were talking, in walked Walter Legge. At that time, Legge was a tsar of the European music scene: He was head of the EMI recording empire, managing director of the Philharmonia Orchestra—England's best symphonic ensemble at the time—and a major force at the Royal Opera and in other important musical organizations. He was a brilliant talent scout: Karajan, Géza Anda, and Elisabeth Schwarzkopf (Legge's wife) were among the many artists whose international careers he had helped to launch, and he had once come to see me in Frankfurt to try to lure me from Decca to EMI by promising me various artistic and financial advantages. I did not take the bait because I did not trust Legge, who was known to play conductors, instrumental artists, or singers off against one another. For purely economic reasons, Legge did not believe in recording much Wagner; with Furtwängler, for instance, he only made *Tristan* and *Walküre*.

Oddly enough, Legge and Culshaw had never met. I introduced them, and then Legge turned to me and asked, "What are you doing here, Solti?"

"I'm recording *Rheingold*. The first session is tomorrow."

"*Rheingold?*" He looked at Culshaw. "A beautiful work, but you won't sell fifty copies."

How wrong he was. We worked long and hard, musically and technically, and when the finished recording came out, it was like a fireball—it created a sensation. It has never been out of the catalog since the day it was issued.

I had hoped that I would be invited to complete the *Walküre* recording, but this was not the case. Moritz Rosengarten was also

RCA's European distributor, and he made almost as much money from distributing RCA as from his entire Decca investment. George Marek, a vice president of RCA, informed Rosengarten that RCA was bringing out a new *Walküre* recording under Leinsdorf's direction, and he pointed out that Rosengarten would be competing with himself if he financed a Decca recording of the same opera. When Culshaw protested that they had already asked me to record *Walküre*, Rosengarten told him to record *Siegfried* with me instead. It was only a few years later, when Rosengarten saw the continuing high sales figures for our *Rheingold* set—and perhaps also when many music lovers and critics began to urge Decca to finish the series—that he finally agreed that Decca should do its own *Walküre* after having recorded *Götterdämmerung*. The whole cycle was completed in 1965. Thus, the grand *Ring* project actually came about in a rather haphazard way. But the results were well worth the effort and heartache. As I prepare this book for publication, nearly thirty-two years after the last notes of our *Ring* were put on tape, the whole set is about to be remastered, with the latest techniques, and reissued for a new generation of listeners. It will also appear on CD-ROM.

Culshaw was an enthusiast and a man of musical vision and taste, but not a technician. The technical mastermind behind the recordings was Gordon Parry, a highly talented engineer. I was lucky to have with me, in my early recording career, these two remarkable men, who gathered around them an outstanding team. Although we inevitably had some differences of opinion, together we created an artistic combination that produced highly successful and interesting records.

At Decca, Culshaw was eventually succeeded by Ray Minshull, whose first recording with me (and the Vienna Philharmonic) was Schumann's Second Symphony. When we sat down to listen to the first playback—a moment when a performer welcomes a glimmer of encouragement—Ray's comment was: "That's awful!" But by the end of his tenure at Decca, he and I were getting along well, and he let me record virtually anything I chose. In the long run, I think I was right to have remained faithful to Decca instead of succumbing to temptations to move to EMI or other companies. Decca has made many mistakes, but none of them were malicious; they were all connected with weakness in marketing. I have always felt the English are not good at selling. I was never given anything even vaguely resembling the promotion that EMI gave Karajan, or that Deutsche Grammophon later gave Karajan, Bernstein, and Karl Böhm. But Decca makes the best-quality, best-engineered recordings, and for real music lovers, this is the highest form of promotion. My recording sessions have been entirely the result of teamwork and I shall always be grateful to my collaborators at Decca. I was never asked to work more quickly than I wanted to work or to compromise on quality in any way. I have made over 250 recordings for Decca, and the international catalogs still contain surprisingly large numbers of them. I'm very proud that I have completed fifty years of international recording with Decca. At a party given by the company at the Royal Academy in London to celebrate the occasion, I was presented with a copy of my first two contracts.

BEFORE the *Ring* project made Wagner one of the central figures in my musical life, I had conducted only five of his ten frequently performed operas. During my years as a répétiteur in Budapest, I had worked on the early operas and *Tristan* and *Walküre*, but not on the other *Ring* operas or *Die Meistersinger* or *Parsifal*. I do not recall being either particularly pro-Wagner or particularly anti-Wagner at the time. Gradually, I conducted all of his main works, starting with my first *Walküre* in Munich, in 1947.

I have never performed Wagner's three earliest operas. Even the composer considered *Die Feen* and *Das Liebesverbot* too primitive, and *Rienzi*, in my opinion, is rather long and pompous. During the single year that elapsed between the premiere of *Rienzi* and the premiere of *The Flying Dutchman*, Wagner made an astonishing qualitative leap. *The Flying Dutchman* is undeniably a work of genius, and I hope that I won't shock dyed-in-the-wool Wagnerites if I admit that I prefer it to its two successors, *Tannhäuser* and *Lohengrin*. Although *The Flying Dutchman* as a whole is not as great as the other two, it has moments of pure genius, such as the Dutchman's monologue and Senta's ballad. I don't feel the other two operas have quite the same qualities. The *Dutchman*'s casting problems are similar to those of Wagner's later operas: It was conceived for big voices that could carry over a large orchestra. The Dutchman himself and Senta are the most difficult roles, thus the hardest to cast. Birgit Nilsson once told me, "Senta is too difficult for me. I don't sing it." That surely is comment enough on the difficulty of the role, coming from a singer who had a most astonishing vocal technique and range.

The vocal writing in *Tannhäuser* is better than in *The Flying Dutchman,* and, with the exception of the role of Tannhäuser, it is easier to sing. Elisabeth and Wolfram are both eminently singable parts. From the conductor's point of view, the main difficulties occur in Act II: Wagner did not handle all of the singing contest with expertise. The danger is that the contest can fall into little pieces, and whoever is on the podium must struggle to keep the musical fabric from falling apart. But the third act is a truly great piece of music. Wagner's choral writing progressed enormously between *Dutchman* and *Tannhäuser* and was to progress even further in *Lohengrin* and *Die Meistersinger;* indeed, *Meistersinger* contains truly outstanding choral writing, in the Bach tradition.

Emil Preetorius, the great German stage designer who had worked at the Bayreuth Festival, and who designed my Frankfurt *Tristan,* once described to me Wagner's color schemes, using examples that he played on the piano. The color that Preetorius saw, Wagner had composed in musical terms. Preetorius described the incredible variety of color in the operas—the blue of the *Lohengrin* Prelude, for instance—and he spoke about the color scheme that Wagner transferred into his orchestration. He told me that each Wagner opera has its own color. *Dutchman,* for instance, is very dark, *Tannhäuser* is a little brighter, and *Lohengrin* is silver—lots of A major, which is the brightest key of all. The *Ring's* "color scheme" is extremely varied but basically dark; *Tristan* is multicolored, built on chromatic scales and half tones, while *Meistersinger* is in very bright, full tones—a diatonic miracle. This variety in color translates itself into an incredible variety in character, which comes across immediately in the various orchestral introductions, before a single note has been sung. Think of the storm in the *Flying Dutchman* Overture, the Pilgrims' Hymn in the *Tannhäuser* Overture, the otherworldliness of the *Lohengrin* Prelude, and the fatal lovesickness of the *Tristan* Prelude; or the atmospheric and seemingly eternal E-flat at the beginning of *Das Rheingold,* the terror of *Die*

Walküre's opening pages, the joyous playfulness of the *Meistersinger* Prelude, and the mysticism of the *Parsifal* Prelude. Compare the passionate Prelude to Act III of *Lohengrin* with the melancholy warmth of the Prelude to Act III of *Meistersinger,* or with the sylvan introduction to *Siegfried.*

Today we tend to look too much into the psychological motivation and character defects of the great composers at the expense of really listening to the music. I am not interested in Wagner's political or philosophical ideas, or his betrayal of friends, including his father-in-law, Franz Liszt. What interests me is the creation of his music—for example, the love motif of *Tristan,* the miracle and completeness of the first four bars, now regarded as a bible of love and beauty. I understand that he wrote several versions, before this motif appeared—a harmonic and melodic miracle. To me, anybody who can create such beauty, whether he be half-Jewish, anti-Semite, revolutionary, liberal, or royalist, is first and foremost a musical genius and will remain so as long as our civilization lasts.

IN APRIL 1959, I made my debut with the Los Angeles Philharmonic in its regular winter series (I had previously participated in summer concerts at the Hollywood Bowl), conducting an all-Beethoven program with Artur Rubinstein as soloist and, the following week, a mixed program with mezzo-soprano Nan Merriman singing Mozart's "*Ch'io mi scordi di te*" and Falla's *Seven Popular Spanish Songs.* I established an excellent rapport with the orchestra, and the concerts went so well that I was invited back for seven weeks during the 1959–1960 season. We worked on a wide range of repertoire, with a strong emphasis on twentieth-century music: Bartók, Stravinsky, Webern, Berg, William Schuman, and *Three Hungarian Sketches* by my friend Miklós Rózsa, a Hungarian-born and -trained composer who was best known for his brilliant film scores, which included those for *Ben Hur* and *El Cid.*

On several occasions, I visited Bruno Walter, who had been living in Los Angeles for years. He remembered me from Budapest, when I had played the piano for his Verdi Requiem rehearsals, and from Salzburg, when I was working with Toscanini, whom he revered. Whenever I came to visit, he would offer me coffee or tea, and we would have a good gossip. Once, he put on a record of Toscanini rehearsing. He found the Maestro's outbursts of anger very amusing, especially when Toscanini would repeatedly shout, "No! No!" without saying what was wrong, followed by a voice in the distance saying, "Maestro, but what should we do?" The "No! No! No!" continued. Years later, in Chicago, I asked my leader of the cello section, Frank Miller, who had played with the NBC Symphony Orchestra in Toscanini's time, whose voice it was I had heard. "It was mine," he said, "because we didn't know what the Maestro wanted." There is an equally amusing recording of Walter himself rehearsing Mozart's "Linz" Symphony. The first reading is excellent, but the more he rehearses, the worse the orchestra plays.

I had the greatest respect for Walter, and during my Munich days, I even adopted the cuts he had made in the *St. Matthew Passion* during his Munich tenure. Later, I decided the cuts were wrong, so I conducted the entire work, uncut. I was much relieved to read in his memoirs that he regarded the cuts as one of the worst musical sins he had ever committed.

When I began to conduct Mahler, I learned a great deal from Walter, who had worked with him. Walter had a strange, not very clear beat, but he was proof that the beat is not an essential part of a conductor. You are conducting with your eyes and with your soul. The German school of conducting taught that the orchestra played not on the beat but after it. This has been the traditional practice for the last hundred years. Furtwängler, Walter, Karajan, and Böhm continued it and so do the Vienna and Berlin Philharmonics to this day. The protagonists of this style feel that a chord after the beat is softer than one that comes on the beat. Rainer Küchl, the Vienna Philharmonic's concertmaster and a first-class musician, tells me, "If we played with the beat, you would never get a soft attack; it would always be sforzato." I don't agree with this. I know from experience elsewhere that precision and gentleness can be achieved simultaneously. Whenever I work with these two orchestras, I ask them to try to play on the beat, not after. But the habit is so ingrained that although they try to please me, we end up with a compromise. I often say, "Please try not to be half an hour late, just fifteen minutes." On the other hand, the Italian school—Toscanini, Victor De Sabata, and others—taught their musicians to play on the beat, and American orchestras and conductors do the same. I follow the Toscanini school. There is a famous joke about Furtwängler conducting Beethoven's Fifth at the Santa Cecilia Academy in Rome, with a large part of the audience sitting behind the orchestra. Before the notoriously difficult first beat of the Fifth, Furtwängler gave an endlessly long upbeat. On this occasion, his arm seemed to move up and up and up, until someone in the audience shouted, "*Coraggio, maestro!*" Somebody once asked a player in the Berlin Philharmonic how they knew when to begin, because Furtwängler's beat was so unclear. He replied, "We watch the double bass player, who counts to five, and then we start." These are apocryphal stories, but they give an indication of the problem.

I sometimes felt that Walter's rhythm was not incisive enough. He also had a tendency, in rehearsal, to talk to orchestras in literary terms, which seemed to me a fundamental mistake: Orchestra musicians need to know which sixteenth note is wrong, why, and how to correct it. When you stand in front of the orchestra, you must never try to show off your aesthetic or philosophical ideas. You must address the musical problems when they arise.

A few years before Walter died (which was in 1962), I found myself aboard a plane with him and his daughter, on a long flight from Copenhagen to Los Angeles. In those prejet days, the larger planes had beds at the back for first-class passengers. On that flight, my bed was near Walter's, and he and I sat up talking about music until the lights were turned off. On our arrival in Los Angeles, Walter and his daughter left the plane before everyone else, because he was quite old and frail. When I went through customs and immigration, the official recognized my name. As I was to conduct the Los Angeles Philharmonic that week, he had seen my photograph in one of the local newspapers. "Aha! You're the conductor!" he said. "Tell me something. Isn't that old guy ahead of you a conductor, too?"

"Bruno Walter is one of the greatest living conductors," I said. "And believe it or not, he has lived in Los Angeles for many years." The official was surprised. But then, even Stravinsky, another longtime Los Angeles resident, used to joke that no one in the city knew him. He said that he was afraid of being hit by a car for two reasons:

it might be the Rolls-Royce of a Hollywood film composer who earned more money than he, and newspaper readers in Los Angeles might discover that he, Stravinsky, was living in their midst.

It was, in fact, a film composer—my friend, Miklós Rózsa—who arranged for me to meet Stravinsky. After I had conducted a double bill of *Oedipus Rex* and *The Rite of Spring* in one of my Los Angeles concerts, Rózsa asked me whether I would like to meet Stravinsky, whom he knew. Naturally I said that I would. One morning, while I was having my coffee, the phone rang. "This is Stravinsky," a voice said. "Rózsa tells me that you would like to visit me. When would you like to come?"

I was totally perplexed. I took a taxi to Stravinsky's home, which was in a pleasant but by no means luxurious part of town. I was dropped off at the corner of the street where he lived, in one of the canyons around Los Angeles. There was a steep path up to a modest bungalow with a small garden. To my surprise, when I rang the bell, Stravinsky himself came to the door, as Strauss had done at Garmisch roughly ten years earlier. Just as I had been reduced to near speechlessness in the presence of Strauss, so I felt equally tongue-tied in front of Stravinsky.

Stravinsky, then in his late seventies, was small in stature, and his English was as strongly Russian as mine is Hungarian. The house was simply furnished. In leading me from the living room to the garden, he took me through his study, and I shall never forget his desk, which was in impeccable order: red pencils in one place, blue pencils in another, black in yet another; pencil sharpener, erasers—everything as precisely deployed as a military battalion on parade. It perfectly matched the manuscripts of his compositions, which were also exceptionally neat and clear. Unfortunately, I remember much less about what Stravinsky said. He mentioned that he had managed to obtain Bordeaux wine during the war, and he talked a little about the Los Angeles Philharmonic, which he, too, had conducted.

The only question I had the courage to ask Stravinsky was why he had changed the orchestration and simplified the rhythms in the score of *The Rite of Spring*, thirty years after the original version was published. "I made the changes because I couldn't conduct the original version—it was too difficult for me," he said.

The answer was charming, and partly true, because, brilliant composer though he was, he was not especially gifted as a conductor. But the real reason, which I learned later, was more practical: At the time of the Russian Revolution, Stravinsky had lost his copyright on his three most popular scores—*The Firebird, Petrushka,* and *The Rite of Spring*—and the only way he could get his royalties was by creating new editions of the works. A few years ago, when I was going to record *Petrushka,* I wanted to base my performance on the original version but to incorporate into it some of the changes from the later one, and I was not sure whether this was a legitimate procedure. I phoned Robert Craft, who had been a close collaborator of Stravinsky's for many years; he told me to do as I thought best, and he confirmed that the revisions had been made because of the copyright problems. "Whatever you do, Stravinsky would have loved it," he said, generously.

I was only with Stravinsky for about an hour. Then his wife, Vera, arrived home. He introduced me, we chatted a bit, and I left. I had been in such awe of this genius, who was a gentle and kind man, that I had felt unable to ask him about his compositions. I also felt I would be able to meet him again, as he had received me so warmly. But all in all, I wasted a unique opportunity.

In 1970 or early in 1971, I was visiting New York, where Stravinsky was living at the time. I knew that he was not well, and I telephoned to ask whether I could visit him. The person who answered the phone told me that Stravinsky was asleep and said that he would phone back, but I did not hear from him before I had to leave the city. A few days later, I received a message from him saying that he had heard about my call only when it was too late, but he asked me to come see him the next time I was in New York. I never saw him again, however, because he died in April 1971.

I have conducted a great deal of Stravinsky's music, at least a dozen works, in addition to the above-mentioned "big three." I still would like to learn and perform *The Rake's Progress* and some of the late, twelve-tone pieces. Every one of his works requires great technical competence and even greater rhythmic precision on the part of its interpreters. I know that comparing Stravinsky to Picasso, his contemporary, has become commonplace, but I feel I must do it too. With respect to their stylistic versatility, their creative longevity, the amazing force and individuality of their artistic personalities, and their cataclysmic impact on the history of the arts in the twentieth century, they are in a class by themselves.

MY WORK in Los Angeles was so well received that Mrs. Dorothy Chandler, the chairman of the Philharmonic's board, asked me to become music director in 1960. I was delighted: I liked the orchestra, the warm climate, the salary, and, above all, the idea of devoting less of my time to opera, which, for a conductor, is far more exhausting than giving concerts. Although symphony orchestras are not without their own organizational problems, the difficulties are infinitesimal compared to those of an opera company. So many components go into even the simplest opera productions, and such vast numbers of organizational headaches and other nonmusical exigencies complicate the procedure, that sometimes the rehearsals and performances seem much simpler than the preparation. Nevertheless, I have never forgotten that I was born with a dramatic musical talent, predestined to conduct operas. As circumstances turned out, destiny pushed me back to opera.

One day in 1957, Alfred Dietz, a Viennese concert agent, came to Frankfurt and said to me, "I want to introduce you to England." By then, my name was reasonably well known abroad, and I had already conducted in Britain. In 1949, I made two recordings with the London Philharmonic, and I gave concerts with the same orchestra almost every season between 1950 and 1957. I performed *The Magic Flute* at the 1952 Edinburgh Festival, as guest conductor with the Hamburg Staatsoper, and I conducted *Don Giovanni* at Glyndebourne in 1954.

Under these circumstances, Dietz easily persuaded David Webster, the general manager of the Royal Opera House, Covent Garden, to send someone to Frankfurt to watch one of my performances. Webster sent Lord Harewood, an important figure in the British musical scene. Harewood attended a performance of *La forza del destino* and gave a good report to Webster, who invited me to conduct *Der Rosenkavalier* at Covent Garden in December 1959. Webster then came to Frankfurt to talk to me about scheduling and casting.

The production of *Der Rosenkavalier* at Covent Garden was a revival, but the cast was exceptional: Elisabeth Schwarzkopf as the Marschallin, Sena Jurinac as Octavian, Kurt Böhme as Ochs, and Hanny Steffek as Sophie. From the start, there was a good working atmosphere. The orchestra played well, the stage personnel were friendly, and I already knew all the singers. The only unpleasant element was Walter Legge, Schwarzkopf's husband, who was then on the Covent Garden board and was able to attend every rehearsal. In my opinion, he tormented Schwarzkopf terribly. At each session, she would start off singing beautifully, but because of his comments and bullying, she became less and less confident. He seemed to tolerate no opinion other than his own, and as a result, his wife became exceedingly tense.

The performances were a great success, although Peter Heyworth, the *Observer*'s critic, wrote that I had led the waltzes as if they had been written for lame ducks. This was my first introduction to the British music critics. One day, during my London stay, I received a telephone call from Ilona Kabos, the Hungarian pianist, whom I knew from Budapest, where she used to come to watch Leó Weiner's chamber music classes. Joan Drogheda, one of her pupils, was married to the Earl of Drogheda, chairman of the Royal Opera. Ilona asked whether I could come to her home in Queen's Grove, St. John's Wood, to have a drink and meet the Droghedas. I accepted, and I remember how impressed I was with her lovely home, never dreaming that thirteen years later I would be living only a few hundred yards away.

"We want you to be music director," Lord Drogheda said, with his characteristic directness. "We can pay only seven thousand pounds a year"—not a princely sum, even in those days—"but you must do it." To his great surprise, I explained to him that although I was honored by the offer, I did not want the job, and that my refusal had nothing to do with the salary. I had accepted the directorship of the Los Angeles Philharmonic because I felt that I had spent enough time as an opera conductor and wanted to concentrate on symphonic music, and privately, I was not certain that I would be able to do justice to both Los Angeles and London if I accepted both jobs.

Lord Drogheda asked me not to make a final decision immediately. "Think it over. We can wait—we haven't got anyone else!"

In January 1960, I went back to Los Angeles for concerts with the Philharmonic. While I was there, I called on Bruno Walter, as I always did when I arrived, and told him about the Covent Garden offer. "You must accept," he told me. "We, the older generation of conductors, no longer conduct opera. You of the younger generation must carry on our tradition and pass it on to the next generation. You are the link." He then made a prophetic comment: "The English will love you—they love talented people—but you will hate the climate."

I thought, What a silly old man! What do I care about the weather, as long as I am working? But he was absolutely right: I intensely dislike the eternal grayness and rain in winter and find the English climate more difficult to take with each passing year. But I love the people and the friends I have in Britain.

I took Walter's advice and sent a telegram to David Webster, who cabled back to say that they would be happy to have me in London. We decided that my tenure would begin in September 1961, one year after my Los Angeles commitment was to start.

In Los Angeles, we had held auditions for the position of assistant conductor of the Philharmonic. Among the candidates was twenty-three-year-old Zubin Mehta, whom I had met in Vienna while he was studying there, and who had come to me for advice about his career. I had invited him to apply for the job, and he was so obviously gifted that we all agreed he was the best choice.

During my first season as musical director, Fritz Reiner had been scheduled to conduct some concerts, but he had a heart attack and canceled all his engagements. Without consulting me, Mrs. Chandler decided that Reiner's concerts should be given to Mehta. In June 1960, while I was in London on Covent Garden business, I received a telegram from Mrs. Chandler, saying, "With your kind permission I have engaged Zubin Mehta as chief guest conductor of the Philharmonic." I was horrified. I had nothing at all against Mehta, who was an outstandingly talented young conductor, but the fact that the chairman of my new orchestra's board had engaged a chief guest conductor without asking my opinion was intolerable. Mrs. Chandler had the reputation of interfering. I knew that if I accepted her intrusion in this matter, she would try to interfere in all other artistic decisions and would undermine my authority. I cabled back to say that under these conditions, I was unable to honor my contract in Los Angeles.

It was a terrible moment for me. I had wanted the Los Angeles position very much. I hoped that Mrs. Chandler would retract her proposal, but she never even replied to my message, and later she made Zubin Mehta musical director.

Within a few years, however, I realized how lucky I had been. If every year I had had to spend three months in Los Angeles and five months in London, the workload would have been too great and might well have restricted my musical development, because I would have had too little time to do anything well. Apart from artistic development, attempting to commute between London and Los Angeles would have been crazy. Even more important, if I had taken over the Los Angeles Philharmonic, I would never have become music director of the Chicago Symphony, which would have been an extremely sad loss.

ABOUT A YEAR before the offers from Los Angeles and Covent Garden, while I was still in Frankfurt, Harry Buckwitz had taken me aside and said, with typical frankness and generosity of spirit, "Solti, you must go now. You're too good for us." Although I have never felt "too good" for anyone or anything, I was beginning to feel that I had outgrown Frankfurt. Throughout my career, I have always had a good instinct for knowing when it was time to move on. And yet, when I made up my mind to assume the direction of Covent Garden, I felt sad to leave a city in which I had lived and worked so pleasantly and fruitfully.

I recall only two problems connected with my directorship in Frankfurt. Early in my stay, the local avant-garde accused me of not giving enough attention to contemporary music, and later on, some detractors complained that I was away too often, guest-conducting abroad. The first accusation was easily answered: In coming to Frankfurt, I had been given a precise mandate to reconstruct the basic repertoire, and in any case, I did not neglect new or recent music: I conducted operas by four living composers—Stravinsky, Hindemith, Gottfried von Einem, and Rolf Liebermann—not to

mention the local premiere of Berg's *Lulu,* one of the most important of all twentieth-century operas. The second accusation was
unjust. During my first eight Frankfurt seasons, I conducted an average of forty performances a year—a large number, in view of the
high percentage of new productions that had to be planned and
rehearsed from start to finish each season. The fact that I was simultaneously developing an international career brought nearly as much
credit to Frankfurt as it did to me. Had I conducted an even higher
percentage of each season's performances in Frankfurt, I would have
been accused of megalomania. There is no satisfying everyone, and I
know opera conductors who have been accused, simultaneously, of
conducting too much and too little in the theaters they direct. And
yet, perhaps my critics were right, because I realize now, while
writing about my Frankfurt years, that I have talked little about
Frankfurt and much more about my work elsewhere.

For my last appearance as music director in Frankfurt—a performance of *Falstaff* on June 19, 1961—Buckwitz had prepared a surprise
for me. At the end of the evening, he went in front of the curtain and
said, "Some people have criticized Maestro Solti for being away too
much. I am now going to show you how much he was here." One by
one, signs were lowered over the stage, each bearing the title of an
opera I had conducted in Frankfurt, along with the cast list. On and
on they went. The audience was amused and appreciative; I was
amused and touched. I realized that in nine years, I had conducted
thirty-three works, nineteen of them new to my repertoire.

I have never stopped being grateful to Frankfurt for the years of
happiness and healthy artistic growth that I spent there.

FIVE

LONDON

D AVID WEBSTER had been the Royal Opera's general manager since 1946. He was a witty, elegant man who could be charming when he wanted but he could also be cold and distant, and at times arrogant. It is not without reason that his biography was entitled *The Quiet Showman.* I remember in June 1960 being driven with him from London to Aldeburgh to attend the world premiere of Benjamin Britten's opera *A Midsummer Night's Dream.* During the entire three-hour trip, David never spoke a word to me.

I later learned that David had been opposed to my appointment as music director, or, to be more precise, that he had been opposed to appointing anyone as music director. Rafael Kubelik, my predecessor, had come to Covent Garden in 1954, the year after Claudia Cassidy had driven him out of Chicago, and he had quickly become the object of harsh criticism. Kubelik had found himself in a similar situation to the one I had experienced in Munich. At that time, he had too little experience in running an opera house; he would have been better off had he started at a house that was less prestigious internationally. I got away with inexperience in Munich for longer than Kubelik did in London because what had been possible in Munich in 1946 was not possible in London in the mid-1950s. The result was that both he and the Royal Opera suffered. Sir Thomas Beecham, the sharp-tongued doyen of English musical life, effectively demolished his young Czech colleague in a letter to *The Times:* "Why are second-rate foreign conductors needed in Britain," he wrote, "when there are plenty of second-rate British conductors available?" (I was spared the lash of Beecham's sarcasm because he died a few months before I moved to London.) Poor Kubelik left Covent Garden in

1958. Fortunately, in his next job, as head of the Bayerische Rund-funk Orchestra, his outstanding talent as a conductor was finally given the acknowledgment it deserved and his musical development there was an unqualified success.

Kubelik had not been immediately replaced at Covent Garden because David preferred to rule alone. Music directors were a nui-sance, he felt, and he was happier without one. It was only after the success of my *Rosenkavalier* in 1959, when Lord Drogheda exerted strong pressure on him, that David finally agreed to engage me. This explained his cold behavior during our trip to Aldeburgh. At the time, however, I knew none of the background to the story, and I felt hurt.

THE PREMIERE of *A Midsummer Night's Dream* took place at the Jubilee Hall. I had never heard anything by Britten—until then he had been little played on the Continent—but I knew of his reputa-tion. After the opera, David and Lord Drogheda introduced me to Britten and I told him how much I had enjoyed the performance and his conducting. But although I had been intrigued by the opera, I had expected a heavier, more Verdian, sound, simply because my experi-ence of Shakespeare had been in weighty German translations. On hearing the music for the first time, I therefore felt that Britten's light orchestration failed to convey the impact of Shakespeare's writing. How wrong I was! I realized very soon that Britten was absolutely right in his setting. The opera is written for a small orchestra and voices, in the style of Purcell, and the transparency of its instrumenta-tion brilliantly catches the transparency of the play's language.

Drogheda joined David and me on the trip back to London, and the liveliness of our conversation on the return journey made up, in part, for the icy northbound silence. The two of them decided to proceed with plans to give the London premiere of Britten's new work the following February. Casting and other details were dis-cussed, and someone proposed that I conduct the production. I wanted the challenge of doing it at Covent Garden, and I accepted.

The Royal Opera pulled out all the stops for *A Midsummer Night's Dream*. The director was John Gielgud and the sets were designed by the painter John Piper. I had seen Gielgud in Los Angeles, in a recital of passages from Shakespeare. Book in hand, and without the assistance of costumes or makeup, he had transformed himself into one character after another. I had never in my life seen such virtuosity.

At the first stage rehearsal for the Britten opera, I was so much in awe of Gielgud's beautiful English that I hardly dared open my mouth. At least that is how it seemed to me at the time. When I later mentioned this recollection to the baritone Geraint Evans, who played Bottom, he said, "Oh, but you spoke all the time."

I enjoyed working with Gielgud enormously. I shall always remember one afternoon, after a stage rehearsal, when Gielgud and I went into a small room to give further coaching to the boy who was playing Puck, who had not quite grasped Gielgud's concept of the part. In particular, Gielgud was not happy with the boy's delivery of the line "Lord, what fools these mortals be!" He demonstrated how to say the line, and in that dingy room this great man of the theater became a naughty little boy before our very eyes. It was breathtaking.

One other incident from this period stays in my mind. During the time of the rehearsals, Gielgud invited Hedi and me to dinner at the Savoy Grill. While we were eating, Winston Churchill, who was then eighty-six, walked in rather unsteadily, accompanied by his secretary. The English used to be quite extraordinary about preserving the privacy of public figures, and no one took any notice of him except me. I behaved badly by English standards: I could not take my eyes off him and kept staring. I thought immediately of those BBC broadcasts of his speeches that had kept my hopes up during the war. He was my idol. And there I was eating my roast beef in the same room with him.

The following August we took *A Midsummer Night's Dream* to the Edinburgh Festival, where we also performed Gluck's *Iphigénie en Tauride*. And it was with this latter work, which was new to my repertoire, that I officially began my tenure as music director of the Royal Opera House in September 1961.

During the previous year, I had worked out the details of my contract with David Webster and had had several meetings to discuss long-term planning. My first intention was to create for the Royal Opera an Italian-style *stagione*—or "season"—system, in which not more than two or three operas are simultaneously in repertoire. Each production is rehearsed thoroughly, one opera at a time, and then presented in a four-to-six-week period, during which the conductor and all, or nearly all, of the cast remain unchanged.

This differed from the system operating at German houses and the Metropolitan Opera, where an opera currently in the house repertoire could appear at any time throughout the season and with any number of alterations to the cast. Under this system, there would be as many as thirty or forty operas performed per season, whereas during my time at Covent Garden, we did a far smaller number, but with greater care.

I found the conditions under the repertory system unacceptable because changes in the cast were made with few or no rehearsals, and this inevitably meant a lowering of artistic standards. One of my main reasons for leaving Frankfurt and wanting to give up opera conducting was Frankfurt's repertory system, with regular revivals performed by different casts. On occasion, I would arrive at a performance to find that a particular role had been filled by someone I had never seen before. I am prepared to overcome the practical and technical difficulties of replacing a singer at the last minute, but it is something that gives me no artistic pleasure.

Introducing and maintaining a revised *stagione* system, in which the same cast was engaged for all the performances, was my first achievement at Covent Garden. It proved to be a success, and over time it began to be imitated on the Continent.

My second priority was the repertoire itself. In the years before I arrived, Covent Garden was like a second-league Italian opera house that played mainly nineteenth-century Italian opera. David Webster was a great devotee of singers such as Maria Callas and Joan Sutherland, and the repertoire was heavily slanted toward works by composers such as Bellini and Donizetti that favored the prima donna. But the prima donnas were not always available. I wanted to arrange more balanced programs. There was practically no German or German-style opera in the repertoire. I changed that by including more Mozart, Wagner, and Strauss. And in this context, it is significant that my first production as music director was the revival of Gluck's *Iphigénie en Tauride*.

A related issue was the rate at which we could bring new productions into the repertoire. At one of our strategy meetings, David strongly expressed the view that we could not cope with more than four new productions a year. I believed that so large and prestigious an ensemble as the Royal Opera could do more. After three hours of discussion, David became tired and wanted to bring the meeting to an end. "All right, have it your way," he said. And this is how we raised the number of new productions to six a year.

However, I do not want to give the impression that David easily agreed to everything I wanted. He could be blunt when circumstances required. Brenda Evans, the wife of Geraint Evans, used to tell about meeting David outside the stage door in Floral Street. "We're going to give Geraint Escamillo next season," he told her.

"But he's not very good at Escamillo," she said.

"I know," he replied, "but he's the best we've got."

During the first month of my directorship, and in keeping with my desire to expand the repertoire, I introduced a new production of *Die Walküre,* directed by Hans Hotter, who also sang Wotan. This was to have been the start of a new *Ring* cycle, but the sets, by Hotter's friend Herbert Kern, did not work. Hotter saw this, and for the revival three years later, we scrapped Kern's sets in favor of new ones by Günther Schneider-Siemssen, who had by then designed the rest of the cycle, as well.

In February 1962, I conducted a new *Don Giovanni,* directed and designed by Franco Zeffirelli. Zeffirelli was a friend of David Webster, and David had suggested that we work together. At our first rehearsal, the entire cast was gathered together onstage, but I soon realized that we were without the director. Twenty minutes later, when Zeffirelli finally appeared, instead of apologizing or even attending to what we were doing, he began opening his mail, which he had brought along with him. I was furious. I turned to him, told him he was late, and asked him if we could now start. But our relations soon improved and our collaboration on this production marked the beginning of a warm and successful partnership that would continue through much of the decade.

The cast of *Don Giovanni* was excellent, but my clearest memory is of the twenty-seven-year-old Mirella Freni as Zerlina. That Freni possessed wonderful talent and a beautiful, golden voice was obvious from the start, but the fact that she is still singing well thirty-five years later demonstrates the great advantages not only of excellent training but also of an intelligently paced career.

I was particularly pleased by the success of a new triple bill that we scheduled for June and July of 1962—three short operas, all directed by Peter Ustinov, and each designed by a native of the opera composer's country of origin: Schneider-Siemssen for the house premiere of Schoenberg's *Erwartung*, Fabrizio Clerici for Puccini's *Gianni Schicchi*, and young Jean-Pierre Ponnelle for Ravel's *L'Heure espagnole*.

Instead of coming to the first rehearsals of each opera with a more or less finished concept and immediately setting out to realize it, Ustinov first had the casts read their lines, as if they were actors in a play. After that, he improvised. I attended his first rehearsal of *Schicchi* and was shocked to hear him say to Geraint Evans, who was singing the title role, "Do something."

"What do you want me to do?"

"Just do what you feel."

I left quickly, convinced that we were on the verge of a disaster. But when I went back a few days later, I found everything proceeding smoothly and all the participants in the best possible humor. Out of unpromising beginnings, something clever and polished was born.

My first Covent Garden season ended with *Otello*, with Mario Del Monaco in the title role. Del Monaco had a splendid dramatic tenor voice, but he was not the most musical of singers. He expected conductor, orchestra, and the other singers to follow him—not an easy accomplishment in *Otello*. Nevertheless, my plans to make the Royal Opera into a great international house were beginning to take effect.

The cancellation of my Los Angeles contract had not left me idle. When Paul Kletzki, a Polish-Swiss conductor, left the Dallas Symphony Orchestra in 1961, I accepted an invitation to stand in as senior conductor for the 1961–1962 season, which coincided with my first Covent Garden season. In two separate periods, roughly a month each in the autumn and spring, I conducted twenty-one concerts in Dallas. My programs included some twentieth-century works that had not yet been accepted into the so-called standard repertoire: the Suite from Bartók's *Miraculous Mandarin*, three pieces from Berg's *Lulu*, and Janácek's Sinfonietta. I also gave an all-Stravinsky program and two performances of Beethoven's Missa

Solemnis. The Dallas Symphony was an excellent provincial American orchestra, by which I mean that it was versatile, quick-thinking, well blended, and generally better, technically, than any but a handful of top European orchestras.

Between my last Dallas appearances in April 1962 and the opening of Covent Garden's Schoenberg-Puccini-Ravel triple bill in June, I recorded *Siegfried* in Vienna. This sort of heavy scheduling was typical of my life in those years. Unfortunately, it is not much different today.

When I returned to London, David Webster said to me, "I have worked with many musicians who have known how to cope with organizational responsibilities, but you are the best I've ever met." From then on, he accepted me fully. We began to call each other by our first names, and we became good friends. Once every week or two, he and I had planning sessions with the Royal Opera committee's other members: Lord Drogheda, who was chairman of the Royal Opera throughout my tenure there; Lord Harewood; Lionel—now Lord—Robbins, the British economist and professor at the London School of Economics; Sir Thomas Armstrong, director of the Royal Academy of Music; and Walter Legge. Legge did not always attend, but when he did, he criticized everything. He did not usually attack me directly, but he was always telling David that this or that project or detail would not work. He was extremely negative, and David loathed him.

George Harewood and Drogheda were David's mainstays within the organization, and they worked well together until George left Covent Garden to become director of the Edinburgh Festival, and later, of the English National Opera. He has a greater knowledge of musical matters and singers than anyone else I have come across in an opera house, and he also has integrity. Lord Drogheda, too, had the best qualities of the British. He was a lovable man who lied to no one and behaved correctly toward everyone. I had a most harmonious relationship with him. Never did he try to tell me what to do. He might question a decision or suggest an alternative, but he never imposed his will, as he could well have done. On the contrary, he protected me and helped me to resolve difficulties. On the day after a performance, he would send out little notes—"Droghedagrams," we called them—to me or other participants, which were usually delivered before breakfast, to tell us what he thought had gone well and what he thought had gone badly. Drogheda was a blessing for Covent Garden because of his savoir faire, his political clout (he was chairman of the *Financial Times*), and also his vast artistic knowledge.

Like other music directors of major opera ensembles, I needed help with my organizational responsibilities, and, in addition, I had to learn to adapt to English practices, many of which were new to me. In Munich and Frankfurt, for instance, we usually rehearsed in the morning, took a long break for lunch, study, and rest, and then reassembled at six for a second rehearsal. I made many people angry when I tried to impose this system at Covent Garden, but no one had tried to explain to me why it would not work. Few musicians can afford to live in or near central London. Most of them commute for an hour or more each way, and they do not want to make two trips a day, or to stay in town for hours and hours with nothing to do. They prefer to have a lunch break of not more than ninety minutes after the morning rehearsal and then proceed with the second rehearsal. Once I understood this, I let them go back to their old system, but in the meantime, I had inadvertently stirred up some ill will.

Besides, I found discipline at the Royal Opera rather slack and insisted on tightening up rehearsal procedures, production practices, and planning, which was split into three categories: weekly, monthly, and long-term. At first, there were masses of complaints; I was called "the Prussian field marshal," and much worse. But in the end, when they saw that my methods brought good results and that standards were rising, they accepted me.

My offices at the Opera House included the same room in which I had met Colonel de Basil during my first London visit in 1938. For my first year, David had engaged a young English conductor, Bernard Keefe, to assist me with administrative matters, but I soon realized that he was not the right man to help make the fundamental changes in organization that the Royal Opera clearly needed. When I had given my first concerts in London in the mid-1950s, my agent had been Joan Ingpen, of Ingpen & Williams. I knew that she had an exceptional organizational mind, and I suggested that she be put in charge of Covent Garden's long-term planning.

Joan was a hotheaded Irishwoman who loved you or hated you, and she could be vicious to the people she hated and wonderfully supportive to those she liked. She and I got along excellently, and she served me and the Royal Opera beautifully. Before I arrived, Covent Garden was scheduling just six months in advance, though Joan later told me that from her experience as an agent with artists working at the Royal Opera House, the planning was sometimes as short as only a month or even a week ahead.

I now understand the horror in David's eyes when I proposed planning three years in advance. But this leap forward in the scheduling was essential. International opera life was becoming more complicated because of the new phenomenon of jet travel: Singers, conductors, and stage directors could fly from London to Milan or Vienna in two hours, or to New York in six, and the temptation to try to be everywhere at once was irresistible for some.

By the end of the 1960s, we had achieved this difficult transition in the Royal Opera's thinking, and Joan had been the key person in the battle to make it happen. She had exactly the right sort of mind for such a task. If anyone asked her, "What will the rehearsal schedule be for the third week of March two years from now?" she would answer correctly and without hesitation. She always carried in her briefcase planning charts neatly filled in in pencil.

Of equal importance to me was the appointment of Enid Blech as my secretary. Enid was the wife of the conductor Harry Blech. Not only was she very musical—at one time, she had wanted to be a singer—but she also knew virtually all the musicians in England and most of the international opera stars. Her office became a sort of club where singers would pop in for a cup of coffee and a chat, and I have a vivid memory of the aroma of freshly ground coffee mixed with the smoke of the small cigars she loved to puff on. She had a strong sense of adventure and enormous joie de vivre: She flew her own small plane, drove a sports car, and built herself a house on a mountaintop in Calabria. Enid, Joan, and I formed an indomitable trio: Together, we made Covent Garden into a place where the best artists wanted to perform, and where the planning was good enough to fulfill almost all of their wishes.

DURING MY SECOND and third Covent Garden seasons, I added *Siegfried, Götterdämmerung,* and Britten's *Billy Budd* to my repertoire; the first two were given new productions, both directed by

Hotter and designed by Schneider-Siemssen. *Budd*, in my opinion Britten's best opera, provided me with an opportunity to get to know the composer better than had been possible at the time of *A Midsummer Night's Dream*. At one of the rehearsals, I hesitantly asked him to listen to some changes in tempo and dynamics that I had made in the introduction. "Oh yes," he said, "very good. I shall call this the 'Solti version.'" He and his companion, the tenor Peter Pears, were always charming, and I wish that my schedule had allowed me to make the long trip to Aldeburgh once in a while. I would have liked to talk to him about some of his works (the *Sinfonia da Requiem*, Variations on a Theme of Frank Bridge, and *The Young Person's Guide to the Orchestra* were also in my repertoire), but this never happened.

I also conducted a number of operas that, although not new to my repertoire, I had not yet performed in London. A new production of *La forza del destino*, directed by Sam Wanamaker, was originally to have been designed by the Italian painter Renato Guttuso, but he and Wanamaker had conflicting ideas and could not reach an agreement. Wanamaker and two assistants designed the sets and costumes themselves, with unsatisfactory results. The rehearsals went well enough, but on the opening night everything that could go wrong did. In the last act, at the culminating moment of the drama, the sword fight between Alvaro and Carlo, sung, respectively, by Carlo Bergonzi and John Shaw, Bergonzi's hat fell off, and his wig came with it. The audience burst into uncontrollable laughter. As we came to the curtain at the end of the performance, Wanamaker and I were actually booed, loudly. I don't know about Wanamaker, but for me it was a first experience. In Italy, *La forza* has the reputation of being an unlucky opera, and I must confess that although I love this masterpiece, I have never again conducted it in the theater. This production was one of my few real disasters at Covent Garden.

My first London *Marriage of Figaro* also had something of a mixed reception, but this time at least there was no booing. It was directed by Oscar Fritz Schuh, designed by Teo Otto and Erni Kniepert, and sung by Geraint Evans, Mirella Freni, Ilva Ligabue, Tito Gobbi, and Teresa Berganza. One critic who took exception to my interpretation of the score described me memorably as a skater skimming over the surface of the music.

Early in 1964, Zeffirelli created a new *Rigoletto* production, which I liked very much. Geraint Evans sang the title role, and his light baritone voice with its deep colors was unforgettable and moving. Carlo Cossutta was the Duke and Anna Moffo was Gilda; both were making their Covent Garden debuts. At the end of Moffo's opening duet with Rigoletto, in Act I, scene 2, she sank to her knees so gracefully in front of her father that it took me a moment to realize that this was more than good acting: She had fainted. We had to bring down the curtain, and there was an interval of an hour and a half until Elizabeth Vaughan, the understudy, could get to the theater and into costume. (The irony of the situation was that Vaughan, who had turned up earlier, had been told that her presence would not be required that evening, and she had gone home to wash her hair.) I heard later that this was not the first time that Moffo had collapsed onstage: She was exhausted and felt that she could not get through the rest of the performance.

Rudolf Bing, who had first invited me to the Metropolitan Opera in New York to conduct *Tannhäuser* in December 1960, invited me back as guest conductor during the 1962–1963 and 1963–1964 seasons. The Metropolitan Opera at Lincoln Center had not yet been completed, and all of my performances took place at the old Met, which I liked very much. My repertoire consisted of *Tristan, Otello, Aida, Don Carlos,* and *Boris Godunov.* During one of the *Tristan* performances, as I gave the upbeat for the delicate beginning of the Prelude, a program slipped out of the hand of someone in the upper balcony and landed on one of the timpani, resulting in an enormous boom. The audience laughed so hard that I had to wait before I could begin the performance. In March 1964, I conducted two special concerts at the Met in memory of President Kennedy, who had been assassinated the previous November; the program included Act III of *Parsifal* and the Verdi Requiem.

I was to have returned to the Met the following year to conduct *Billy Budd,* but Bing, in his dictatorial way, tried to force me to conduct *Peter Grimes* instead, with Jon Vickers in the title role. For some reason, Vickers and I had never got on well, which was a pity, since he had an excellent tenor voice; we could have done some very good work together. More important, however, was the fact that *Grimes* was not in my repertoire at that time, and given all my prior commitments, I would not have had time to learn it properly for the following season. Bing was adamant. But so was I. (I have never conducted again at the Met, with the exception of guest performances of *Figaro* and *Otello* with the visiting Paris Opéra at the new Met in 1976.) During the 1960s, despite the many first-rate singers who performed at the Met, the company as a whole was far below the high standard that it has since reached under James Levine's direction. The orchestra is now one of the finest opera ensembles in the world. After a gap of more than thirty years, I am looking forward to conducting them in a concert of Mahler's Fifth Symphony in 1998.

WHEN I ARRIVED in London in 1961, the Royal Opera bought a house for my wife and me in Lexham Walk, Kensington. It proved to be a shrewd investment, for by the time I left, the administrators found that the property had appreciated—to such an extent that they made more money on its sale than they had paid me in salary throughout the decade. In effect, my work had cost nothing. It was a lovely house with a small fenced-in garden, and Hedi, who admired elegance and the upper-class English way of life, was in heaven. She was a fanatic Anglophile, much more than I ever was or will be. I love the English as individuals—an English friend is a friend forever—but their love of amateurism—"hobbyism," I like to call it—is something which has always been strange to me. Hedi had no such doubts. She was thrilled with her broad, diverse social life in London, and she was much liked. Aided by Frau Zador, our guardian angel, she became a successful hostess, constantly entertaining, and when Frau Zador had to leave temporarily for family reasons, Hedi engaged a Spanish couple to look after us: José, the chauffeur and butler, wore gloves when he served us, and Maria did the cooking and cleaning. It was so formal that I felt uncomfortable, but my wife believed that we had to "look right."

For the first time in my life, I was able to save money, thanks to the increased number of my guest appearances, and after a terrific holiday in Mexico, we decided to buy a holiday home of our own. We placed an advertisement in the *Neue Zürcher Zeitung,* the *Corriere della Sera,* and the *International Herald Tribune;* one answer came from a property speculator who offered a home at the Pineta di Roccamare, a residential area that was being developed on Italy's west coast, near Castiglione della Pescaia. Enid Blech had met the architect, Ugo Miglietta (who, by chance, was related to Dieter Satt-ler, a friend of mine from Munich days), and she and Hedi went to have a look at the place. Hedi was enchanted but worried. "It's won-derful, but we can't live here," she shouted at me over a bad phone connection. "It's full of the wealthiest Swiss!"

"If we can afford to buy it, of course we can live there!" I shouted back. And buy it we did. Roccamare is off the beaten track for some-one who has to travel as much as I do, but the setting is astonishingly beautiful, and in the summer it is usually sunny and hot enough to suit my taste for subtropical temperatures. The house, which is mod-est, is hidden away in an evergreen grove, surrounded by a private garden, and is only a minute's walk from a wonderful stretch of Mediterranean beach. On the first occasion that I drove to Cas-tiglione, I had the clear feeling that I had been there before, that I knew the landscape. This always puzzled me over the years, but hav-ing just visited my ancestral village in Hungary, I realize that the vegetation of the landscape is very similar—finally the mystery of my sense of homecoming is resolved. From my perspective today, buying the house was one of the best things I have ever done. I love the place. The relaxation and regeneration I gain from it every year, I believe, is the source of my energy and, I feel, has augmented my lifespan. I study, play tennis, ride my bicycle, swim, see friends, play bridge. The entire place is becoming rather like a United Nations holiday center, as we have friends and neighbors here from all over the world. I love the nearby village of Castiglione, and the honorary citizenship they bestowed on me means more than any other honor I have received. The landscape is very beautiful and unspoiled and there are many wild animals and, particularly, singing birds. Recently, I was working on my score of Bach's *St. John Passion* and one of the little birds was sitting in a pine tree and singing the most wonderful accompaniment to Bach.

Despite my growing success, or perhaps because of it, during my third Covent Garden season, Hedi and I separated, after twenty years together. The basic problem was a subtle psychological one: Hedi could not accept me as an adult. For her, I remained the overgrown Hungarian émigré wunderkind she had met in Zurich, the boy-man who had to be told how to behave in society and who could never be allowed to make his own choices in any sphere except the musical one. The day came when I could no longer bear the lack of personal independence, and I moved out of the house in Kensington and into the Savoy Hotel. Although the divorce was difficult, we managed to part amicably. She later married an Irish landowner and military man, but soon after that, she developed cancer of the liver. It was discovered too late. She died in her late sixties. I shall always be grateful to her for the love, support, and guidance she gave me during the most difficult period of my personal and professional life. Her courage and strength have been a constant example to me.

Shortly after Hedi and I separated, but before we had divorced, I became seriously involved with a young businesswoman whom I had met in New York while I was working at the Met. After we had spent a month together at Roccamare, however, we both realized that we were not meant to have a permanent relationship, and we went our separate ways.

A few months later, in September 1964, Valerie Pitts, a young journalist and television personality, came to the Savoy to interview me for the BBC. As usual, I was a little behind schedule, and I had to shout from the shower, "Wait a moment. I'm not dressed." I eventually went to the door in my bathrobe, and I asked Valerie to help me find my socks, which I had mislaid. I think we both fell in love within minutes. After the interview, I invited her to lunch, and a passionate love affair began. We very soon decided that we wanted to live together, but we were both married. Understandably, the situation created great difficulties, not only with her husband but also with her parents, who at the time did not approve of her love affair with a man twenty-five years her senior—nearly their age—and still, technically, married. She wanted to end everything, but I would not let her go; I pursued her determinedly.

In February 1965, I had to go to Tel Aviv, to guest-conduct the Israel Philharmonic, and I continued to pursue Valerie, phoning her at least twice a day, despite the complicated, time-consuming connections that had to be made by an operator in those days, and begging her to join me there. It was a difficult feat for her to bring off, but she did it, arriving early in March. I had delayed the start of a concert so that I could see her before it began, but unfortunately, her flight had had to stop in Athens, and she did not arrive until the intermission. When Ken MacDonald, the soloist, asked Valerie how long she was staying, I replied, "For the rest of her life."

I cannot recall Valerie's decisive flight to Israel without also mentioning a heart-stopping incident that occurred during our stay there. I was conducting two different programs, each repeated several times; the soloist on both was the British pianist John Ogdon. He played Tchaikovsky's First Concerto on one program and Liszt's First on the other. As music lovers know, in the first movements of most traditional concerti there is a substantial cadenza—a virtuosic, unaccompanied passage for the solo instrument—during which orchestra and conductor stay still and listen. On the evening of April first, in Haifa, in the hot, stuffy, smelly cinema where the orchestra used to perform, and in the middle of what seemed like the hundredth repetition of the Liszt Concerto, I suddenly realized that Ogdon had strayed into the cadenza of the Tchaikovsky. At first, I thought I was dreaming, but the more I concentrated, the more clearly I perceived that my soloist had indeed switched concerti in midstream. Panic overtook me. What will happen in forty-five seconds, I asked myself, when he gets to the end of the Tchaikovsky cadenza and I have to bring the orchestra in with the end of the Liszt movement—in a different key? It was a nightmare come true. But at the last instant, Ogdon invented a transition back into the right concerto, and the rest of the piece went smoothly. Afterward, I wanted to rush to his dressing room and strangle him—until the truth was revealed to me: The "accident" was really an April Fools' joke that Valerie had instigated and that Ogdon had carefully put into play.

Valerie and I married on November 11, 1967—Armistice Day. Our friends always ask us whether one war began on the anniversary of another war's end. The answer is, decidedly, no.

MY 1964–1965 COVENT GARDEN season was frantic. It began with the first complete *Ring* cycle I had ever conducted. Hotter and Schneider-Siemssen created new productions of *Das Rheingold* and *Die Walküre* to complement their existing *Siegfried* and

Götterdämmerung. The new designs for *Walküre* were a big improvement over the 1961 sets. Musically, I was at a tremendous advantage because by then I had recorded three of the operas and therefore knew the scores intimately. We also had at our disposal a splendid array of singers. And these separate factors combined to make it a very strong *Ring,* the proof of which is that it was repeated five times during the following six seasons.

For Christmas of that year I conducted a revival of a Rennert production of *The Tales of Hoffmann.* Many people don't realize that I love French music—especially *Carmen* and *Hoffmann.* I had last conducted the Offenbach score in Frankfurt in 1955, but I chose to use the original version of the opera for my first London production. During these performances, I worked for the first time at Covent Garden with two excellent young sopranos, Reri Grist and Heather Harper.

The following month, I had an extraordinary cast for a new production of *Arabella,* including Lisa Della Casa, Dietrich Fischer-Dieskau, and Joan Carlyle. Fischer-Dieskau was a classical singer more suited to Schubert recitals than to singing a Mandryka type, but he had the ability to create a wonderful, strong Mandryka sound; and Joan sang Zdenka brilliantly. It was a particularly happy production. This was in part because of my affection for *Arabella.* Although it is not in the same class as *Elektra* or *Rosenkavalier,* as a conversation piece I find it most enjoyable. For me, it is the first collaboration between Strauss and Hofmannsthal in which the librettist has the upper hand, and the poetry of the piece shines through.

There have been three great collaborations between composers and librettists in the history of opera. The first, between Mozart and Lorenzo Da Ponte, produced *The Marriage of Figaro, Don Giovanni,* and *Così fan tutte.* The next, between Verdi and Arrigo Boito, included not only a beautiful correspondence but also the 1881 version of *Simon Boccanegra* and the new masterpieces *Otello* and *Falstaff.* Strauss and Hugo von Hofmannsthal collaborated on many more works, including *Elektra, Der Rosenkavalier, Ariadne auf Naxos, Die Frau ohne Schatten, Die ägyptische Helena,* and, last of all, *Arabella.* It is a testament to Hofmannsthal's importance to Strauss that after Hofmannsthal's death, Strauss wrote a moving letter to his widow in which he said that he had lost not only a collaborator and a friend but his life, as well. It was a prophetic statement: Strauss lived for another twenty years, but he never again wrote a great work.

But *Arabella* was a happy production also because it was directed by Rudolf Hartmann, a good friend from my time at Munich and Frankfurt, who had also been a personal friend of Strauss. Hartmann was a wonderful director, the sort of director I would like to be myself. He had a natural, no-nonsense approach to the staging, he knew the score, he knew the music, and he understood the singers' point of view; out of this came a natural and joyful production, which I shall not forget.

My last production of the season, in June 1965, was one of the most difficult tasks I have ever undertaken: the British premiere of Arnold Schoenberg's uncompleted opera, *Moses and Aaron*. The world premiere, conducted by Hans Rosbaud, had taken place in Zurich in 1957, six years after the composer's death. It had made a strong impact on the public, but it had rarely been performed since. Walter Legge pressed Lord Drogheda to present *Moses* at Covent Garden, and the whole board eventually agreed that we must do it. I felt too ashamed to say no. Although I had conducted works by Bartók and Stravinsky, I had never before conducted twelve-tone music of such complexity. *Moses* is a much harder work than, for example, *Lulu*. There is a bel canto, legato quality to *Lulu* that is in contrast to the predominantly spoken and contrapuntal *Moses*. I remember feeling depressed as I grappled with the score during my 1964 Christmas holiday: I simply didn't know how to learn the piece, how to get it into my bloodstream. Eventually, I succeeded, but the further I forged ahead, the more I became aware of the enormity of the practical task ahead of me. Schoenberg's written indications of main theme and secondary theme, for instance, help performers to grasp what is going on, but bringing those indications to life is anything but easy.

Many of the parts, including the role of Moses, are spoken rhythmically rather than sung. But although there are difficult rhythmic problems, the problems of intonation are even harder. I took great pains at rehearsals to make the textures clear and to ensure that the solo voices were always audible, although the orchestration is sometimes too heavy and the individual orchestral parts are sometimes so demanding that the players are hard put to think about anything except playing the right notes at the right time. The same difficulties of rhythm and intonation also exist in the choral writing. Schoenberg's attitude toward singers seems similar to Beethoven's in the Missa Solemnis: The singers must sing what has been written down, no matter how difficult it is technically. But in the Missa, the notes are at least embedded in a harmonic context that is easy to understand; in *Moses,* there is no harmonic help, and every note is hard to find. I discovered that the solution to such atonal music was to approach it expressively, to play it like a Brahms symphony, so that it sounds simple, rather than harsh. And in this expressive quality lies the connection between Schoenberg and German Romantic music.

Peter Hall directed the production—the opera has so many spoken parts that it seemed logical to turn to the dramatic theater for a director—this was the first of several successful collaborations between us. Peter is intelligent, he has a sense of humor, and he is a professional; he takes time to learn an opera and he is well prepared every time he comes to the stage. But in the staging, too, major difficulties had to be overcome. Like *Fidelio, Moses* is a parable. But whereas *Fidelio* has a strong narrative, *Moses* sometimes feels like a philosophical treatise set to music. The rehearsals were spread over many weeks. I remember it vividly as the only time in my life when everyone—myself, Peter Hall, and the singers—was afraid of the rehearsals. My approach was nebulous; I just didn't know where to start or how to bring the sounds together. I had to lose my fear of the piece, and the only way to do this was to master the material. Looking back, I now feel that I should have started with a concert performance and gone on to do the opera once I had become familiar with the score. But the stage rehearsals were also dispiriting for a practical reason. Because of the complete lack of space at Covent Garden, David Webster had arranged for us to rehearse at the new Opera Centre, a former cinema on the Commercial Road, in the East End of London. It was not the ideal place that David had described, and it certainly took a great deal longer to get to from Covent Garden than the twenty minutes that David had told me to allow.

In the event, the acting was fine, but the production was too realistic for my taste. In the Golden Calf scene, for instance, everyone was covered in blood, and some local strippers had been hired to play naked virgins. This particular scene upset David so much that he could not bear to look at it, and every night at this point, he used to retreat to his habitual corner in the Crush Bar. It upset me, too, but for a different reason, since I was too busy conducting to be able to watch and enjoy this historic event.

We resolved the worst problems that *Moses and Aaron* posed, and it was so well received that it was repeated the following year. In the midst of this success, however, there occurred an incident that nearly brought about my resignation from the Royal Opera. David, who was very friendly with Maria Callas, had persuaded her to come to Covent Garden early in 1964 to sing *Tosca* in a much-admired Zeffirelli production; she enjoyed a triumph and agreed to return for a revival of the production in July 1965, with Georges Prêtre conducting. Shortly before the first performance, she decided that she did not feel well enough, vocally, to sing all four evenings. She would sing only the second performance, she said—a royal gala at which the queen would be present.

I found her attitude intolerable. Although I was not conducting *Tosca*, I felt that, as music director, I was responsible. "Either she is in or she is out," I told David. "If she can sing one performance, she can sing all of them." Marie Collier, an excellent young Australian soprano with whom I had worked many times, was prepared to sing *Tosca*, and I would have been delighted to let her perform at the gala as well as at the other performances if Callas refused to yield. David, however, took Callas's side.

I was so upset that I sent David a letter of resignation. "I can't take this," I said to Lord Drogheda. "This is not a serious opera house— no serious house would allow such nonsense." I told him that to allow Callas to have her way would set a dangerous precedent.

"Please reconsider," Drogheda said. "It's not worth it. There is so much important work to be done here. You mustn't give it all up over one little incident." He assured me that no precedent was being set, and he said that by offering my resignation, I had made my point.

So I stayed, and Callas sang her gala performance. I appeared at the beginning of the evening, to greet the queen, but did not remain for the opera. Everyone considered Callas a law unto herself, and, as Drogheda had predicted, no precedent had been set. The truth is that she had not been behaving whimsically: Her voice really was deteriorating. And that single London *Tosca,* on July 5, 1965, was her last performance of a complete staged opera. Collier stepped in for the remaining performances—thereby giving her own reputation a great boost. She was well on her way to a brilliant career, but it ended abruptly a few years later when she fell to her death from an open window in Leicester Square, only a few minutes' walk from Covent Garden.

I met Callas just once, when she was visiting London some time after the *Tosca* incident. David and I had been nurturing a sensational plan for her to sing the title role in *Lulu* at Covent Garden. We went to see her at the Savoy Hotel, and he told her about his dream project.

"*Lulu?* What's *Lulu?*" she asked.

"It's a major opera by Alban Berg," I said.

"Berg? Terrible music!" she said. "Why don't we do Bellini?" And that was the end of that.

People often talk about the Callas legend, but in my opinion, she did not have as great a voice as her rival Renata Tebaldi. Callas, though, had a magic about her; when she was onstage, you could not take your eyes off her.

Apart from the *Tosca* story, the only truly unpleasant episode that I recall from my Royal Opera years was the brief existence of an anti-Solti claque in the gallery, when some young people decided that I was no good and must go. After one particular performance, a cabbage was thrown onto the stage when I came out for a curtain call, and on another occasion, I found that my car, which I used to park in a reserved space on Bow Street, had been scratched and smeared with the message "Solti must go." This campaign, which lasted about half a season, reminded me of an old Nazi tactic: In Dresden in the 1930s, the Nazis regularly engaged a claque to disrupt performances by the anti-Nazi Fritz Busch. Every time he came into the pit, the mob would boo and whistle until he had had enough. The Covent Garden gang never explained what they did not like about my leadership; they simply hit and ran. However, although I am a worrier by nature, this particular situation, disagreeable as it was, never caused me real anxiety.

The press was a different matter. In Frankfurt, no one had harassed me, and there had never been any question of my artistic authority. In London, everyone felt free to tell me his or her likes and dislikes, and my authority was always being questioned. The professional critics were divided about me: William Mann, of *The Times*, was well disposed toward me; Andrew Porter, of the *Financial Times*, never quite decided whether to like me or hate me; and most of the rest maintained a basically negative attitude. I gradually learned to cultivate voluntary censorship: If Valerie or someone else I trusted told me not to read a certain newspaper review, I usually followed the advice. This saved me so much anger that I still adopt the same system. The funny thing is that even if I know someone has written a bad review about me, I am not upset unless I read it. But I need a great deal of self-discipline not to read a review, as I am always curious to know what has been written.

Generally speaking, performers pay too much attention to the press. Serious artists know much better than their critics when they have done their job well and when they have not. I have never overestimated either my talent or my accomplishments, and I know that whatever I have achieved has been the result of hard work—study, thought, experimentation. I have also learned that my musical taste develops faster than my ability to put it into operation, so I am forever trying to catch up with my taste. This has placed great demands on me all my life, but I hope and believe that it has resulted in growth. The enemy, for a musician as for any other artist, is not this or that negative remark by an outsider, but rather, laziness and self-complacency.

DURING the 1965–1966 season, I conducted new productions of *The Flying Dutchman;* an imaginative *Magic Flute* staged by Peter Hall; and *Der Rosenkavalier*, directed by Luchino Visconti. Visconti was one of the great film and stage directors of this century. His *Don Carlos*, in my opinion, was one of the most successful productions ever mounted by Covent Garden. He should, however, never have tackled *Rosenkavalier*, because he didn't speak German and arrived at the rehearsals with a pocket translation of the libretto in order to follow the text. Consequently he had great difficulty in keeping up with the rehearsals; he never really knew where we were. But despite all this, he did make a very good, if controversial, production.

In February 1967, I added *Fidelio* to my Covent Garden repertoire. A few years earlier, Otto Klemperer had conducted this production, and I had found his performances amazing, musically. He had difficulty in making his way to the podium because of semi-paralysis, and one could hear him muttering to himself during the spoken dialogue, but the musical intentions were strong and clear. Before the war, when he was in full command of his powers, I heard him give brilliant performances of some Beethoven symphonies in Budapest. There was vast power in his music-making, but the manic depression from which he suffered all his life made everything he did unpredictable. After the war, on one of my first return visits to Budapest, I heard him conduct *Figaro* at the State Opera, of which he was then principal conductor. He was in one of his manic phases, and whenever anyone in the audience coughed or made any other sound, he would turn around and shout, "*Schweigen Sie!*"—"Shut up!" At the end of the performance, when he came out for a curtain call, one of his dress shoes was bothering him, so he took it off in front of the audience and held it in one hand. During that visit, I called on him at his hotel. When I entered his room, he was lying half-naked on a sofa, with lipstick marks all over his body. The first thing he said to me was: "I hear you like Toscanini."

"Yes, very much," I answered.

"Oh," he said disapprovingly, "he has no taste. And besides, what sort of family life must he have? His wife stays over here in Europe while he's working in New York. How terrible!" This from a man who at that moment did not look like a model of domesticity. But during his last years, when he was conducting the Philharmonia Orchestra, his behavior became somewhat more sober. He was friendly to me whenever we met.

I tried to invite as many first-class conductors as possible to Covent Garden, and to encourage and further the careers of young conductors and singers. I invited Carlo Maria Giulini several times and another Italian, a young conductor, Claudio Abbado, who appeared there for the first time in his career. I found that Edward Downes, who had been an assistant conductor at the Royal Opera long before I arrived, was a talented man, and I gave him a great deal of work; I am pleased to say that he later developed an excellent international career. The great British Wagnerian, Reginald Goodall, was also a member of the music staff. He had an amazing understanding of Wagner's works and coached all the young singers in the roles. Although I esteemed him as a musician, I felt that he lacked the basic technical conducting skills that are necessary in order to transmit his love of the score to the performance. I know many people felt differently, and raved about his performance and criticized me for not giving him a chance to conduct at Covent Garden. I may have been wrong, but that was my opinion. Another member of the music staff who has made an excellent international career is Jeffrey Tate.

My only real problem in England was that I am not an amateur. I am a professional, I know what I am doing, and I want to do things well. The English have traditionally found professionalism in the arts suspect. I feel to this day that they have never completely accepted me, because when I want something, I want it forcefully. I do not apologize continually to the orchestra. Of course, if I make a mistake, I'm the first person to say "Sorry." Musicians want to hear a conductor admit to a mistake rather than gloss over it and try to press on as if nothing had happened. Besides, if you have a bad conscience, you cannot ask the orchestra to perform to its limits. I believe it was the composer Ralph Vaughan Williams who said that the English attitude toward music making is this: "Anything that's worth doing is worth doing badly."

My 1966–1967 season ended with a new production of Strauss's *Die Frau ohne Schatten*. Surprisingly, since the opera was then nearly fifty years old, this was its Covent Garden premiere. *Die Frau* is an amazing masterpiece and is quite unlike *Rosenkavalier* or even *Elektra*. Not every part is perfect, but it is genuinely dramatic and sometimes purposefully Wagnerian. No other piece by Strauss is so expressive, and this is why I like it. The opera is constructed from a strange and wonderful idea by Hofmannsthal, and is, in my view, the finest product of the great relationship between librettist and composer, in which words and music are beautifully balanced. The story is centered on two couples: the Emperor and Empress, and Barak, a dyer, and his wife. Both marriages are barren, and the outward sign of the Empress's childless state is that she casts no shadow. The opera's main theme is the fulfillment of both unions through the birth of children. *Die Frau* was first performed in 1919 in Vienna, and it can be seen as a celebration of peace and a reaction to the terrible slaughter of a whole generation in World War I. Its central themes are forgiveness and the recognition of suffering.

Strauss was important to my Covent Garden repertoire, and during each of the following three seasons I conducted one of his operas. In March 1968, I revived the Visconti *Rosenkavalier*, with a young Yvonne Minton in the role of Octavian; and in June 1970, I conducted a new production of *Salome*, directed by August Everding, in which Grace Bumbry was memorable in the title role. But it was my first London *Elektra*, in May 1969, that I remember most vividly. I had a dream cast that included Marie Collier as Chrysothemis, Regina Resnik as Klytemnaestra, and Donald McIntyre as Orest. Most extraordinary of all, however, was Birgit Nilsson as Elektra, a role that poses enormous challenges—vocal, musical, and dramatic. Nilsson is the only soprano who was magnificent in all three ways. Her Salome and Brünnhilde were extremely good, but it was as Elektra that she achieved her peak. I remember in particular the Recognition scene, in which the wild chromatic upheaval of the music gives way, after the revelation of Orest, to the A-flat major chord. The calm that follows was sung by Nilsson with a masterly tonal beauty and the passion, suffering, and sense of vengeance she conveyed were deeply moving. Nilsson has an indestructible voice: I hear that she can still sing today, and she is in her mid-seventies.

During the 1969–1970 season, I also gave my first London performances of *Don Carlos*. Giulini, who usually conducted our much-praised Visconti production, was unavailable for that engagement and I happily took his place. Later in that same spring of 1970, we took *Don Carlos* and *Falstaff* to Berlin, and *Falstaff* to Munich. These were my only tour performances with the Royal Opera ensemble. But I remember the tour mainly for a nonmusical event: While the company was in Berlin, Valerie gave birth to a baby girl, and I made a special trip back to London to see Gabrielle a few minutes after she was born. At the age of fifty-seven, I had become a father, and when I held the baby in my hands, I felt I was looking into my mother's eyes again. Three years later, a second daughter, Claudia, was born. The existence of these two dear creatures, who came into my life when I was old enough to be a grandfather, altered me profoundly and gave me so much joy that I cannot be grateful enough to Valerie and to my God for them. And just when this change in my private life was taking place, an equally important change transformed my professional life.

WHILE CONDUCTING in Dallas, during the 1961–1962 season, I had received a visit from Dr. Oldberg, an eminent surgeon who was chairman of the Chicago Symphony's Orchestral Association, and Seymour Raven, the orchestra's general manager. Our meeting, which had been arranged by Siegfried Hearst, my American manager, was short and anything but sweet. Oldberg and Raven told me that Fritz Reiner had announced his retirement, effective at the end of the 1962–1963 season (as it happened, Reiner died in 1963), and they asked me whether I was interested in succeeding him. I thanked them but also reminded them about the cutthroat review that Claudia Cassidy had given me in 1957. "I don't want to face any more of that sort of thing," I said.

"Don't worry, I can deal with her," Dr. Oldberg replied. "But I must tell you that we would need you in Chicago for sixteen weeks of concerts each season."

I said, "I can't give you that much time, because I am already committed to Covent Garden for six months of the year." I was about to add that by reorganizing my schedule I could give Chicago twelve weeks a year, which was as much time as most of the other major American orchestras' music directors spent with their respective ensembles. But I was not allowed to say another word.

"This is an insult to the Chicago Symphony," Dr. Oldberg blurted out. And with that, he stood up abruptly and marched out of the room, with Raven in tow.

I thought that this collision had ended whatever chances I had had for ever working again with the Chicago Symphony, but Hearst managed to arrange a two-week Chicago engagement for me in December 1965. I was in heaven conducting Schubert's "Great" C

Major Symphony with this magnificent ensemble, and the experience repeated itself the following week, when we rehearsed and performed Bruckner's Seventh Symphony. Indeed, I enjoyed the whole engagement so much more than another guest appearance I had made during the same period that I told Ann Colbert, Mr. Hearst's successor (he had died in the meantime), that although I did not want to come for any more one- or two-week engagements, because of the travel involved, I would love to return for a three- or four-week engagement with the CSO.

In 1967, John Edwards, who had replaced Raven as the Chicago Symphony's executive director, came to tell me that Jean Martinon, Reiner's successor, would be leaving the orchestra the following year and to ask whether I would be willing to become music director. I was certainly willing, but I thought that the job might be too much for me, inasmuch as I was still committed to Covent Garden. I suggested sharing responsibilities with Giulini, who had worked often in Chicago and was much liked there: One year, I would be music director and he principal guest conductor; the next year, our roles would be reversed. I now realize that the plan would never have worked, but at the time I thought it a good one. Giulini offered a more practical solution. "I am no good as an organizer, but Solti is," he told Edwards. "Make him music director, and I'll be happy to be principal guest conductor."

So it was that in the autumn of 1969, fifteen years after my debut with the Chicago Symphony, I became the orchestra's music director. And I let my friends at Covent Garden know that I would leave them in the summer of 1971—the end of my tenth season—because I did not want to face a crushing double workload for more than two years.

THE LAST two new productions I conducted during my directorship of the Royal Opera were *Eugene Onegin,* in February 1971, and *Tristan und Isolde,* in June, both directed by Peter Hall. At my last performance as music director, Birgit Nilsson took the part of Isolde. After ten years at Covent Garden, I knew that it would be an emotional occasion for me and I was worried that I might become overwhelmed. But the night itself was incredibly hot and I needed all my concentration just to get to the end of the opera.

After the performance, there was a reception in the Crush Bar, attended both by Queen Elizabeth the Queen Mother and by the prime minister, Edward Heath, who made me an honorary Knight of the British Empire. (It had to be honorary, because at that time I was still a German citizen.)

My time at Covent Garden had changed me enormously. I had grown a great deal and learned so much from the British: their style, subtlety, sense of humor, and above all, fairness, the latter a concept I had never really known before I worked in Britain. I had been feted, honored, had the privilege of associating professionally and socially with many outstanding people, and generally experiencing a far more sophisticated life than I had ever known before. I think I can say that Covent Garden turned the middle European musician into a cosmopolitan. Ten years of my life were over, and it was the end of an era at Covent Garden. Very sadly, toward the end of my tenure, Enid Blech had been diagnosed with cancer, and she died a few years later. I remember her with great fondness and gratitude. Joan Ingpen left with me and went to Paris to help Rolf Liebermann amalgamate the Paris Opéra and the Opéra-Comique. David Webster had retired shortly before I left, and he died soon afterward. My choice to replace him would have been Lord Harewood, but he had already taken over the English National Opera, and so it was David's assistant, John Tooley, who took his place. John was the logical choice as he had been running the house virtually on his own during David's last year. We had a good relationship, and he was always very helpful to me.

For the following nine years, until 1980, I returned to Covent Garden almost every spring or summer. Usually, I would conduct a revival of one of my old productions, but occasionally I took on something new. In 1973, for instance, I conducted my first *Carmen* in London, with an outstanding cast that included Shirley Verrett in the title role, Plácido Domingo as Don José, Kiri Te Kanawa as Micaëla, and José Van Dam as Escamillo. Verrett was a truly outstanding mezzo-soprano, and she did herself a great deal of damage when she began to sing soprano roles. Domingo is a phenomenon: Not only is he one of the most *musical* singers I have ever known; he is also capable of singing virtually anything well. When he performs Wagner, he produces the right kind of sound, just as he does for Verdi, Puccini, Bizet, and Spanish music. Kiri, who had made her Covent Garden debut only a year and a half before our *Carmen* production, is also a wonderful singer. I have worked with her many times since, in the theater and in the recording studio, and she is a much loved family friend.

I conducted my first Covent Garden *Parsifal* in 1979, in a new production directed by Terry Hands of the Royal Shakespeare Company. It looked very strange: The entire stage appeared to be covered in long-haired green moss. A repetition of *Parsifal* in 1980 was followed by a four-year silence, during which I wasn't invited. I've never understood why, since the general director, John Tooley, and the new chairman, Sir Claus Moser, were both close friends of mine. But in 1984 my friends remembered me again, and between then and 1995 I conducted new productions of *Der Rosenkavalier, The Abduction from the Seraglio, Elektra, Simon Boccanegra,* and *La traviata,* as well as a revival of *Otello.*

IN RETROSPECT, I would distinguish my three principal opera directorships in terms of a period of struggle (Munich), a period of calm development (Frankfurt), and a period of mature productivity (London). At my first press conference, on taking over at Covent Garden, I dared to say that I wanted to make the Royal Opera into the number-one opera company in the world, and I now have the temerity to say that I think I achieved just that. By the mid-1960s, daily performance standards at Covent Garden were probably higher than at other leading opera houses, including the Vienna State Opera and the Metropolitan.

At Covent Garden I have conducted eight operas each by Wagner and Verdi, five by Mozart, four by Strauss, and one or two each by Britten, Gluck, Schoenberg, Puccini, Ravel, Offenbach, Beethoven, Tchaikovsky, and Bizet—quite a list! I am proud of it. Tchaikovsky's *The Queen of Spades,* Stravinsky's *The Rake's Progress,* Berg's *Wozzeck,* and perhaps Verdi's *Macbeth* are the important operas that I have not yet conducted and would still like to do. But my pride in what I accomplished at Covent Garden has little or nothing to do with the

With Harry Buckwitz: A chance encounter on a Munich street in 1951 led me to join him at the Frankfurt Opera.

BELOW: Playing table tennis in the garden at Schwannheim

BELOW, LEFT: Emilie Zador outside the house at Schwannheim

With the soprano Claire Watson, Frankfurt

With Hedi and John Scott Trotter
(second from left) en route for
America in the mid-1950s

At the old Metropolitan Opera
House in the early 1960s

With Clifford Curzon at the time of my New York debut, 1957

BELOW: Enid Blech, my invaluable secretary at Covent Garden

BELOW LEFT: Hedi and John Gielgud at a party for *A Midsummer Night's Dream*, my first production at Covent Garden, February 1961

With Lord Drogheda, Chairman of the Royal Opera throughout my tenure

Studying beneath the pines at
Roccamare, 1962

With Valerie on our wedding
day, November 11, 1967

Die Walküre: the playback of Act III, 1965. With (from left) Hans Hotter, John Culshaw, and Birgit Nilsson

RIGHT: As a Valkyrie

At a party held by Enid Blech in 1971 to mark the end of my term at Covent Garden, with Jess Thomas and Birgit Nilsson, who sang *Tristan und Isolde* in my last performance as music director

With Valerie,
Claudia, and
Gabrielle at Oak
Street Beach,
Chicago, in 1974

With the Chicago
Symphony at
Orchestra Hall

With Michael Tippett, discussing the score of his Fourth Symphony. I conducted its world premiere in Chicago in 1977

With John Edwards, the general manager of the CSO

BELOW: At the rehearsals of *Otello*, my last production as music director of the CSO, 1991. With (from left) Kiri Te Kanawa, Luciano Pavarotti, and Leo Nucci

Portrait by Karsh

amount of repertoire I got through. It is based on my knowledge that all of these productions were thoroughly rehearsed, despite the old-fashioned stage and the poor facilities available to us at the Royal Opera House. Today, there is a mania for modernizing opera houses, but a much more worrying factor than inadequate facilities is the ever-diminishing number of conductors who have grown up in opera and are capable of achieving all-around excellent performances. And one of the reasons for the increasing influence of stage directors is the diminishing talent of music directors. The real opera conductors of my generation—Karajan, Giulini, Kempe, Keilberth, Krips, Fricsay, Leinsdorf, and quite a few others, including myself—have either disappeared or are well past eighty. Carlos Kleiber, Lorin Maazel, Colin Davis, Charles Mackerras, Claudio Abbado, Zubin Mehta, and Bernard Haitink are in their sixties and seventies; James Levine, Daniel Barenboim, and Riccardo Muti are in their mid-fifties; and Riccardo Chailly is in his mid-forties. I welcome with great relief the arrival of Valery Gergiev, who has grown up with the opera tradition at the Mariinsky (Kirov) Opera in St. Petersburg, and my former Salzburg assistant, Philippe Augin, who is now the music director of Braunschweig, and will soon be music director in Nuremberg, where hopefully he will become a "Meisterconductor." There are also Franz Welser-Möst and Daniele Gatti, so I am rather positive about the opera tradition continuing.

A good music director of a major opera company needs many more qualifications than musical talent, and the most important of them is organizational ability, because even the basic task of planning a season comprises many complicated elements. The shortage of international singers, for example, makes it increasingly difficult to maintain standards at an international house such as the Royal Opera. With fewer international singers and more international houses, the demand for singers is that much greater, which in turn makes planning essential. If you do not plan ahead, you will not get the best artists. You also need clever judgment. You must ask yourself which operas in the house repertoire can be presented again, in viable but not new productions; which areas of the repertoire need to be strengthened; which operas one would like to insert into the repertoire—and of these, which ones can be inserted, given the singers, conductors, and other material conditions at one's disposal.

I always tried to be well informed about the international vocal situation, through auditions, live performances, recordings, and the opinions of people I trust. Experience has taught me not to engage singers without having heard them myself. Whether or not a voice is well trained can usually be determined fairly objectively, but whether or not one likes the sound of a specific singer is a matter of taste. Nor should a music director be afraid to cast a young singer in a major role. A good example of this was my casting Angela Gheorghiu as Violetta in my Royal Opera production of *La traviata* in 1995. During roughly the first half of my Covent Garden decade, one could still insist on keeping singers, conductor, and director together for five or six weeks of rehearsals and six or eight performances in a row. But this has since become impracticable, because advance planning isn't good enough and not enough money is available to satisfy the celebrity singers. Music directors must decide which works to conduct themselves and which ones to distribute among other house or guest conductors, and they must never be afraid to invite the best available guests. To attempt to run a one-person show is ultimately self-destructive. In a big ensemble, a second cast and two or three house conductors must be on hand for any emergencies. Ideally, young singers who cover roles ought to be allowed to sing some of the later performances in a run.

Early in the twentieth century, stage directors and set designers were completely subordinate to conductors such as Mahler and Toscanini, who had the final say on everything. The situation changed after World War II, when all the great old opera conductors concentrated on the symphonic repertoire, retired, or died: Toscanini, Walter, Klemperer, Kleiber, and Victor De Sabata all gradually disappeared from the orchestra pit. Although this gave my contemporaries and me some wonderful opportunities to step into the breach, we did not yet have the authority of the older generation. The stage directors quickly occupied what had been the conductors' territory, on the assumption that if the musical component was no longer especially interesting, at least the staging could be more attractive. This was fair enough: The visual aspect of opera badly needed to be modernized, and the directors were right to try to revitalize the art. But revitalization soon became provocation. Some of the abominations that go onstage these days sadden me. I am sorry that the conductors of my generation have not had the courage to stand up to the more far-fetched concepts of certain directors. The solution will certainly not be a return to naturalistic productions, which are no longer acceptable; what we need are productions that are imaginative and in the spirit of the music. In the last ten years, I have seen a few new productions in which the director seemed to be ashamed of the music and thought that he could improve on it.

But let us assume, for the sake of argument, that conductor and director have agreed on the basic principle of a production. They should discuss stage action together and the coloring of the opera— the scenes and sets—and the conductor must give the director clear tempo indications well in advance so that pacing does not have to be grossly revised during ensemble rehearsals. They must communicate with one another and they must be flexible, because opera is an endless compromise. Conductors should not demand that every singer stand at the front and center of the stage for every important passage, just to make the balance easier to achieve, but by the same token, directors ought to learn that placing Madame X behind a column is of no use if part of the audience will be unable to hear her.

Stage directors should choose their set designers; the conductor may not always like the choice, but a harmonious relationship between director and designer is the first consideration. Together, conductor, director, and designer must figure out how much time is needed to create the sets and costumes. Covent Garden's administrators are now trying to create proper rehearsal facilities so that preliminary rehearsals can take place in a space that simulates conditions on the big stage. In the 1960s, we compromised on this matter, and the compromise did not do us any real harm. Although opera houses need up-to-date modern facilities, the quality of what happens onstage is what makes for success. The danger of the mania for "bigger and better" is that opera houses could return to their former roles as casinos and eating places in which the opera was put on merely for the benefit of the diners.

Another of the music director's responsibilities is to engage talented young coaches who play the piano well, and to help them master their craft through watching, listening, and participating. This is the best way to create new generations of opera conductors. When I rehearse singers, I rarely play the piano myself; an assistant plays, thus allowing me to listen carefully. But if there is a phrase or some

other detail that I do not like, I go quickly to the piano to demonstrate how I want it done. This sort of illustration is useful, because
few singers react well to complicated verbal explanations. I prefer
explaining at the keyboard to explaining by singing: I may not play
the piano as well as I once did, but I still play it better than I sing.
How many piano rehearsals are necessary depends on various factors. Is the work under preparation already in the repertoires of most
of the singers? Does the work present great technical difficulties, in
addition to purely musical difficulties? Have the principal singers
worked together before? Has the conductor worked often with most
of the principal singers?

Similar questions apply to an opera conductor's approach to
orchestra rehearsals. Has the orchestra played the work within the
last season or two? Has the orchestra played the work *with me*
within the last season or two? If so, the players will know my working methods and the rehearsals will take less time. Very soon after
I have begun the staged ensemble rehearsals for a new production,
I follow the advice that Strauss gave me in 1949: I ask my most
trusted assistant to conduct for the first twenty or thirty minutes of
a rehearsal while I listen from the auditorium. Since the singers
cannot sing their parts full voice twice at one rehearsal, I tell them
"sing out now with the assistant conductor, so that I can hear the
balances." From this new perspective, an experienced conductor
will quickly discover any basic weaknesses in the overall balance
and will be able to make corrections accordingly. When the orchestra is ready, we have what the Germans call a *Sitzprobe* and the
Italians a *prova all'italiana:* The singers sit on the stage and sing
their parts, accompanied for the first time by the orchestra, without having to worry about movement and acting. This allows
the singers to accustom themselves to projecting their voices over
the orchestra—totally different from the experience of projecting
over a piano—and it allows the conductor to begin to judge balances between singers and orchestra. Then come the ensemble
rehearsals—singing and acting, with orchestra, chorus, and everything else—which conclude with a pre–dress rehearsal and a dress
rehearsal. Finally, we are ready to perform—or so we hope.

· · ·

WILLIAM BUNDY, who was the Royal Opera's technical director throughout my musical directorship, resented me terribly during my first season or two because he thought I was trying to interfere. After two or three years, however, he became much friendlier: He appreciated the fact that I cared about coordinating rehearsals, about lighting, about how the stagehands carried out their tasks, and, indeed, about the entire technical side of opera production, which was becoming increasingly complex in those years. One day in 1971, when I was about to leave the Covent Garden directorship, Bundy dropped in to see me. "I want you to know," he said, "that you taught me how to make a theater work properly—how to create a proper production. I hated you at first. I called you a Prussian field marshal, because you enforced discipline. But now I know what you were aiming at. It's become part of me, and I'll never lose it. And I just want to tell you that I am grateful to you."

Of all the tributes I received when I left the Royal Opera—tributes from famous singers, powerful administrators, and even royalty—this is the one I still cherish the most.

DESPITE MY MARRIAGE to an Englishwoman and my decade-long directorship of the Royal Opera House, every time I landed at London's Heathrow Airport after a trip abroad I had to go through the foreigners' immigration queue, while my family joined the queue for British subjects, which was usually shorter. After I had been made an honorary KBE, I applied for British citizenship. I asked Robert Armstrong, now Lord Armstrong, who was the secretary of the Covent Garden Board, son of Sir Thomas, and a leading Civil Servant, to help me, and a few days later an official came to my home to examine my documents and ask a few questions. Within a short time, in 1972, British nationality was granted to me, and I was able officially to add the title Sir to my name. Needless to say, the first time I flew back to England with my new passport, the queue for British subjects was much longer than the one for foreign nationals. But never mind: Three nationalities in one lifetime are enough. I have a British wife and two British daughters, and British I shall remain.

SIX

CHICAGO

M Y TERM AS music director of the Chicago Symphony Orchestra was the happiest time in my professional life. I had completed twenty-five years of conducting opera and I decided that for the foreseeable future I wanted to concentrate more on symphony work, of which I had done comparatively little. To be in charge of the Chicago Symphony was the fulfillment of my dreams, but at the same time it was a new learning experience for me, a master class in musical directorship.

The orchestra represented the height of professionalism; the players were always prepared and arrived at rehearsal having studied and practiced their parts well, and consequently I had to work at the same level, or, indeed, beyond it. I had to prepare myself so that I knew every score in depth and had a very clear idea from the first rehearsal of what I wanted from the orchestra. Many of the players were not only outstanding musicians but also outstanding leaders. Frank Miller, principal cello, had played with Toscanini in the NBC Orchestra; Adolph Herseth, the principal trumpet, was the éminence grise of the entire brass section and perhaps the most revered and respected orchestral brass player in the world; Dale Clevenger, a brilliant young musician, headed the horn section; Milton Preves led the viola section as a benevolent dictator; Ray Still, the first oboe, was an outstanding player and teacher, and Donald Peck was a brilliant flute player. The joint concertmasters were Victor Aitay and Sidney Weiss, and Arnold Jacobs was a sort of father to all tuba players; young musicians from all over the world flocked to him for advice and guidance. The musicians of the Chicago Symphony in 1969 were masters of their profession and, despite personnel changes in the intervening decades, they still are today. I sometimes say that an orchestra is made up not of a hundred players, but rather of the fifteen players who lead the various sections. If these fifteen members are first-rate, the rest will be stimulated to play well, and Chicago was the best example of seeing this theory in practice. Many of the musicians in the orchestra have their own chamber groups, so that there are probably more conductors in the CSO than in any other orchestra in the world.

The Chicago Symphony was founded in 1891 by Theodore Thomas, a German-born musician who had arrived in New York with his parents in 1845. As a teenager he started playing violin in the pit for opera performances, and he later founded his own orchestra, which toured the eastern cities and Chicago. He went bankrupt and was forced to disband his orchestra, but he was rescued by an acquaintance who was a Chicago businessman. Unexpectedly encountering a depressed Thomas on Fifth Avenue, and discovering the reason for his gloom, the businessman asked whether Thomas would be prepared to come to Chicago if the money could be raised. Thomas is reputed to have replied, "I would go to hell if they would give me an orchestra." Thomas was not only a good musician but also a wonderful human being who was devoted to the well-being of his orchestra members.

After Thomas died in 1905, Frederick Stock, a violinist in the orchestra, took over as music director and remained there until 1942. From then until 1969, when I arrived, there were five music directors from five different countries: the Belgian Désiré Defauw, the Pole Artur Rodzinski, the Czech Rafael Kubelik, my compatriot Fritz Reiner, and the Frenchman Jean Martinon. My term as music director of the Chicago Symphony was longer than that of anyone except Stock.

At the beginning of my Chicago life, I had two personnel problems: The first was of my own making, the second not. In the spring of 1969, a few months before I started as music director, Tom Willis, the chief music critic of the *Chicago Tribune,* was sent to interview me in Vienna, where I was recording at the time. In the course of the interview, I looked through a list of the musicians and their dates of birth, and I made the mistake of saying that there were too many elderly players in the Chicago Symphony's string section. Had I been more diplomatic, done my work, and then gradually made changes, there would have been no trouble, but instead, when I arrived in Chicago and began to rehearse for my first concert, I found the players tense. I asked the Hungarian-born Victor Aitay, who was co-concertmaster of the orchestra, what was wrong and why the musicians never smiled at me.

"They are scared of you," he said. "They remember that Reiner fired players all the time, and they worry that you may be another Reiner."

"I am not going to fire anyone," I said.

"Then the best thing to do is to tell them."

At the next rehearsal, I explained the misunderstanding. My aim was to engage young players gradually, as the older ones retired. "I know how well this orchestra plays," I said, "and I have no intention of changing things." Two of the older members asked to audition for me, to prove that they could play as well as the younger members. I said that this was not necessary, but they insisted—and both played very well.

As a matter of fact, later, when the first string vacancies appeared, it proved difficult to find young players of a sufficiently high standard. In the early 1970s music was not yet regarded as a serious means to earn a living. In the case of string players, it took many years and a substantial financial commitment on the part of the parents to train a child to play a violin, cello, or viola. A whole generation was turning to safer and more practical professions such as medicine and law, in which they could earn a good living. I remember many fruitless auditions at the end of which I had hired no one. In desperation, I once engaged a particular young musician, simply because I felt I had to take on someone, but I soon realized that this was a mistake and that she was not right for the job.

Years later I held my last audition at the CSO for six violin vacancies, which I filled with the greatest of ease. The financial situation has improved so much that today a string player in a leading orchestra can earn more than a high-ranking government employee. Unfortunately there are more talented musicians coming out of music schools than there are job opportunities in the United States; this has been beneficial to European orchestras, which have been able to employ some of them. Unemployment among young American musicians has been aggravated by new federal laws that have raised the pensionable age, resulting in fewer vacancies. This is a matter that urgently needs to be addressed.

The second personnel problem was something that I inherited. A few years before I arrived, Jean Martinon had clashed with one of the orchestra's leading players and had dismissed him. The player, feeling that he had been unfairly dismissed, took his case to court, where he won and was subsequently reengaged. Unfortunately, during the trial certain colleagues had testified against him, with the result that the reengaged musician was not on speaking terms with certain members of the orchestra, despite the fact that they all sat together for rehearsals and concerts. During one rehearsal in my first season, one of these players stood up and walked out, saying, "I can't take any more of this!"

I knew that this was a major test for me: If I did not act immediately, the orchestra's internal discipline would fall apart. I called a break and asked both of the gentlemen concerned to come to my office. "It is intolerable for two such excellent musicians to make a scene like this during a rehearsal," I said. "If you don't make peace at once, forgive each other for whatever differences there have been between you in the past, I shall leave the orchestra immediately." I meant what I said. However sad I would have been to leave Chicago, I would have kept my word.

They were both silent for a moment, and then they shook hands. The break ended and they took their seats in the orchestra. From then on life became more harmonious.

I HAVE HAD quite broad experience with American orchestra musicians, not only in Chicago but in many other cities as well, and most of them have been outstanding. One must not forget that they have optimum working conditions: workable schedules and decent salaries. The only comparable conditions in Europe are found in the Berlin Philharmonic and possibly in Amsterdam's Royal Concertgebouw, whose musicians are well paid and have a restricted number of services each week. I am much in favor of this method, because only when players are not overworked can the conductor justifiably ask them to give their best and to practice regularly. Alas, this is not always the case in Europe. The brilliant Vienna Philharmonic, although financially secure, is at times desperately overworked, as the musicians play operas and concerts in the evenings and make recordings mornings and afternoons. Fortunately, their punishing schedule has not undermined the outstanding quality of their playing. The situation in London is bad, because orchestra players have to accept crippling schedules in order to survive. The British government gives neither the generous subsidies that many other European countries contribute to arts organizations nor the substantial tax writeoffs for private donors that the American government allows. As British orchestras unlike their American counterparts, lack the "cushion" of endowments, most musicians can survive only by running constantly from one job to another, and personnel managers are forever telling conductors, "The second flute will be late today," or "The third trombone won't be at this afternoon's rehearsal." I am anything but Prussian in my approach to life and work, but I do believe that musicians have a responsibility to the public, to themselves, and, above all, to the music to give their best—and this requires good organization, basic discipline, proper working conditions, and adequate pay and pensions.

There is another reason, and a fundamental one, why musicians should not have to play too much: The best of them must have time for teaching, so that they can pass their knowledge and experience on to the most talented players of the next generation. The American system makes this possible, but in many European countries it is not possible and this demonstrates a sad short-sightedness.

It is a shame that the Latin countries do not produce really first-rate orchestras, as there is at least as much talent in Italy, France, and Spain as elsewhere. Badly paid teaching and lack of discipline are the reasons. In the United States, on the other hand, training is excellent, and it is no longer fair to refer only to the traditional Big Five orchestras—Boston, Chicago, Cleveland, New York, and Philadelphia; one ought to refer to the Big Eleven, including also Dallas, Houston, Los Angeles, Pittsburgh, San Francisco, and Washington, D.C., and probably others as well.

Many conductors complain about the toughness of the American musician unions' regulations, but at the Chicago Symphony I learned a great deal about the organization of one's time in rehearsals because of these requirements. The musicians are disciplined about starting on time (tuned and ready to play) and ending on time, according to the rules. The two-and-a-half-hour rehearsal, with a twenty-five-minute break in the middle, seems to me to be the right length. If you concentrate intensely and work hard during the time available, you do not feel like continuing for longer. Also, the rehearsal order has to be given a week in advance so that the players know ahead of time when they will be needed, and this schedule cannot subsequently be altered: If Beethoven's Fifth Symphony is posted for the rehearsal on Tuesday morning at ten, you must stick to it. For some of my European colleagues this kind of scheduling can be difficult, but I quickly got used to it, probably due to my experience in opera, where planning is paramount.

Every system has its disadvantages, and to my mind, a common disadvantage in the United States is the subscription series, which is needed because there are no state subsidies. If well over 90 percent of the seats for an entire concert season are sold many months in advance by subscription, as was the case in Chicago during my time there, the organization enjoys a wide margin of financial safety; but subscriptions do not always create the best atmosphere for music-making. An ideal audience is made up of people who see that a certain program is going to be given, are interested in hearing those pieces, and buy their tickets accordingly. Many subscribers attend concerts simply because they have already paid for their ticket. Regardless of the works being performed or who is performing them, they go every Tuesday, Thursday, or Saturday, even if they aren't in the mood. Many are easily distracted and cough or clear their throats during soft passages or long, held notes. I found this so annoying that I once turned to the audience and said: "If you knew how long we worked on that pianissimo phrase, you would control your coughing."

The lack of attention is also expressed by the perfunctory applause at the end of each piece. And no sooner has the last note sounded at the end of the concert than many of the subscribers make a dash for the door. During my first years in Chicago, I used to turn to the concertmaster and joke, "Fire! Fire!" But deep down, I felt sad. Although I knew that the Chicago public liked me, I could not help thinking that many people came to our concerts feeling bored even before we had begun to play. I wanted to change the orchestra's concert series from a social ritual into a musical occasion. There were moments during my first years in Chicago when I felt that I would rather have people boo me than hear their tepid applause and watch their backs hurry through the exit doors.

The audience response improved as the years went by, not least because recordings enabled listeners to become more knowledgeable, which in turn made them more attentive. In fairness to the American symphony orchestra subscribers, many of them display great curiosity about new or unfamiliar works. They are less attentive when they are listening to a Beethoven symphony for the hundredth time than when they are listening to a new work for the first time. When I arrived in Chicago, the taste for Bruckner and Mahler was just becoming widespread in the United States, and what we now call twentieth-century classics—works of Stravinsky, Bartók, Alban Berg, and a few others—were not always readily accepted. This attitude changed during the 1970s, as a new generation of listeners began to dominate the audience, so that we even had great success with a concert performance of Schoenberg's *Moses and Aaron*. Many people came purely out of curiosity and discovered, to their surprise, that they liked the work.

During my early years in Chicago, each program was performed three times: Thursday evening, Friday afternoon, and Saturday evening. I hated Friday afternoons. These concerts were a trying institution left over from the "heroic" era of American orchestras in the early decades of the twentieth century, when an ensemble's survival depended on the support and hard work of its women's committee, which was made up of the wives of local businessmen and industrialists. Many of the ladies who managed to persuade their husbands to give money to the orchestra wanted a chance to attend concerts in the afternoon and had to leave at a certain time in order to get a lift home to the suburbs with their husbands. I didn't like those concerts because I went to bed late after the Thursday evening concert, and when I got up the next morning I had to prepare for the afternoon concert, which took place when I normally had my nap and then studied. Finally, one year we experimented by splitting the Friday series into ten afternoons and ten evenings. As attendance proved better in the evenings, the following year we moved the entire series to the evenings. Eventually, a Tuesday-evening series was added, and this I found exhausting, as it added up to eight services a week—four performances of that week's concert and four rehearsals for the next week's—in addition to a great deal of studying. However, it was a great improvement on the Friday afternoon series.

I do not mean to complain, however. The artistic pleasures that the orchestra gave me were enormous. And this is why I spent twenty-two years in Chicago.

WHEN I ARRIVED in the autumn of 1969, Chicago was like a sleeping beauty. The buoyancy of the postwar years had faded, and the city had turned inward and in some ways had become isolated from the east coast of America and indeed from the rest of the world. There were few direct flights to Chicago from Europe—you had to change planes in New York or Montreal—and European newspapers usually arrived days later. The spectacular architecture of the city had become run down and gloomy and several magnificent buildings were being torn down. The atmosphere at Orchestra Hall was far from dynamic. The orchestra still had its supporters and benefactors, but as far as the city was concerned, it was rather like a beloved but neglected piece of old furniture. There was a wind of change in the air, however, and within a few months of my arrival Chicago began to awake from her sleep. The first sign of this was the building of the John Hancock Center by the architects Skidmore, Owings & Merrill, which was completed in 1970. If you arrive by air, it is the first thing you glimpse, like a great lighthouse on the edge of the lake. Suddenly, there was a rush of spectacular new modern buildings enhancing the architectural gems of the past. There was a zip in the air and it was my good fortune to arrive at this time.

My job was to bring a similar change of air to Orchestra Hall. Martinon's five-year directorship had not left a lasting imprint on the Chicago Symphony; the orchestra I found before me in 1969 was more or less the same orchestra that Fritz Reiner had left in 1963. But morale was low, because Martinon had been a weak music director. Fortunately, Reiner had had a firm hand in selecting musicians, and his hard work had created a first-class orchestra. I was able to build on what he had done.

Reiner, however, was not interested in his orchestra's place in the world. I was. I am especially proud of three of my achievements in Chicago: I raised the musical standards, increasing international respect for the orchestra; I made the people of Chicago proud of their orchestra; and I helped to give the musicians financial security, so that they could count on better salaries during their working years and good pensions when they retired. These three accomplishments are closely related.

In 1969, the Chicago Symphony was the only one of the Big Five American orchestras that had not toured Europe; it did not even tour much in America. Again, I was enormously fortunate. The chairman of the Orchestral Association, the controlling organization of the orchestra, was a real-estate king named Louis Sudler. Louis was a keen singer and loved music, and he was also a man of vision. When I mentioned to him that it would be good for the orchestra to go on foreign tours in order to build up its reputation, he seized on the idea. John Edwards, the orchestra's manager, was equally enthusiastic, and within eighteen months we were in Vienna recording Mahler's Eighth Symphony on the first leg of a ten-city European tour. Chicago's Mayor Richard Daley had given us a check for $100,000 and on our return he welcomed us home with a ticker-tape parade. Until then, so strong a reaction from the local public had been unthinkable. I later took the orchestra on numerous long and short tours within the United States and on nine overseas trips: five to Europe (including one to Russia), three to Japan (the second included Hong Kong), and one to Australia, for the country's bicentennial celebrations in 1988. When we arrived in Sydney, we were all moved by a banner stretched across the road that led into town from the airport. It read: "Sydney has waited two hundred years to welcome Solti and the Chicago Symphony!"

The growth in Chicago's pride in its orchestra translated into concrete terms: When I took charge, the Symphony was $5 million in debt and near bankruptcy; when I left, twenty-two years later, it had a very substantial capital fund. America's Second City had become third in population but first in music; by then it was generally accepted that the CSO and Solti were the best musical team in the United States. We were proud that within the city of Chicago we became as well known and as well loved as the famous Chicago sports teams. Instead of being renowned as the home of the 1920s gangster Al Capone and the site of the brutal 1968 Democratic convention, Chicago soon became known worldwide as the home of the Chicago Symphony. I persuaded Decca to give the orchestra a recording contract and my conducting colleagues brought in their own companies, such as EMI and Deutsche Grammophon. The defunct radio broadcasts began again, the subscriptions increased, donations were up, the players had larger pensions, better health care and paid holidays, and we soon came to be regarded as the front-runner in the American orchestral scene.

John Edwards could be described as a twentieth-century Mr. Pickwick. He was a bachelor and bon vivant, and he was enormously well read. He loved people, attending parties, and talking about the orchestra. On concert evenings he would stand in the entrance hall greeting the patrons. The orchestra was his entire life and his office on the seventh floor of Orchestra Hall was both home and work-space to him. He liked to work with people he knew and at his own pace. His correspondence tray was legendary for its height. We used to say that he never answered his mail unless it was really urgent, because after a few months the mail answered itself. He was a very dear friend, but the friendship could be ruffled if you tried to alter his way of going about things, and there were some minor storms between us, though they never lasted for long. We were the joint parents of a large family, and whatever else we may or may not have achieved, we gave the orchestra the feeling of being a family.

The most enjoyable times we had were on tour. We set off like a circus troupe or medieval army, with orchestra members accompanied by their families, from small babies to grandparents, and some of the trustees and supporters. We would eat together, go sightseeing together, and laugh a great deal, as well as rehearse and perform. Rehearsing on tour is always a valuable experience, particularly when you are playing in different halls and have to adjust the dynamics to the acoustics. There is also the pleasure of playing in some of the great halls in the world, such as the Concertgebouw in Amsterdam, the Musikverein in Vienna, the Musikhalle in Hamburg, and the Philharmonic in Berlin. One of the key people on the tours was the stage manager Bill Hogan. He and his team got the instruments from A to B, loaded them up after the concerts, shipped them off to the next port of call, and then set up the stage for the following day. In all my years of touring, I never saw any of the stagehands in bad humor.

Among my great delights in Chicago were the Art Institute and the city's private art collections. A close friend of mine, Harold Joachim, grandson of the great violinist Joseph Joachim, was director of the Art Institute's Prints and Drawings collection. He was a quiet, discreet man who became poetic and passionate when talking about drawings and paintings. It was always a joy for me to visit him. He would show me the treasures in the vaults of his department. "Now I want you to look at this," he would say as he lifted out an early Goya or a Van Gogh drawing. He loved music and I love paintings, so our visits together were always enjoyable.

Valerie and I entertained a great deal, as I felt that visiting artists should be looked after. It can be lonely for a soloist, after the applause has died down, to go back to a hotel room and order room service. When we lived at the Drake Hotel, we had a large reception room overlooking the lake and it was there that we gave the parties, usually after the Saturday evening concert. We used to see many of the artists from the Lyric Opera, in particular Luciano Pavarotti and Geraint Evans. (Luciano used to come and eat spaghetti with us— he even prepared it with his famous sauce.) I remember Luciano visiting us once, at the beginning of his career, when he was giving a concert at the large Auditorium Theatre in Chicago. He had been billed as the new Caruso, but he was very worried that the concert would not be sold out. It seems unthinkable today that he should ever have had such doubts. Victor Borge was another frequent visitor. Apart from being an excellent pianist and comedian, he liked to conduct, and over supper he would ask me technical questions about conducting *The Magic Flute*. Another Chicago friend was the great astrophysicist S. Chandrasekhar from the University of Chicago. Beethoven was his passion and he had an amazing understanding of the composer.

The Chicagoans themselves could not have been warmer and more generous to us. They opened up their homes and their hearts. As a family, Valerie, our daughters, and I think of Chicago as our second home, and are grateful for all our friends there. It was a very happy place in which to live and work. The climate was dreadful in winter, but public and players struggled through the elements to come to the concerts. I believe I only had to cancel once, and there was also a recording session of Mahler's Fifth Symphony which had to be postponed for three hours because of a freak snowstorm. On sunny days I loved to walk along the lake and look back at the breathtaking skyline. One day when I was walking with Gabrielle (then four years old), a lady came up to me and said, "You are Mr. Solti, aren't you?" to which I replied, "No," as it was rather cold and I didn't want to stop and talk. Gabrielle was horrified and as we walked off quickly, she hopped at my side, whispering, "But you are, you are!"

DURING MY TIME in Chicago, I felt a clear commitment to conduct works by American composers. In my first season, I performed Charles Ives's *Three Places in New England,* which was in the program of my first concert as music director, on November 27, 1969; Elliott Carter's Variations for Orchestra, which was a Chicago premiere; and Gunther Schuller's *Seven Studies on Themes of Paul Klee.* I also felt strongly about introducing new pieces by leading European and American composers, and I eventually conducted world premieres of works by Marvin David Levy, Alan Stout, Hans Werner Henze, David Del Tredici, Sir Michael Tippett, Easley Blackwood, Witold Lutosławski, Morton Gould, George Rochberg, Karel Husa, Gunther Schuller, Ellen Taaffe Zwilich, and Andrzej Panufnik.

During my first season I also performed three works by Mahler: the *Lieder eines fahrenden Gesellen* and the Fifth and Sixth Symphonies. But it was Mahler's Fifth which I shall always associate with the Chicago Symphony. It was part of our first tour program together, to Carnegie Hall in New York. We went with a certain trepidation, not knowing how New Yorkers would receive us, as we were still an unknown quantity. When we finished the last movement, the audience stood up and screamed hysterically as if it were a rock concert. The applause seemed endless; they had fallen under the spell of our exceptional performance. I had never experienced such an overwhelming phenomenon in my life and probably never will again. From that time on, we enjoyed success in New York. Every time we went there, which was once or twice a year, and sometimes with the chorus, it was more than a concert; it became a musical happening.

I missed only one concert in all those years: Mahler's Eighth, which was conducted by our chorus master Margaret Hillis. I had tripped getting out of an elevator in Chicago, and suffered what can only be described as spectacular bruising. I was so shaken that I was unable to move and had to stay in bed for several days, so the orchestra had to leave for New York without me. I arrived with some difficulty two days later. Although I had trouble walking, once I was on the podium, all my stiffness and discomfort disappeared until the end of the performance, when I could hardly walk to the dressing room. It was astonishing.

The New York concerts were particularly agreeable because I was able to see many old friends who were either living in New York or had come especially for the concerts. Freddy Fellner, the man who had persuaded me to leave Budapest and consequently saved my life, was now living in California with his wife, Clary, and they used to make the trip to New York for the Chicago concerts. Terry McEwen, who at that time was running London Records in New York, was always a most generous host. He gave parties after the performance and invited all my friends, visiting celebrities, and any musicians and singers who happened to be in town and had become part of the CSO fervor.

Whenever we were in New York, Valerie and I used to go to the Broadway theaters as often as possible. Nor was our time in New York ever complete without a visit to our dentist, CSO groupie Dr. Walter Goldstein, who gave us all the latest New York music news while he took care of our teeth. Another regular stop was the Fifth Avenue toy shop, F.A.O. Schwarz. On one visit just before Christmas, I bought a rocking horse for Gabrielle. It was too late to deliver it, so I had no alternative but to take it with me and walk down Fifth Avenue to my hotel with a rocking horse tucked under my arm.

MY CHICAGO CONTRACT required me to conduct twelve weeks of concerts each year, as well as domestic and international tours.

Valerie and I continued to maintain our bases in Switzerland, Italy, and London, and in 1973 we moved into the house in North London that remains our main residence to this day. When we first went to Chicago, we took an apartment in the Drake Hotel, but after Gabrielle was born we rented a rather depressing little flat not far down the street. We soon returned to the Drake and occupied the same suite for several years. At one point, we rented a beautiful house near Ravinia, the big park where the CSO's summer concerts take place. Unfortunately, it was an hour's drive from Orchestra Hall, which meant that I spent two to four hours a day in the car, and when the traveling became too much for me, we again moved back to the Drake. Then, one day, Marco Torriani, manager of the Mayfair Regent, sent us a message via our friend Biba Roesch about a suite he had created to lure us away from the Drake. We looked at it and moved in. We remained there for ten years, until the Mayfair Regent was sold. These days when we visit the city, we stay at the Four Seasons.

If I dwell on the matter of our residences, the reason is that Chicago was the first city in which I was music director without making it my main home. I needed to provide a place for my wife and myself, and later for my daughters, that at least felt like home, even if it was not our principal residence. Gabrielle was born just after I had completed my first Chicago season, and Claudia arrived three years later. When they were little, they usually traveled with us, accompanied by Jill Ferguson, their nanny, and Pat Hughes, our housekeeper and secretary, both of whom we engaged shortly after Gabrielle's birth and who are still working for us today.

The girls loved Chicago—the neighborhood playground, the afternoon visits to Baskin-Robbins, and their many friends. When Gabrielle was ten, however, Valerie and I had to make a decision about her future, and Claudia's as well. If we made Chicago our permanent home, the girls would be left behind when we returned to Europe for concerts. They would be Anglo-Hungarian children living six months a year in the United States, without their parents. The alternative was to educate them in Switzerland or England, where their grandparents lived. For this reason, we finally settled in England; at least they wouldn't be as rootless as I am.

Whether my decision was right or wrong only time will tell, but I am very proud of the fact that both of my daughters went to Oxford, and that they have a sense of the world, of politics, and of the arts. But as a parent, I am not at all sure I did the right thing. I tried to organize my working schedule around their holidays, by splitting my twelve Chicago weeks into three four-week groups; but this did not always work, and our family life was continually disrupted. Between Chicago and my various tours and guest appearances all over the world, I was away from home nearly nine months a year, and to this day I regret the sacrifices that we all had to make.

Valerie divided her time: two to three weeks with me, then two to three weeks with the children. Jill was absolutely faithful and reliable—she loved the girls and they loved her—and the loving grandparents weren't far away. Nevertheless, children do need their parents. Gabrielle went to boarding school when she was sixteen, and Claudia, who was thirteen at the time, later told me that when Gabrielle first went away and she was at home without her sister or her parents, she often cried herself to sleep. It still hurts me to think about that, because it makes me feel that I failed as a father. I can only hope that neither of them was scarred by their upbringing. Our lifestyle clearly was not ideal from the domestic point of view, but professionally, the joy of working with the Chicago Symphony was immeasurable.

DURING THE 1970s, I combined my Chicago duties with a substantial commitment to two Parisian ensembles: the Opéra and the Orchestre de Paris. My first engagement in France had taken place in the 1950s, when I conducted the Orchestre de la Société des Concerts du Conservatoire. That had been a shocking experience. At rehearsals, the concertmaster had sat with his legs crossed and a cigarette dangling from his mouth. The rank-and-file members had argued, chattered, and carried on in an anarchic manner until we started to play, when they became passive and lethargic; the strings, for example, wouldn't move their bows more than five inches. And every time I stopped to make a correction or to ask for something to be played differently, the noise would begin again. The concert was awful, and for many years I did not work again in Paris, except with touring ensembles from abroad.

In 1967, André Malraux, President de Gaulle's minister of culture, gave the conductor Charles Munch an order to create a great national orchestra. The idea was excellent, but Munch was not well and did not take the trouble to form a completely new orchestra. Instead, he used fifty-six players from his old Orchestre du Conservatoire, which he led during World War II, as the core (roughly two-thirds) of the new Orchestre de Paris. This worked well enough for him, because he knew many of the musicians personally, but it worked less well for Herbert von Karajan, who, after Munch's death, took charge of the orchestra in 1969, and who gave up after only a year. Roland Bourdin, the orchestra's manager and Decca's former representative in France, asked me to take over. I attended one of Karajan's concerts with the orchestra, found the ensemble good but not great, and accepted the conductorship.

After the first few sessions, I understood why Karajan had left: To go to the Orchestre de Paris from the Berlin Philharmonic must have been a shock to him, just as going to it from the Chicago Symphony was a shock to me. In short, the orchestra was not good enough. It lacked discipline, and the overall level of quality was uneven. I tried very hard, but after having served three of the five years stipulated in my contract, I recommended Daniel Barenboim as my successor and left. I told Daniel that he would have to fight hard with the orchestra, but I believed he was the right man for the job. And so he was. He kept at it for fourteen years, gradually improving the quality of the players, so that when I returned later as guest conductor, I found a far better orchestra.

One incident that I remember from my tenure with the Orchestre de Paris was a concert performance of *Salome* in the Théâtre de Champs-Elysées. Grace Bumbry had sung the title role with me in London with great success, and I had recommended her for Paris. She flew in from the U.S., arriving just in time for a rehearsal, but not feeling well. Although she knew the role and did not herself need much rehearsal, the orchestra needed to rehearse with her. It was not an opera orchestra, and most members had never played *Salome* before. I insisted that she take part in the rehearsals, but I told her to mark (to sing softly) so that she would not strain herself.

At the first performance I noticed that Bumbry was having considerable difficulty. She got through the opera, including the difficult final scene, but part of the audience booed. She immediately canceled the second performance, which was to take place two days later at the Palais des Congrès; she said that she was ill. I recommended Anja Silja to replace her, but she was unavailable. While we were wondering whom to ask next, Bumbry phoned to say that she was feeling better and would do the performance.

The following evening, during Salome's scene with John the Baptist, Bumbry had even more trouble than she had had at the first performance. At the end of that scene, as the Baptist sang his curse, "*Du bist verflucht,*" Bumbry walked off the stage. Salome has a few minutes' pause at this point in the opera, and I assumed that Bumbry had gone off to have a drink of water. The performance proceeded, but she did not return. When the time came for her next entrance, "*Ich bin nicht durstig, Tetrarch,*" we went on without her. We continued through her next scene and on into the Dance of the Seven Veils, in which there is no singing. While I was conducting, I became preoccupied with how to end the performance. I knew that it would be ludicrous to attempt to get to the end of the opera without Salome; it seemed there was nothing to do but finish the dance and stop there. Toward the end of the dance, I made desperate attempts to signal to Gerhard Stolze, our Herod, that he must not stand up to sing his first line. But by then, he was a nervous wreck, like the rest of us. He jumped up and sang, "*Ah! Herrlich! Wundervoll, wundervoll!*" ("Oh, marvelous! Wonderful, wonderful!") The first "*Wundervoll*" was loud; the second came out softly, and it was followed by total silence.

Some members of the audience thought the opera had ended and began to applaud, but others started to boo loudly. I left the stage. The exit door was locked, but I shook it until someone opened it— and I found Bumbry in her dressing room, being looked after by a doctor. Meanwhile, part of the audience was storming backstage. They poured into my dressing room and demanded their money back. The manager was nowhere to be seen, and there I was, facing an angry crowd. Valerie, who had also rushed backstage, stood in front of the people and said, "*Il faut s'adresser à la direction*" ("You must take this up with the management").

I thought they would lynch me. "Now you know what it must have been like at the Bastille in 1789," I whispered to Valerie. I could only tell people I was sorry that we could not continue. Finally someone else arrived to say that ticketholders could either have their money back or be given tickets to another event.

This was the only time in my career when a leading character abandoned the stage in the middle of a performance. Bumbry wrote me a letter a few days later, accusing me of having shown no sympathy toward her. But how could I have shown sympathy under those circumstances? She should not have sung if she did not feel well. She was a wonderful mezzo-soprano, but Salome is a role better suited to a dramatic soprano. Several years later, Bumbry wrote again to apologize; she said that she had been going through a difficult spell at the time. (It is said that at one occasion in a *Salome* performance, Anja Silja felt she could not get through the final scene and solved the problem by jumping into the cistern with John the Baptist.)

At about the same time that I took over the Orchestre de Paris in 1970, Rolf Liebermann was appointed plenipotentiary director of the Paris Opéra and invited me to become artistic adviser. I did not want to give up opera conducting entirely, and the prospect of transforming the dusty old Opéra was enticing; I accepted. Liebermann closed down the Palais Garnier, the opera house, for renovations, and he tried to create a new orchestra and chorus by selecting the best players and singers from the old Opéra and Opéra-Comique. Hundreds of people auditioned for the new chorus, which was excellent. It destroyed the myth that there are no good choral singers in France. The orchestra was another matter. The musicians from the two old orchestras protested about the mass auditions, and in the end Liebermann weakened and agreed to give them all new contracts without any auditions. In so doing, he lost a unique chance to form an opera orchestra from scratch.

At my insistence, Liebermann hired Joan Ingpen to do the Opéra's planning, and she worked out a system whereby approximately half of the double-sized orchestra was rehearsing one production by day while the other half was performing another production in the evening. On paper, the system was as efficient as the one Joan had worked out for Covent Garden, and at first it worked well. But the French orchestra musicians were too clever for her. I soon noticed that players were missing at some rehearsals or performances, and every time I demanded an explanation I was told, "*Malade, monsieur.*" This state of affairs became so bad that I asked absent musicians to produce medical certificates to prove that they were ill. The truth was that many players skipped rehearsals or performances in order to earn extra money—that is, in addition to their state-subsidized salaries—by playing recording sessions or other jobs elsewhere. And at the Opéra, as with the Orchestre de Paris, each problem was exacerbated by the fact that I speak French badly.

Our first production was *The Marriage of Figaro,* which we produced first at the Palais de Versailles and then at the freshly restored Palais Garnier in Paris. Giorgio Strehler, the founder-director of Milan's Piccolo Teatro and an experienced opera producer, created a beautiful production, but I had an unfortunate personal experience with him. Shortly before the stage rehearsals began, I had taken an overnight flight from Chicago to London. When we landed, Valerie, Gabrielle, and I could not hear. After two or three days Valerie and Gabrielle were fine, but it took me three weeks to recover fully. By the time I was able to go to Paris, the stage rehearsals were finished and the ensemble rehearsals had begun. During one of them, I asked Strehler to make a small change in one scene. "You want me to make changes *now?*" he shouted. "Why didn't you come to the rehearsals?" And he walked out. I have not seen him since. He had assumed that I was one of those conductors who are too lazy to attend stage rehearsals; he simply did not believe that I had been ill. I regret never having worked with him again, because he is a brilliant director.

I was scheduled to conduct a complete *Ring* at the Opéra, but we never got past *Rheingold* and *Walküre.* Peter Stein's *Rheingold* production had some fascinating features. At the beginning, for instance, you could see Mime and Alberich working and swimming, deep down in Nibelheim, and this was very effective. But as a whole, the production was forced. After the *Rheingold* dress rehearsal, Stein left Paris and sent me a telegram that said, more or less, "I love and appreciate you very much, but what a pity that you don't love me."

The *Walküre* also had its difficult moments. The director was Stein's colleague Michael Gruber. One day, as he demonstrated something to Christa Ludwig, our incredibly gifted Fricka, she interrupted him. "Herr Gruber," she said, "everything you're telling me is shit, but I'm doing what you say because I'm well paid."

For me, the last straw was the dress rehearsal of *Die Walküre*. When I walked into the pit, I discovered that the first trombonist and the bass trumpet had not taken part in any of the previous rehearsals. Because these two instruments play the leitmotifs all the time, they are essential in *The Ring*. The results were terrible, and the production was my swan song at the Opéra.

DURING THE SUMMER of 1983, I conducted *The Ring* at Bayreuth, in the festival theater that Wagner himself had created and in which most of the great Wagner conductors had worked. Performing at Bayreuth ought to have been a particularly gratifying experience for a conductor who has dedicated as much time to Wagner's music as I have, but in the end it caused me endless suffering.

Since its opening in 1876, the Bayreuth Festival has always been run by members of the Wagner family: first the master himself; then his widow, Cosima; followed by their son, Siegfried; and then the son's British-born widow, Winifred, who was a friend and supporter of Hitler. After the war, Winifred was succeeded by her sons, Wieland and Wolfgang. Wieland, a brilliant man, died prematurely in 1966, and Wolfgang, the younger brother, assumed control by himself. He has considerable administrative ability, but his artistic talent is not equal to the task.

The festival has two outstanding features: the phenomenal acoustics of its theater and the excellence of its chorus, directed by Norbert Balatsch. But the basic musical standards were low because there was not enough money to pay for the stars. And in the 1980s this was as true for the orchestra as it was for the singers. For some years, the festival's administrators had been able to engage good East German musicians at relatively low rates: The players would come to West Germany, eat decently, buy clothes, and return home at the end of the summer having been paid in hard currency. Then Erich Honecker, the East German leader, toughened exit restrictions and put an end to what had been a mutually beneficial procedure. As a result, by 1983 the Bayreuth orchestra was fundamentally West German. But because they could not afford the best West German musicians, who earned enough at home during the main season and preferred a holiday by the sea or in the mountains to a two-month stint in rainy Bayreuth, the orchestra had become decidedly second-class.

My biggest problem, however, was casting. Twenty years earlier, when I recorded *The Ring*, I had had Nilsson, Hotter, and Windgassen at my disposal. The singers available to me in 1983 were not in the same league. Hildegard Behrens, our Brünnhilde, sang well, and some of her results were good. Siegmund Nimsgern, our Wotan, had a beautiful voice, but it was too small for a part that requires tremendous power. Siegfried Jerusalem also had a lovely, lyrical voice, but he should have stuck to Mozart and other, lighter repertoire; his Siegmund was not outstanding. But the main difficulty was with Reiner Goldberg, whom I had engaged to sing Siegfried. I had auditioned him first at Covent Garden and then in the Bayreuth Festspielhaus, with Wolfgang Wagner present, and both times I had said to myself, "This is *the* voice. Not since Melchior has there been such a natural Heldentenor." Lauritz Melchior, a Dane, was the most admired Wagner tenor of the 1930s and '40s, though he was not very musical. I was once amazed to hear an early recording in which he sang the "*Winterstürme*" aria from *Die Walküre* in 10/8, although Wagner had written it in 9/8. Years later, I was amused to hear Melchior perform the same piece with piano accompaniment in a charity concert in Los Angeles: He still sang it in 10/8.

What I did not know about Goldberg was that he was unable to master text. Since the days of my tribulations with Max Hirzel in Zurich, I had never worked so hard with any singer as I worked at the piano with Goldberg. At the first stage rehearsals he was magnificent vocally, just as I had hoped, but then he became frightened and shrank away to nothing. During the dress rehearsal, he was afraid to look at me. I never saw his face—he kept turning away from me and from the audience, hoping that no one would notice that he did not know the words. There was nothing to be done: We had to replace him. Manfred Jung was called in at the last minute and sang all three performances of *Siegfried* and of *Götterdämmerung*.

At my suggestion, Peter Hall staged the entire *Ring* that year. I admired Wieland Wagner's abstract productions, but I felt that it was time to do something different. I thought it would be interesting to have a modernized, naturalistic production—one that would keep to the spirit of Wagner's instructions without being ridiculously literal. Peter and William Dudley, the designer, created a fine production, but there were many technical problems. The stage crew was made up largely of Czechs who did not understand German well, let alone English, and Peter and Bill had considerable difficulty in communicating with them. This slowed down the entire staging process, and even at the performances there were some ludicrous technical problems. In one of the *Götterdämmerung* performances, for instance, the curtain went up late at the beginning of the second act, and the words "*Schläfst du, Hagen, mein Sohn?*" ("Are you sleeping, Hagen, my son?") were sung from behind the curtain. Someone, certainly, was asleep.

Nevertheless, the main problem remained the singers. It is possible to cast *Meistersinger, Tristan,* and *Parsifal* these days, although with difficulty, and you can probably cast *The Flying Dutchman, Tannhäuser,* and *Lohengrin,* but you cannot cast *The Ring*—and I say this despite the fact that all performances at the festival are sold out years in advance. I am not nostalgic about the old days. Generally speaking, Mozart operas are sung better today than in previous generations, and many works by Verdi, Puccini, and others can be cast better than ever. Where, three generations ago, was there a tenor with Domingo's versatility, musicality, and intelligence? And today there are many promising young singers, from Ben Heppner to René Pape, from Angela Gheorghiu to Renée Fleming. But with respect to *The Ring,* I stand firm in my opinion. There are no dramatic sopranos capable of singing Brünnhilde, no Heldentenors capable of singing Siegfried, and no Wagner bass-baritones capable of singing Wotan as the parts should be sung.

What, then, should Wolfgang Wagner do? Close the Festspielhaus? On the contrary, he ought to open it further. Wagner intended it as a center not only for his own works but for German opera in general. Why not perform Weber's, Strauss's, Henze's operas, Pfitzner's *Palestrina,* Hindemith's *Mathis der Maler?* Abolish Wagnerism as a religion and let some fresh air into the theater, as Wagner wanted. Try to rejuvenate the audience. The Wagner Festival as such has outlived its time, and new thinking is needed.

In 1984, when John Edwards died, I recommended Kenneth Haas, the Cleveland Orchestra's manager, to replace him as general manager of the Chicago Symphony. For personal reasons, Ken was not interested in changing positions at the time, although he later took charge of the Boston Symphony. The orchestra's vice-president suggested instead Henry Fogel, who was managing the National Symphony Orchestra in Washington, D.C. I phoned my friend Mstislav Rostropovich, the National Symphony's conductor, for an opinion. Slava told me that Fogel was a very good manager, but he warned me that if Fogel came to Chicago he would probably try to do what he had done in Washington: replace the entire management personnel with his own people, so that he could hold total control. In the end, the Chicago Symphony's board of directors hired Fogel, who did exactly as Slava had predicted. The only key management people left from Edwards's time are Martha Gilmer, the artistic administrator, and William Hogan, the stage manager. When I go back to Chicago these days, I know hardly anyone in the administration, and the numbers have swollen, enormously; I have been told that the administration is now more numerous than the orchestra.

Henry and I worked well together, but he was indirectly a contributing factor in my decision to leave Chicago. I felt clearly that I was the only remaining major part of the old guard. Because of my position, he would have difficulty in changing that, so I decided to make his task easier. The approaching hundredth anniversary of the orchestra seemed the moment to depart. I had long since passed my seventy-fifth birthday and although my appetite for work was unabated, the six-hour time difference between London and Chicago had become taxing, and I no longer wanted to travel so much. It took me a week to recuperate from the jet lag, and three trips a year meant six weeks wholly or partially wasted.

The decision was not made easily. When I had arrived in Chicago in 1969, I thought I would fulfill my three-year contract and then leave, but twenty-two years later, my heart was heavy. I had fallen in love with the orchestra, the city, and the American people. During my Chicago years, the center of town had been transformed into a cleaner and more beautiful place. There was tremendous choice in the shops and a general feeling of prosperity and well-being. (In 1969, Europe was a much cheaper place to live than the United States, but now it is the other way around.) At first, I had been disturbed when people came up to me in the street and said, "Hi, Solti, how are you?" But later I came to enjoy it. I like the Americans' friendliness and openness—so much so that Valerie and I flirt with the idea of spending my last years in a warm part of the United States. Above all, I left a public behind in Chicago; I think they liked me, and I certainly liked them. And when I return, my concerts are always sold out, which gladdens me.

The idea of engaging an American conductor to replace me was immediately raised, but no one could come up with a viable candidate. Leonard Slatkin was then considered too inexperienced, and Jimmy Levine was so busy at the Metropolitan Opera that he was not even considered. The two leading foreign candidates were Claudio Abbado and Daniel Barenboim. I had no personal preference, as they both seemed good to me; but when the players took a vote, they rejected Abbado, on the grounds that he rehearsed details in a fussy way, without giving the orchestra an overall vision of each work. By seventy votes to thirty, they chose Barenboim over Abbado, and their preference matched Fogel's.

Taking over from me was hard for Barenboim: The "Solti handicap" was a burden, and some of the critics were mean to him. Barenboim himself remarked that I was a hard act to follow, and that whatever he did would be wrong. I told John von Rhein, of one of the city's main newspapers, that when I first came to Chicago the critics wrote harsh reviews about me, but that by the time I left it was as if I were the greatest conductor of all time. I am glad that they have become accustomed to Barenboim too.

WHAT HAPPENED to me in Chicago repeated my experience in Frankfurt and at Covent Garden. When I arrived, the institution was better than I was, but, thanks to hard work and my evolving talent and taste, by the time I left I had well and truly caught up. I do not mean this boastfully: I had developed steadily and quickly, in a way in which an institution cannot. When I began in Frankfurt, I had only six years of conducting experience behind me and needed to do a great deal of catching up, but by the time I left Frankfurt I had worked with many great orchestras and singers and had made great strides. When I took over at Covent Garden, I was thrilled that London wanted me, but when my tenure ended I had the sound of the Chicago Symphony in my ears and was less happy with an opera orchestra. And at my first Chicago Symphony rehearsal, the orchestra seemed so near perfection that I thought I could never have anything better in my life, but by the time I left my musical vision had progressed.

And yet, the durability of my love affair with the Chicago Symphony was extraordinary. My tenure there was by far the longest of my music directorships—twenty-two years, as opposed to six in Munich, nine in Frankfurt, and ten at Covent Garden. The Chicago Symphony always was and still is the most "German" of the major American orchestras, because of its splendidly rich low string and brass sections. Initially, I found the brass too heavy—proportionally, they outweighed the strings and woodwinds—but over time I modulated and lightened their sound. There is no limit to the orchestra's technical ability; the only limit is the conductor's imagination, and the musicians love to be stretched to the limit, to improve the performance. This special quality of the orchestra changed my working methods.

Until I came to Chicago, I had been used to many rehearsals, because the technical ability of the orchestras I had worked with was mostly low. So when I first arrived I held my customary four or five rehearsals, in which I would concentrate on all the essential elements of music-making—phrasing, form, balance, rhythm. But I soon found that in Chicago I needed less rehearsal time than with European orchestras, and that I did not need to speak as much. My philosophy became "Let them play." Today, I still aim not to do too much in the first rehearsal; instead I let the orchestra play and I listen until the end of the rehearsal, when I introduce my ideas. During the second and third rehearsals I interrupt and make changes, and in the fourth rehearsal we play the piece through. In Chicago, once we had studied a work I did not need to think about the technical side. When I performed and then recorded *Moses and Aaron,* I required only a third of the time that I had previously taken. This was partly because I knew the answers to many of the questions that the score raises, but it was also because of the orchestra's technical skill. I lost the fear I have with all other orchestras—will their technical ability match my vision of a piece?—and I stopped having to worry about whether a particular phrasing we had rehearsed would happen in performance. The CSO never let me down, and this gave me the courage and tranquillity to perform.

MY CHICAGO SYMPHONY directorship ended in April 1991 with performances of Verdi's *Otello* in Chicago and New York. Luciano Pavarotti sang the title role for the first time in his life, Leo Nucci was Iago, and Kiri Te Kanawa took the part of Desdemona. Pavarotti and I shared the same publicist in America, who told me that Pavarotti would like to do it. I had already worked with Domingo in this role and I thought a change would be a good thing.

In the summer of 1989 Pavarotti came to my house in Italy two or three days in a row. I shall never forget his arrival, driving himself in his red Mercedes, in the trunk of which was a large pot and various plastic bags—his spaghetti-making utensils. We always had to break our rehearsals in time for him to prepare his pasta, which we all enjoyed greatly.

Pavarotti's voice was as beautiful as ever and he sang the heroic and lyric parts with equal distinction, but the whole enterprise turned out to be troublesome in many ways. He developed a cold, which I then caught from him and, consequently, I had to conduct my final performances as music director of the CSO with a high fever. I had no time to be sentimental about the end of my twenty-two-year tenure, and the farewell wasn't really difficult because I knew that in six months I would be returning to my orchestra again in the role of conductor laureate.

DURING MY ENTIRE time in Chicago I never had any serious disagreements with anyone in the orchestra, and I was proud when in 1987, on my seventy-fifth birthday, the musicians gave me a framed declaration, which they all had signed, and which read: "Through all these years, you have been not only our maestro but also our friend." I really did think of myself as their friend, and I still do. The Chicago Symphony's approach to music-making is extremely serious. I had always been a serious musician and a hard worker, but the Chicago Symphony made me even more so. The musicians' attitude was so stimulating that *they* made *me* love the rehearsals more than the actual performances. And this is a great compliment for a conductor to give an orchestra.

SEVEN

THE WORLD

I N JUNE 1991, I arrived in Roccamare with a heavy heart, and missing Chicago terribly. But after a few days, thanks to the recuperative powers of the pines and the sea, I began to feel more cheerful and started to study *The Magic Flute*, which immediately restored my spirits. I was to conduct a new production of the opera at the Salzburg Summer Festival, the first major engagement in my career as a freelance conductor.

In 1954, shortly before his death, Wilhelm Furtwängler had invited me to conduct *The Magic Flute* in Salzburg. I had accepted with pleasure, conducting in 1955 the beautiful production directed by Herbert Graf, with designs by Oskar Kokoschka, who made multicolored sets for the Felsenreitschule. I was enchanted by him as a person and also by his designs and paintings.

Herbert von Karajan was appointed the festival's artistic director in 1956, and for the following thirty-three years I conducted no operas in Salzburg—although I gave a few concerts there with the French National Radio and Television Orchestra in 1959, with the Vienna Philharmonic in 1962 and 1964 (during the four-year period when Karajan was not part of the festival's administration), and with the touring Chicago Symphony in 1978 and 1981. Christoph von Dohnányi told me that once, during a meeting of the festival directorate, someone had raised the possibility of my conducting *Elektra* at Salzburg, and that Karajan had leaned back in his chair and said, with a smile, "Just what I want for Christmas!"

When people asked me why I did not conduct at Salzburg, I answered that I had not been invited; when they asked why I had not been invited, I said that I did not know the reason, but that I regarded Karajan's attitude toward me as a great compliment. He was, obviously, a man of genius, capable of absorbing scores like a sponge; his repertoire was enormous. Beyond his musical talent, he possessed a tremendous appetite for power—indeed, he was probably the greatest musical power-broker since Wagner. I had little personal contact with him. In the early 1960s, when he was head of the Vienna Staatsoper, he invited me to conduct an opera at Salzburg, but the work was by a contemporary composer whose music I did not like; I declined the offer. A few years later, when I conducted a tour performance of the Vienna Philharmonic in Berlin, Karajan's Berlin Philharmonic gave a party in a restaurant for their Viennese colleagues; he and I were both present, and we had a polite little chat. So far as I can recall, there was no further direct contact between us for twenty years.

In about 1986, Franz Willnauer, the general secretary of the Salzburg Festival, phoned to invite me to conduct the Berlin Philharmonic at the 1988 Salzburg Easter Festival. I asked, "Does Karajan know about this call?," Willnauer assured me that the invitation had come from Karajan himself. I said that I was already booked to tour Australia with the Chicago Symphony, but that I would come with pleasure the following year. Willnauer, however, invited me to conduct a Vienna Philharmonic concert at the summer festival in Salzburg in 1988, and I accepted. At Easter 1989, when I was in Salzburg for my Berlin Philharmonic concert, I attended an excellent performance of *Tosca* conducted by Karajan. I went to congratulate him afterward and found him so frail that he could walk only with assistance. While there, I was also asked to conduct Strauss's *Die Frau ohne Schatten* at Salzburg in 1992; I imagine Karajan realized that he had grown too weak to undertake such a massive task. To this day I do not understand why I was suddenly in favor with Karajan.

In the summer of 1989, John Schlesinger, who was staging Karajan's new production of *Un ballo in maschera* for the Salzburg Festival, told me that Karajan was much better and that he was active and attending all the stage rehearsals. I was therefore shocked when, on July 16, my daughter Claudia phoned Roccamare from London to tell me that she had just heard on the news that Karajan had died. The next morning, Willnauer phoned to ask me to take over the *Ballo* production, which was to open a week later. I said no, because I had not conducted *Ballo* onstage for more than twenty years, and I suggested that he ask Claudio Abbado or Riccardo Muti, both of whom were working in the festival that summer, but they didn't want to do it. Then Plácido Domingo, one of the production's stars, called. "Maestro, you must come," he said. "You are the only person who can help us. We are desperate." So I agreed, despite the difficulties of the undertaking at such short notice. I immediately arranged to have my score sent from London by air courier. It arrived in Roccamare the next evening, having been picked up from the courier's drop point in Livorno, a hundred miles away, by our gardener and caretaker. I had two days to work on it, and then I left for Salzburg. To save time, Dimitri Pappas, one of Salzburg's most devoted supporters, offered to send his private plane to pick me up and the commandant at the local NATO base allowed us to land there.

That evening in Salzburg I was shown the models for the sets. The next morning was the "piano dress" rehearsal, when I first saw the costumes, the movement, and the lighting. As the production was a lively one, with a good but complicated staging, I gave several cues in wrong directions until I became accustomed to the singers' positions. Fortunately, the principal cast members—Plácido Domingo, Leo Nucci, Josephine Barstow, Florence Quivar, and Sumi Jo—were quite splendid and helped me to find my way around. I particularly remember that in the last scene, when the stage was full of masked figures, I desperately looked around to find my Riccardo; Plácido kindly waved his hand to show me where he was, and everything worked out fine in the end. Given that I had just over a week between receiving the score and conducting the first-night performance, it had been a risky and potentially unrewarding task for me to take on.

The festival administration was grateful to me for having saved the day, and Willnauer invited me to conduct *Ballo* again during the 1990 Summer Festival. Beate Burchhardt, Karajan's administrative assistant for the Easter Festival, came to me after the last performance and offered me the music directorship of the Easter Festival. Delighted with the opportunity to have an official function at Salzburg for the first time, I accepted. Dr. Kupper, a Zurich lawyer who was president of the Easter Festival, got in touch with me, and we discussed my responsibilities—artistic planning, not finances—and we worked out an initial, three-year agreement, effective from

1991. There was no written contract, but I was certain that the program we had decided on would be honored: I was to conduct *The Magic Flute* in 1991, *Die Frau ohne Schatten* (as previously scheduled) in 1992, and *Falstaff* in 1993. Each production would be repeated at the summer festival, but with the Vienna Philharmonic instead of the Berlin Philharmonic, and under the artistic directorship of Gérard Mortier.

By 1991, however, Claudio Abbado had been appointed to succeed Karajan as music director of the Berlin Philharmonic, and as the Berlin Philharmonic was the main orchestra for the Easter Festival, logic dictated that I share the leadership with Abbado. Hans Landesmann, who was part of the summer festival's administration and a close friend of Abbado, suggested that Abbado and I discuss the matter and come to some form of agreement. But not until 1993 did Abbado and I meet in my office at the Festspielhaus.

We knew each other well since Covent Garden days and I had frequently invited him to Chicago, where he was a major guest conductor. At our meeting, I suggested that we take turns during the following three years of the Easter Festival: One year he would conduct the annual opera and I would conduct the concerts; the next year we would swap roles. He said that sooner or later he ought to take charge of the Easter Festival, because he was music director of the festival's orchestra, and because he had already turned sixty. I saw his point and suggested that we work closely together for the following three years, up to and including the 1996 festival, after which he would take charge.

Abbado said that this seemed like a good solution, and that he would think it over. I asked him to send me a letter to confirm this agreement. The European postal system must be slower than I ever imagined, because four years have passed and I have still had no reply. The consequence is that I have conducted no operas at the Easter Festival since 1993. I did not then understand what was going on, but I learned recently that as early as 1991, the Directorate of the Easter Festival, Frau von Karajan, Dr. Kupper, and Frau Burchhard, had come to a private understanding with Abbado, which they had failed to tell me about. If they had, I would have agreed to be a guest conductor, but I would not have taken on the responsibilities of music director for only a three-year period. I am glad to be free of the politics of the Salzburg

Festival and to have no more administrative responsibilities, but it saddens me that at the time, none of the people who were my colleagues in the administration had either the courage or the decency to tell me what was going on. Had I been directly and immediately informed, I would have been the first person to understand.

A friend of ours who is a Salzburg insider and knows all the intrigue, said, "You know the problem with Solti? He turned out to be too good. The administrators needed someone to fill in the time until Abbado was able to take over." They had expected me to be a slightly dotty old Kapellmeister whom they could easily chuck out, but instead I was a success, and my personality was probably too strong to fit in with their post-Karajan planning. Many people were astonished when they learned that I was not coming back. The Austrian television network smelled a rat and asked me to speak about the situation, but I refused, as it seemed to me unhelpful to create a scandal. This is the first and the last time that I am making a statement on the subject. I continue to work regularly at the summer Salzburg Festival and to have a good working relationship with the Vienna Philharmonic and the Berlin Philharmonic.

AN EXTRAORDINARY event that took place during the first months of my freelance career was a performance of Mozart's Requiem in Vienna on December 5, 1991, the two hundredth anniversary of his death. In anticipation of this important commemoration, I had had endless discussions with my friend H. C. Robbins Landon, the eminent Haydn and Mozart scholar, about which edition of the work to use.

Mozart had died before he could complete the Requiem; he had composed and orchestrated only the first two movements in full. Parts of the third movement are by Mozart—the choral part and all the solo parts were written by him but not orchestrated. In the introduction to the Lacrimosa only four bars are by Mozart. His widow, Constanze, had asked Joseph Eybler to complete the Requiem, but in the summer of 1792 Eybler was commissioned to write a musical entertainment similar to *The Magic Flute* and handed back, unfinished, what he had done. The manuscript then went to Franz Xaver Süssmayr, a former pupil of Mozart's, who finished it.

Originally I had not wanted to use Süssmayr's edition, which is the most commonly performed, because I was convinced that too much of it was by Süssmayr and too little by Mozart; I had intended to use Eybler's version. But Landon told me to stick to Süssmayr's, and I am glad I followed his advice, because I found that, after all, Süssmayr kept his own interjections to a minimum, with the result that there is more of Mozart in his version than in any other.

The performance of the Requiem, which was to be televised all over Europe, took place in the late afternoon at St. Stephen's Cathedral, and was officiated by the Cardinal Archbishop of Vienna. That morning, I was informed that Arleen Augér, our soprano soloist, had lost her voice and could not sing the performance. We at once tracked down Judith Howarth, a young soprano, who lived in the north of England. The Austrian Broadcasting Corporation sent a private plane to pick her up from Newcastle, and by early afternoon she was in Vienna. At three o'clock, while Howarth and I were running through her part at the piano, there was a telephone call to say that Augér had had an injection and was now feeling well enough to sing. I asked Howarth to sit in the front row of the cathedral during the performance, so that if Augér lost her voice or could not continue, Howarth would be able to take her place. Through the two days of rehearsals, I had been troubled by the thought that Mozart had died only a short distance away and that his funeral had been held in this very church. I felt that his spirit was there, somehow, and I feared that this would unsettle me during the performance and I would start to cry. But in the event, I was so worried about Augér that I had no time to be affected by that. In the end, she sang the whole performance beautifully.

On returning to Holland, she discovered that she had cancer, and she died not long afterward—a sad end for a great talent. In a sense, she had sung her own requiem.

THE FOLLOWING year, 1992, marked an anniversary of my own: my eightieth birthday. On an October evening, Valerie, Gabrielle, Claudia, and I were whisked off to Buckingham Palace, where Prince Charles was hosting a dinner in my honor. What I did not know was that he, Paul Findlay (the director of opera at Covent Garden),

Valerie, and Charles Kaye (my assistant) had planned some surprises. We were not taken to the main entrance of the palace, but to a side entrance, and from there we were shown into an empty drawing room. At this point I should have realized that something unusual was happening. As I turned to Valerie to ask where everyone was, the door opened and in walked Prince Charles and Princess Diana, followed by fifteen other members of the Royal Family. We greeted each other and started chatting over a drink. A few minutes later, Princess Diana announced: "I think we should open the doors now." I suddenly found myself in a huge room with about two hundred guests, all of whom had been invited for a concert and dinner. Prince Charles made a charming speech in which he joked, "We want to make a little music for you, but if you get bored you can go home at any time."

The evening began with a three-piano arrangement of the *Figaro* Overture played by my Hungarian friends Tamás Vásáry and Peter Frankl, with Charles Kaye. Slava Rostropovich played a movement from a Bach suite. There was also a small orchestra that performed Wagner's *Siegfried Idyll*. It was made up of solo players from each of the orchestras with whom I had performed in the previous year and included Adolph Herseth, who had flown from Chicago to play the trumpet (the part played by Hans Richter in the premiere on Cosima Wagner's birthday); Rainer Küchl, the leader of the Vienna Philharmonic, who had flown back from the orchestra's Japanese tour; Rudolph Watzel, the chairman of the Berlin Philharmonic, who played double bass; and members of the Royal Danish, Royal Concertgebouw, Royal Opera Covent Garden, London Symphony, London Philharmonic, BBC Symphony, Zurich Tonhalle, Orchestre de Paris, Bayerischer Rundfunk, and Chamber Orchestra of Europe. Solos were sung by Hans Hotter, Anne Sofie von Otter, and Philip Langridge, and the concert ended with the finale of *Falstaff*, sung by a double cast that included Plácido Domingo, Leo Nucci, and Birgit Nilsson. Afterward there was a supper, where I discovered many old friends who had come to London for the event, including two representatives of my student days, George Feyer and Edward Kilenyi. It was a beautifully organized and unforgettable evening.

Nineteen ninety-three proved to be even busier than 1992. There were more concerts in Europe and North America, and *Falstaff* performances at Salzburg's Easter and summer festivals. The older I get, the more I love *Falstaff,* which is my favorite opera of all, at least at the moment. Gérard Mortier, the festival's new director, and I had invited Luca Ronconi to stage the opera. The production was brilliant, but the distances onstage were so great that keeping the ensemble together was often difficult, particularly in the fast passages.

During the summer, I worked with the young players of the Schleswig-Holstein Festival Orchestra, which was a strange ensemble. The predominantly Russian and American string section was very fine, and the woodwind playing was fair, but the brass section was mediocre. Nevertheless, I arranged for the orchestra to come to Castiglione della Pescaia, the town nearest my summer home at Roccamare. I had been made an honorary citizen of Castiglione, and I wanted to show my gratitude by giving a concert outside the castle that dominates the village. Unfortunately, a strong tempest blew up; the opening scene of *Otello* would have been appropriate, but all I was able to salvage was a reduced version of the *Fledermaus* Overture, played twice in a tiny sheltered courtyard.

In 1994 I conducted the Israel Philharmonic concerts in Frankfurt, Stuttgart, and Munich. The Israel Philharmonic could now be called the Russian Philharmonic, as a high percentage of the players are emigrants from the former Soviet Union, and this has tremendously improved the orchestra's quality.

Also in 1994, I went on a Japanese tour with the Vienna Philharmonic. I particularly recall that the Viennese horn players did not want to perform *Till Eulenspiegel* as fast as I wanted it to go. The reason is that the Vienna horn players still play old-fashioned F horns, which have no valves, and produce a distinctive mellow tone. But a particular skill is required for playing them, since they are neither as easy nor as flexible as modern horns. We have worked together for a long time now, so we reached a compromise: I conducted the tempo they wanted. But until we got to that point in the rehearsals, there were several slips which are referred to in the business as "fishes," so at one point I said to the leader, "I feel as if I am in an aquarium."

In 1992 or '93, I had a phone call and then a visit from Judith Aaron, the executive director of Carnegie Hall. She explained that although the New York Philharmonic had made Carnegie its base for the first seventy years of the hall's existence, Carnegie Hall had never had its own orchestra. She wanted to create one, she said, and she thought that it should have a six-month season. I suggested a more modest start: a two- or three-week season in the summer, to see whether the project would work. We agreed that the orchestra should be made up mainly of young American players, and my idea was that the section leaders be chosen from among the top players in the best American orchestras. We made a list, and everyone we invited came: Sidney Weiss, who had been my first concertmaster in Chicago and is now with the Los Angeles Philharmonic, filled the same role with the Carnegie Hall Project orchestra. The principal second violin came from Boston; the viola, cello, bassoon, and trumpet from Cleveland; the double bass, flute, and oboe from Philadelphia; and the clarinet, horn, trombone, and tuba from Chicago. It was the musical equivalent of an all-star football team, and the results were wonderful. The principal woodwind and brass players chose the other members of their own sections on the basis of auditions; the string section leaders accepted tapes from young players, and on the basis of what they heard, invited the best candidates to audition for us in Chicago. The quality of the two hundred young American string players was extraordinary: All of the people who auditioned were good enough to be accepted. I remembered how difficult it had been to find good players during my first seven or eight years in Chicago and I thought, Too bad I'm not starting my Chicago career now.

Everyone gathered at Carnegie Hall in June 1994 and prepared two programs, with pieces by Beethoven, Wagner, Strauss, Bartók, and Shostakovich. We worked hard, and the recording that we made bears witness to the excellent results. I told Judith Aaron that the following year we should take the orchestra on a short European tour, to demonstrate what brilliant young musicians America produces. She liked the proposal, but Isaac Stern, president of the Carnegie Hall Corporation, was against it. I stood firm: "If I can't show off the orchestra, I'm not coming back," I said. And sadly, that was the end of that.

In the autumn, after a brief Italian tour with the London Symphony, I returned to London to rehearse a new production of *La traviata* at Covent Garden. The director was Richard Eyre, artistic director of the Royal National Theatre. This turned out to be one of my happiest collaborations: The production was contemporary and fresh, but contained nothing that was not in the spirit of Verdi. It was also a sensational success. The part of Violetta was sung by Angela Gheorghiu, a comparatively unknown young singer from Rumania. I had wanted to give her a chance, because I thought she had the right qualities, and from that moment her career rose meteorically. I had not originally planned to record the production, but at the first stage rehearsals with orchestra, when I realized how wonderfully Angela sang and played the role, I changed my mind. You never know with an opera just how it will turn out. But this was a good one. I asked Evans Mirageas from Decca to attend a rehearsal. Within three days he had arranged to record the last two performances. I also called Avril MacRory at BBC television, who brought BBC executives to a rehearsal, and the seemingly impossible was achieved: The schedules on BBC2 were cleared for an entire evening at less than two weeks' notice so that there could be a live broadcast. As a result, we have a permanent visual record of the production, as well as a wonderful CD. There were never enough tickets to go around, since there were only five performances. As one friend remarked at the time, the only way to get a ticket was either "to kill or to steal."

The following year, 1995, was a particularly busy one in terms of international travel. At the beginning of the year I returned to the United States for a series of events: my first appearance in more than forty years with the excellent San Francisco Symphony, some concerts with the Chicago Symphony, and two performances with the Vienna Philharmonic in New York.

In July I conducted a special concert at Victoria Hall in Geneva to commemorate the fiftieth anniversary of the creation of the United Nations. I was delighted to be involved in this event, as the UN is an organization in which I firmly believe, although I wish it could have more power and be allowed to function more effectively. Fittingly, the orchestra's seventy-nine outstanding musicians came from forty-five orchestras in twenty-four countries. There was an introductory speech by Secretary General Boutros Boutros-Ghali, after which we played Rossini's *William Tell* Overture as a tribute to Switzerland, our host country; Bartók's Concerto for Orchestra, to commemorate the fiftieth anniversary of the composer's death; and the final scene from *Fidelio,* for its theme of liberation.

Concerts in Vienna, Berlin, and London were followed by a tour of Spain, Switzerland, and Italy with the excellent Budapest Festival Orchestra. This was the first time I had toured with a Hungarian orchestra. After further performances of *La traviata* at Covent Garden, I spent the summer in Roccamare, restudying *Die Meistersinger* and learning Bruckner's Symphony No. 0, "Die Nullte" ("The Zero" —so-called because it predates the nine symphonies in the composer's own official canon), both of which I was to record in Chicago that September. While in Italy I tried to make up for the concert that had been canceled at Castiglione two years earlier by accompanying the soprano Adelina Scarabelli and the baritone Stefano Antonucci in a recital of lieder and Italian songs, not in a castle this time, but in a farmyard. When heavy rain forced us to call off the first evening's performance, I began to think that my well-intentioned project was doomed to failure. But to my great relief we managed to bring off the event the next night without opposition from the elements.

I had not expected to be able to persuade Decca to let me rerecord *Die Meistersinger,* as its length and large cast make it very expensive to produce. But I had never been satisfied with the recording of it that I had made in the 1970s. I had disliked it even as we were making it. The cast, most of whom had been engaged on the recommendation of the record company, was not right. At the beginning of 1995, I heard on my car radio Pogner's monologue from Act I of *Die Meistersinger.* Usually I turn off the car radio immediately—I don't like background music—but the monologue moved me so deeply that it brought tears to my eyes. I thought, I have to do the opera again, soon. I had recently conducted *Così fan tutte* and I wanted to bring to *Meistersinger's* conversational parts something of the light style of Mozart's opera. After rehearsing the entire opera with the CSO that September, we recorded three live performances, and from these the finished recording was put together. Only an exceptional orchestra and chorus could have brought off such an achievement. As a result of its success, I plan to rerecord *Tristan* in Vienna in 1998 and 1999, because I was too inexperienced when I conducted the 1960 version. Besides, the acoustical balance was not good. John Culshaw and Gordon Parry believed, correctly, that Furtwängler's

EMI recording of *Tristan* had been badly balanced, with the singers singing directly into the microphones and the orchestra swamped in the background, but our 1960 recording had gone to the opposite extreme, with the orchestra swamping the singers—even Birgit Nilsson.

While I was in Chicago for the *Meistersinger* project, I also recorded "Die Nullte," which completed my set of all the Bruckner symphonies. I have mentioned how, in the 1950s, Theodor Adorno had communicated to me his enthusiasm for Bruckner, a composer I had previously found long-winded. I had started by recording the Seventh Symphony, and then the Eighth, in Vienna in the 1960s. Then there was a gap until I began in Chicago, where, over a period of years, I recorded the Fifth, the Ninth, the Sixth, the Fourth, the Third, and the Second. I did not come to Nos. 0 and 1 until much later, when I had determined to finish recording the whole series. And the "Nullte," which I had regarded as a young man's symphony, was last of all. The truth is that I had serious reservations about it until I talked the matter over with Robbins Landon. "Is it essential to include it?" I asked him. "There is no question," he said. "You must do it—it is a major symphony. Parts of it are better than either the First or Second Symphonies." How right he was. Of course, "Die Nullte" has its imperfections, and Bruckner's melodic invention was not yet as rich as it later became; but it is a beautiful work, a classical symphony of large proportions. The orchestration is transparent, and the piece as a whole presents only one basic problem: The conductor must sense where there should be major tempo fluctuations in order to avoid rhythmical monotony.

Only about a year elapsed between the completion of "Die Nullte" and the start on the Symphony No. 1, but Bruckner's orchestration had progressed and thickened considerably during the intervening time. In this symphony, as in the later ones, the conductor must take care not to let the brass cover everything else; he should not hesitate to change their dynamics drastically when necessary. The brass need to be brought to the fore when they have solo parts or other important lines to play, but in accompanying chords they must not be allowed to drown out the strings or woodwinds, just as a good opera orchestra should not drown out the singers. An orchestra performing Bruckner ought not to sound like a brass ensemble. Another general problem is Bruckner's fixation with symmetry: Four-bar phrases follow each other, one after another, and motifs are repeated over and over. Mozart and Beethoven would never have allowed such things, but Bruckner evidently believed or sensed that monotony has a certain majesty—as indeed it can have.

The Third, Fourth, and Fifth symphonies were all written during the 1870s and show an impressive development. Bruckner wanted to dedicate his Third Symphony to Wagner and went to Bayreuth to ask his permission. When he presented the great composer with the score, Wagner asked him what his name was. Bruckner replied that it could be heard in four notes of the trumpet solo in the first movement: *"An-ton Bruck-ner"* (D-A-A-D). This delighted Wagner, and he allowed the dedication.

Bruckner's next symphony, the Fourth, is his first great work. Along with the Seventh, the Fourth enjoyed a degree of popularity even before the composer's international revival after World War II. The reasons are obvious: The thematic material is beautiful, and the proportions, although large, are not gigantic.

The Fifth is longer and more complex than the Third or the Fourth, and its orchestration is the thickest of any of Bruckner's symphonies up to that point. In this symphony the conductor must take particular care to balance the sections of the orchestra. In addition, the finale of the Fifth presents a formal problem. It is particularly difficult because there are very complex contrapuntal elements in the score, and because it is hard for the strings to maintain rhythmic sharpness through the long stretches of dotted figurations. Fear of this huge movement—which is longer than an entire Mozart symphony—is the main reason for my having avoided conducting this work for more than ten years. It tends to become fragmented.

The Sixth Symphony is enigmatic and very different from the others. It is not as good as the Fifth and the Seventh, but it has some interesting, experimental features, such as its unusual opening. It begins immediately with the main motif, on high violins, without any introductory bars. But it is probably the least popular of the symphonies, as it does not yield easily to either performers or listeners.

The Seventh is not only the first Bruckner symphony I conducted but also the one I have conducted most often. Even many non- or anti-Brucknerians concede that it has one of the most beautiful openings of any symphony in the literature. The cello and horn theme, which Bruckner said came to him in a dream, is so simple and at the same time so mysterious. Among its other fine qualities, the Seventh has a decisive, well-proportioned finale.

Bruckner's melodic invention is revealed at its highest stage of development in the Eighth Symphony. As to the Ninth, although Bruckner's declining health did not allow him to compose the finale, the three existing movements show no lessening of his powers. I once visited Vienna's Staatsbibliothek to consult the original manuscript of this symphony, and the librarian also showed me a pile of sketches for the finale. It was a moving experience, because the sketches, which to begin with are well written and cover thirty or forty bars each, become ever more fragmentary and less and less logical, until they dissolve into single bars.

The Ninth, like the Fifth, is another beautiful work that I have neglected for a decade and that I would like to return to soon.

FOR THE FIFTIETH anniversary of Béla Bartók's death, in 1995, I conducted *Bluebeard's Castle* in Paris and Lille, and in London I did three all-Bartók concerts with the London Symphony. One of them included not only *Bluebeard's Castle* but also the immensely difficult Second Piano Concerto, with András Schiff as soloist. If the pianist's rhythm is not absolutely precise in this work, the whole piece can easily fall apart. The second movement of the concerto has a very fast tempo marking, and the conductor and pianist must keep the same tempo instinctively, so fast do the player's fingers move. From the podium, the conductor cannot hear the piano's sound at that moment; it is covered by the woodwinds. András was outstanding. It was a joyful collaboration.

The last major event of my musical year was Haydn's *Creation* in Munich, with the Munich Radio Chorus. I admire this group enormously and I hope to record Bach's *St. John Passion* with it in the near future. Having never conducted the work before, I am looking forward to this exceptional new musical experience.

Early in 1996 I gave my first performance of the opening movement of Mahler's Tenth Symphony, with the Tonhalle Orchestra in Zurich and on tour in Spain. Just as my late discovery of Bruckner's early Symphony No. o had fulfilled my forty-year love affair with his works, so my late discovery of Mahler's last, unfinished masterpiece completed my equally long study of this great composer. For thirty years, from the 1950s to the 1980s, I had conducted a large number of Mahler's works. Then I felt I needed to distance myself, in order to develop a fresh viewpoint. The break is now coming to an end, because I am about to conduct the Fifth Symphony again.

Mahler was a great conductor as well as composer, and the dynamic instructions in his scores are more precise than those of any nineteenth-century composer except Verdi. These instructions must be followed. Although Mahler did not often use metronome marks to indicate tempo, he did use written descriptions of tempo— including warnings not to rush or not to drag—and these give a clear indication if you have a sense of Mahler's style.

The First Symphony is nearly program music—it evokes scenes such as dawn and awakening—and in this sense it is Wagnerian. The first movement, in particular, is childlike, wide-eyed, enchanting, with strong hints of folksong and birdsong. The Second Symphony is more reminiscent of Beethoven. It is direct and dramatic, and not as tortured as some of its successors; it speaks to me more clearly than the Third, the Sixth, or the Seventh, for instance. For the conductor, the offstage band in the finale is hard to coordinate, and the unac-companied choral singing can be dangerous. The structure of the Second is heavier than that of the First, but the Third is even more massive. The Fourth is lighter and shorter and closer in nature to the First. Then begins the big crescendo in Mahler's work: Five, Six, Seven, Eight, each more grandiose than its predecessor. What I espe-cially like about the first movement of the Sixth is that it begins in medias res, with an introduction of only five bars—and even those five bars contain essential thematic material.

I have conducted the Seventh fewer times than any other Mahler symphony. It is a strange piece of music. The first movement, in particular, seems to represent a nightmare, and feels like the work of a madman. I hope to study and perform it again. In the Eighth Symphony Mahler often changes meter. Although the ending of the second part strongly anticipates Schoenberg and Berg, I think of the Eighth as Mahler's last great nineteenth-century work. For the conductor, most of the problems in this symphony stem from its massiveness. In a sense, the Eighth is a vast opera whose visual aspect remains in the imagination. Opera conductors have a tremendous advantage in conducting this and other big choral-orchestral works.

With *Das Lied von der Erde* and the Ninth Symphony, Mahler leaped from the nineteenth century into the twentieth. The middle movements of *Das Lied* display a Schubertian Mahler, rather than a Beethovenian or Wagnerian Mahler. It is not a grandiose work, and even the last movement, although long, is liedlike; in the closing "*Ewig, ewig*" section, one feels profoundly that the composer was saying farewell to this world.

In the Ninth Symphony, there are moments when tonality virtually disappears. The beginning, dominated by horn and harp, is followed immediately by one of the most beautiful of all Mahlerian melodies. The Ninth is an amazing piece: Structurally speaking, it returns to the relative simplicity of the earlier symphonies, but it is exceptionally difficult, and requires a virtuoso orchestra. I conducted this work for the first time in Frankfurt in 1959, but have not conducted it since the Chicago Symphony's Australian tour in 1988. As I looked over the score in preparing my comments for this book, I burned with desire to conduct it again soon. Wonderful though *Das Lied* is, the Ninth seems even more consistently remarkable and remains for me Mahler's greatest work.

My performances of the opening movement of the Tenth Symphony made me want to attempt to conduct a reconstructed version of the whole work. Mahler completed and orchestrated only the first movement of the symphony, which is twenty or so minutes in length. The melodic invention of the movement is heartbreakingly beautiful. It was written when he was already fatally ill and after his wife, Alma, had confessed that she was having an affair with the architect Walter Gropius, and Mahler's desperate suffering can be heard in the endless cry of the first violin. The long second and third movements exist in draft form only, in Mahler's handwriting. But the fourth movement was never written. The English musicologist Deryck Cooke made the first reconstruction of the symphony, but I have not used it, as I think it lacks the contrapuntal element in Mahler's writing. Three further versions of the Tenth Symphony exist or are in preparation, and in the summer of 1999 I would like to work on a solution to the symphony, putting together the different reconstructions that are available and adding points of my own.

And yet, despite my admiration of Mahler, I reached a point at which I felt I had to turn away, for a while, from these huge symphonic pronouncements and return to the miraculous world of Mozart. It is not by chance that Mahler has become the idol, the cult figure, that he is today. Regardless of how good or how bad a performance is likely to be, the hall is always full for a Mahler symphony. Maybe his appeal to today's audiences derives from the fact that the music is charged with anxiety, love, suffering, fear, and chaos—states that characterize our age. Mahler once said that his time would come, but he could not have imagined his music enjoying the success it does today.

It is easy to understand why, after the public had absorbed Mahler's symphonies and other massive orchestral works of the late nineteenth and early twentieth centuries, many composers opted for smaller structures and ensembles, down to the minimalists of our own day. I prefer the music of early minimalists such as Haydn and Mozart, whose music is simple but full, to that of their modern counterparts. Think of what Haydn achieves in the first few pages of *The Creation*. He describes the creation of the world out of chaos and pain, and when he arrives at the words "And there was light!," the final, forte C major chord of the phrase—if it is performed well—feels louder and mightier than all the massive chords Wagner or Bruckner or Mahler ever wrote.

IN MARCH 1996, I conducted two concert performances of *Don Giovanni* in Paris to reopen the renovated Palais Garnier. Then I went to Russia for my debut with the St. Petersburg Philharmonic. It was love at first sight—a repetition of the experience I had had with the Chicago Symphony more than forty years earlier. The orchestra is magnificent (particularly the sound in the lower strings—violas, cellos, and basses), and the Tchaikovsky and Shostakovich Hall, the nineteenth-century hall where it plays, not only looks beautiful but has wonderful acoustics. The language barrier posed no problem: The musicians and I understood each other at once, and they got used to hearing me say "Good boy!" whenever one of them achieved something I had asked for.

One of the pieces we were performing was Tchaikovsky's "Pathétique" Symphony. In the second movement, the main theme consists of a series of two-bar groups. I wanted a slight emphasis on the first note of the second bar in every group, but they played it with a crescendo through the first bar and without an accent in the second bar.

"Maestro, this is the way we always played it with Mravinsky," the first cellist said to me, in broken English. (Evgeny Mravinsky had been the orchestra's principal conductor for fifty years, until his death in 1988.)

I checked the score; the crescendo was there, but so was the accent mark, as I pointed out.

"All right," said the principal cello, "we'll make a Solti-Mravinsky compromise: crescendo plus accent."

I thoroughly enjoyed our concerts and our recordings of the "Pathétique" Symphony and the soundtrack for the film *Anna Karenina*. There are moments when even the most experienced performer is overcome with awe, and that is how I felt as I walked up the steps of the hall that Tchaikovsky had walked up when he conducted the "Pathétique" for the first time, more than a century earlier. Tchaikovsky died just ten days after the premiere, so that in the last movement of the symphony, in effect, he composed his own funeral music.

Following our St. Petersburg sessions, I took the orchestra on a short tour to Rome, Barcelona, Strasbourg, and Luxembourg. After the last concert I gave a supper for the musicians at their hotel. As my wife and I were leaving, they all stood up and shouted after me: "Good boy! Good boy!"

A concert with the London Symphony in Dresden gave me the opportunity to visit the beautiful Semper Opera, rebuilt from the ruins of the city, which had been pulverized during World War II. It struck me immediately that this is undoubtedly the most magnificent opera house in the world. As I went up the main staircase, which is as glorious as that of the Palais Garnier in Paris, the general manager and the technical director both explained that some of the marble from the old building had been preserved and had been mixed together with marble from Carrara and artificial marble in a small factory that had been created specifically for this purpose, by order of Erich Honecker. Giuseppe Sinopoli was rehearsing *Erwartung* in the auditorium, and the orchestra sounded marvelous. I have never heard opera house acoustics to equal these.

I made a trip to Lübeck, in northern Germany, to conduct a charity concert to raise funds for the reconstruction of Turkish immigrants' houses that had burned down. Then, in July and August, I rehearsed and conducted *Fidelio* at Salzburg. Herbert Wernicke's production was modern and very strong—an excellent solution for this notoriously difficult-to-produce opera, which is really neither opera nor oratorio. The singing of Cheryl Studer, Ben Heppner, René Pape, Ruth Ziesak, and Roberto Saccà was wonderful. After *Fidelio,* during my short holiday period in Italy, I worked hard to rethink the Beethoven Ninth, which I performed in September with the Chicago Symphony at the Proms in London. I was happy to be working again with my old orchestra after nearly a year's separation, and I think the pleasure was mutual. The following month, I gave concerto performances of the Paris *Don Giovanni* at the Royal Festival Hall in London. The cast now included Bryn Terfel, who was singing the Don for the first time, and Renée Fleming, an outstanding Donna Anna. Terfel is a wonderful talent, and Renée Fleming has the vocal and musical potential to dominate the leading dramatic soprano roles in the next ten years.

THE ADVANTAGES of being a freelance conductor are obvious. If you are not the music director of a major organization, you do not have to cope with personnel troubles, financial problems, programming requirements and audience demands. The disadvantages of being a free-lance conductor are less obvious. When I work with orchestras that are not absolutely first-class—youth ensembles, for instance—the difficulty lies in putting the players at their ease, so that they are not afraid of me. When I work with first-class orchestras, I always feel that I must prove myself, every time. I am not referring to the fact that when orchestra musicians are about to work with a conductor who is past eighty, and whom they have not seen in a year or more, they ask themselves, "Does he still have the ability?" Yes, they are all amazed that at my age I can conduct with full vigor, because I am lucky enough to be in good physical shape, but they get over that amazement in the course of the first rehearsal. I am talking about proving myself *musically*. In this sense, working for one or two weeks as a guest conductor is more tiring than working many weeks with my own orchestra. On the other hand, rising to the challenge of proving myself every time I step before an orchestra has contributed greatly to my development since I left Chicago. And I have probably advanced more during the last five or six years than in the previous fifty. I have reworked many, many pieces, and I realize that I function much better today than in the past. My vision is broader. I dare more. I grew up like a good foot soldier, a follower: If Mahler or Nikisch or Furtwängler or Toscanini did something a certain way, I felt I should do the same. Now, I proceed in my own way.

I listen carefully to my recordings before I allow them to be issued, but I never listen to them when I am preparing to perform or to record the same piece again. I do not want to be influenced by my old way of thinking about a work; I want my approach to be as fresh as possible. Occasionally, I listen to other people's recordings of pieces I am studying, letting them act as catalysts, but I am primarily interested in developing ideas directly from the printed score. In my mid-eighties, I feel more strongly than ever that I have an endless amount of studying and thinking to do in order to become the musician I would like to be.

EIGHT

MUSIC, FIRST AND LAST

ALL MY LIFE I have been preoccupied with how to be a good musician—not merely a musician with a successful career, which is also important, but how to develop and improve my talent. Recently, while I was studying Strauss's *Also sprach Zarathustra,* I said to myself, "I do not know this piece, after fifty years!" I was in despair. People think conducting is simple: You beat the air and everything comes out naturally and easily. They do not understand how much work must be done before one arrives at something that can be called an interpretation.

In my case, the entire learning process is slow, because I have no visual memory. I cannot look at a score and absorb it as Toscanini and Karajan were able to do; I have to learn each note individually. This does not mean that conductors with excellent visual memories work less hard than I do; but they have a tremendous advantage over those of us who are forced to spend so much time studying every note of every score. When I was younger, I did not study as thoroughly as I do now. I studied form, which has always interested me, in both symphonic and operatic music, but I did not master detail as carefully as I have since the age of seventy. I believe that today I study scores more thoroughly than if I had a good visual memory. Some conductors I know master the outlines of a score, tell themselves that they have done enough, and then depend on their orchestra to bring out the details. But learning and conducting go hand in hand. You cannot be a first-class conductor unless you know the score in the greatest detail. After all, a conductor must be a teacher, first and foremost. How can you teach something you do not yourself know well? As I said earlier, I think I can make any orchestra, good or bad, perform to the best of its abilities. This is probably my greatest talent, and in fifty years of hard work, of teaching myself and orchestras, I have acquired the technical knowledge and the experience to do this.

When you go before an orchestra, you need to have a clear idea in your mind—a sound-image—of what you are trying to achieve. And then you must try to realize it. When I start a movement, I know the shape of it from beginning to end. I am an architectural conductor; I cannot improvise as Nikisch and Furtwängler did. In the first movement of the "Eroica" Symphony, for instance, I know at which point I will slow down for the second theme, and at which point I will return to the original tempo. With any symphony, a conductor must have a clear idea of how to make the main "voice" dominate and when to bring the other elements—contrapuntal, harmonic, rhythmic—to the foreground; he must know when secondary "voices" ought to be more audible than the primary ones; and he must understand how to draw this out of the players. A conductor's aim is to make the orchestra produce what he imagined during the weeks and months when he was studying the score. Toscanini once told his orchestra, "I hate you all, because you destroy my dreams." It was an overstatement, not least because he really loved his musicians, but it perfectly expresses the conductor's plight: You have a dream and you try to realize it; if your dream is destroyed, you suffer. Rehearsals exist in order to try to realize dreams.

Then comes the obvious question: What are you doing wrong? If you do not realize your dream, it is because you did not communicate it well enough. The shortcomings usually will not be technical, because the best orchestras have seen enormous technical progress in the last half-century. I remember how much time we used to waste in European orchestras, fighting over intonation. These days, music students play a great deal of chamber music, and they learn to listen to one another. In all my years with the Chicago Symphony, I hardly ever had to tune the woodwinds or brass, because the players detected bad intonation as quickly as (or quicker than) I did.

Conductors whose beats are not clear, like Bruno Walter, one of the great conductors, lead a difficult existence. Walter, an extreme example, eventually grew very anxious about this, until his conducting arm became so stiff that he could not lift it. At this juncture, he went to see Dr. Freud, who recommended a month's holiday, after which, Freud said, everything would be all right. And it was.

Aside from wielding the baton, a basic necessity for a conductor is to know exactly how a certain passage should sound. If your imagination is clear, then you will communicate with the orchestra even if your beat and technique are not first-rate. If a conductor believes in what he is doing—if he is convincing and does not vacillate—the musicians will always follow him. For me, the fight is with myself, not with the orchestra. If I can solve an interpretive problem in a way that satisfies me, then I am able to get the orchestra to achieve it.

The inexplicable miracle of conducting is that the body, eyes, and soul of a conductor transfer something intangible and unique to an orchestra. If an orchestra plays the same sixteen bars of music under different conductors, those bars will sound different on each occasion.

Early in my career, when I was working mainly with second-rate orchestras, I learned that they generally played below the level they were capable of achieving, and that they were happier when I made them play at their highest level. A sense of accomplishment is the best gift that any conductor can bestow on an orchestra.

ABOUT TWENTY YEARS ago, I held a competition in Chicago for young conductors. We had more than one hundred young American applicants, ranging in age from eighteen to thirty-five. I watched and listened to all the candidates, each of whom initially conducted two pianos in a preselected program. After five minutes I could tell whether they had any talent for conducting. Most of them didn't know how to start by giving an upbeat before the music began, and once they had started, instead of leading, they swam along with the pianos. Out of the hundred, only fifteen went on to the final rounds. This was the clearest proof for me that conducting cannot really be taught or learned; you either can lead or you cannot. A conductor has to be able to anticipate the sound and give the beat a split second ahead of the orchestra. In addition, you have to have imagination and the talent to communicate what you have in your soul and mind.

When I was studying at the Liszt Academy, conducting classes began during the final year. As I mentioned earlier, we learned a completely wrong technique using the wrist, which took me years to forget. We didn't have too many orchestras to conduct, but there was the student orchestra at the academy, and I was fortunate enough to conduct the post office orchestra; my conducting it must have been a disaster, but at least I was given the opportunity. I once conducted the trio from *Così fan tutte*—Fiordiligi, Dorabella, and Alfonso. I didn't know how to start the orchestra in the first two bars, but once the singers joined in, I was all right.

Actually I learned conducting from watching the great conductors when I was a coach in the 1930s at the Budapest Opera: Erich Kleiber, Issay Dobrowen, Fritz Busch, and Bruno Walter, for whom I played the piano rehearsals for the Verdi Requiem; later, my Salzburg experience with Toscanini was a revelation, for the magnificence of his interpretation and the clarity of his conducting. One of my first opportunities as a coach in Budapest was to conduct the off-stage band in Friedrich von Flotow's *Martha*. I was a beginner in my second year; I had never conducted it before and had had no rehearsal. The scene onstage was a marketplace, and I was responsible for the village band. In order to keep in time and take my cues I had to look through a hole in the scenery with one eye, while watching the band with the other, a first for me. I watched like a hawk, took my cue, started off, and was so thrilled that it was going so well, that I stopped looking at the conductor and concentrated entirely on conducting my band, with the result that when that particular episode ended, I was a full bar behind. "You had better go home quickly," the senior coach warned me.

Serving as a coach at the Budapest Opera was invaluable training. I don't believe that anyone can be a true opera conductor without that kind of experience, although in the end, why some can and some cannot conduct remains a mystery. Beyond the importance of training and experience, above all, we conductors should always remember our role as interpreters; we are there to serve with the best of our technical abilities the wishes of the composers, who are the creators.

LIKE ANY OTHER profession, conducting has its physical hazards, which range from bursitis to injuries sustained from falling off the podium. I have twice stabbed myself with my baton. The first time, I was recording *Parsifal* at the Sofiensaal in Vienna when I struck my left hand with the baton, the tip of which broke off under the skin. My assistant conductor, Jeffrey Tate, who is also a medical doctor, suggested that I have the hand X-rayed immediately. The X-ray showed no damage, and the doctor told me not to worry: "If it doesn't hurt, leave it alone. The bit that broke off will work its way out." Sure enough, during a rehearsal in Chicago a few weeks later, I turned to Valerie, who was sitting in the auditorium, and shouted, "Look! Look! It's come out!"

A more serious incident occurred while I was conducting a performance of *Figaro* at the Met in 1976, with the visiting Paris Opéra ensemble. We had had only one rehearsal, the dress rehearsal, and I had not gotten used to the conductor's light being higher than usual; to compensate, I was raising my arms higher than I normally do. During the Count's aria, at the beginning of Act III, I stabbed myself in the head with the point of the baton. I went on conducting, but blood began to run down my face. At first I tried to stop it with my handkerchief, and during the harpsichord-accompanied recitative that follows the aria, which lasts for about twenty seconds, I left the pit, wet the handkerchief in a drinking fountain backstage, replaced it firmly on my head, and returned to the pit. The stage manager, who had noticed the empty podium, had given the order to lower the curtain; but when he saw me reenter the pit, he made the curtain change its course in midair. I arrived just after the sextet had begun and took over from the concertmaster, who had stood up to conduct. It all happened so quickly that not even Valerie had noticed that anything was amiss. After the performance, the house doctor bandaged my head, and the next day I went to another doctor for stitches. "You're lucky," he told me. "If the point had entered one centimeter to the left, it would have hit the main vein, and you wouldn't have stopped bleeding." Since this second mishap, I have always used batons with rounded tips.

My "core" repertoire spans well over two hundred and fifty years in the history of musical composition, but I have conducted little music by composers prior to Bach's generation: a few performances of Purcell's *Dido and Aeneas* at the Margrave's Theater in Bayreuth in 1949, and not much else. When I was a young piano player, Bach's music was considered important to perform for mechanical reasons—for improving technique—but not for the profundity of the musical content. This attitude was as prevalent in Hungary as in many other countries. I studied parts of *The Well-Tempered Clavier* and the Two- and Three-Part Inventions, the "Italian" Concerto, and, later, the C Minor Partita, but I really had no idea what Bach's music meant. I understood the construction and the way in which the voices linked together, but I did not understand the substance; I played it mechanically.

The *St. Matthew Passion* was the first major Bach work I conducted, in Munich, and I have performed it many times since. To me, this is not only a religious work, but also an "unoperatic opera" that relives a tragic story of human suffering from beginning to end. It is among the greatest masterpieces ever written. The musical descriptions of Christ surpass any of Wagner's musical descriptions; maximum dramatic effects are achieved with the simplest orchestration.

The Mass in B Minor is more specifically religious but no less wonderful than the *Passion,* and I regret that I have performed it only twice. Over the years, I have also conducted the "Brandenburg" Concerti and some of the other concerti, and suites; but I know very few of the cantatas, and I am saddened to think that there are so many great ones I will never know. It is a pity that I shall die without having learned much more of his music.

As with Bach, I have performed little of Handel's vast and marvelous output. I have conducted only *The Messiah* among the oratorios, but I have conducted none of the operas and know but a handful of the concerti grossi and a few of the other concerti. Bach and Handel seem to me opposites, in many ways. There is a spiritual quality even in Bach's secular works, whereas in Handel, even the religious oratorios are operatic. Handel was an opera composer par excellence.

Chronologically, the next composer who figures at all substantially in my repertoire is Gluck, although I have conducted only two of his operas: *Orfeo ed Euridice* and *Iphigénie en Tauride.* As his music is at times static, productions of his operas require not only fine singing and playing but also lively, intuitive stage direction and excellent corps de ballet. I would like to restudy *Orfeo,* because I am sure that I would fall in love with it again.

In my day, Haydn was a great favorite of Hungarian piano teachers—perhaps because of his long connection with the princely house of Esterházy, who were his patrons for many years—and in my boyhood I played more Haydn than Mozart. I adore Haydn, but I have conducted only about fifteen of his symphonies, which number more than a hundred. I have also performed several of his concerti; the Sinfonia Concertante for violin, cello, oboe, and bassoon; and the two great oratorios, *The Creation* and *The Seasons*. I consider *The Creation* to be one of the greatest masterpieces of the oratorio literature, if not the greatest. I admire Haydn also for his generosity of spirit and for his unselfish admiration of Mozart's ability. It is well known that Haydn told Mozart's father, Leopold, "Before God and as an honest man I tell you that your son is the greatest composer known to me either in person or by name."

I came to Mozart's music at an early age and have conducted a great deal of it throughout my professional life. During my years at the Budapest Opera, we performed all three of the Da Ponte operas as well as *The Abduction from the Seraglio* and *The Magic Flute*. But the general standard was not high. The operas were sung in Hungarian translation, and I was young and unaware of how great these works are. Then I went to Salzburg, where I heard Bruno Walter conduct *Don Giovanni,* with Ezio Pinza in the title role, and worked with Toscanini on *The Magic Flute.* I understood for the first time the greatness of these operas. Working with Toscanini was like having a spotlight on the opera, and at the time, I thought his *Magic Flute* was the most wonderful thing in the world. Thirty years later, in America, I heard a pirate recording of one of those performances and found the tempi strange: The fast tempi were too slow, the slow tempi too fast—everything was a little awry. And yet there is great authority: You feel that whatever Toscanini did, he believed in it at that moment, and so did we, who worked with him, and the public. Tastes change, but my great love for the work remains.

I sometimes read that a particular conductor once performed a piece at a particular speed. Nobody should believe it. Often, when I hear a recording of a performance I thought I had remembered well, I am surprised at how different it is. What you really remember is not the performance itself, but whether a performance touched you, and the best example of this for me was Toscanini's *Magic Flute.*

When I began to conduct Mozart's operas, I immediately felt at home with them. I always thought that I had clear ideas about these works, but this does not mean that I did them well. Indeed, those early performances cannot have been good, stylistically, because in those days the average professional orchestra, like those of the Munich and Frankfurt opera companies, had too many strings and did not have the lightness of sound or the technical ability to play fast enough, so that they could not carry off a piece like the Overture to *The Magic Flute,* for example. Gradually, however, I found my way. I began to understand that "andante" means "moving at a natural tempo," not "slow," and that Mozart must never be heavy or slow. I had great success with Mozart's operas in Munich and Frankfurt, even though my interpretation of *The Marriage of Figaro* at Covent Garden in 1964 was criticized for being too fast. But today, quick tempi have been adopted by nearly everyone.

The stylistic issue in Mozart interests me greatly, and my present opinions are based on having conducted about ten of the twenty-seven marvelously varied piano concerti, at least half a dozen of the concerti for other instruments, the Sinfonia Concertante for violin and viola, many of the symphonies, the Requiem, the "Great" Mass in C Minor, and several miscellaneous pieces, in addition to six of the operas (all of them from *Idomeneo* onward, excepting *La clemenza di Tito*). I have come to the conclusion that in Mozart as in Bach, Haydn, and Beethoven, there is only one correct, natural tempo for each piece, and every other tempo feels and sounds wrong—whereas in the works of Wagner, Bruckner, Mahler, Strauss, and many other Romantic or post-Romantic composers, many different tempi are possible. Therefore I firmly believe that the tempo question is more crucial in eighteenth-century music than in nineteenth-century music.

The question of texture runs parallel to the question of tempo. I inherited the nineteenth-century and early-twentieth-century habit of playing eighteenth-century music with a full string section (sixteen first violins and so on)—a practice that was prevalent until well after World War II—and I thought that to do otherwise would be a sacrilege. I labored under the delusion that a reduced string section would not "sound" in a big hall. Slowly, after years of experience, I learned that this is not right. How can the wind instruments balance all those strings? One must either double the winds or reduce the strings—and I came to the obvious conclusion that the strings must be reduced. In Mozart operas the reduction should be rather drastic: depending on the size of the theater, there should be no more than twelve first violins for *Don Giovanni,* and fewer, perhaps ten, for operas such as *Figaro* and *Così.* This not only helps the wind-string balance; it also makes the overall texture more transparent. Even in this matter, however, there are no absolutes. I recently conducted *The Creation* using a full complement of strings in the big choral pieces, but reducing the section to half or even less in the arias and other thinly scored pieces.

The "original instrument" movement may have helped to lighten our approach to eighteenth-century music, but I never listen to these "authentic" groups. I have reached my conclusions through experience. I see the point of the research and appreciate the good intentions, but I do not understand why people want to make and play on reproductions of old instruments that were difficult to tune when modern instruments can be easily and properly tuned. I agree that Beethoven's piano music should not be overpedaled or pounded out too heavily, but I do not see the point in playing the "Hammerklavier" Sonata on an old fortepiano that was considered inadequate even in the composer's day, rather than on a magnificent modern grand piano. Likewise, why try to play the horn solos in Leonore's aria and cabaletta in *Fidelio* or at the end of the third movement of the Ninth Symphony on an old-fashioned instrument instead of on a modern one that can handle the task more dependably and no less beautifully?

Having mentioned Beethoven, I want to express some of my thoughts about his works, because they are the backbone of my instrumental repertoire. If you consider the road Beethoven traveled, from the playful opening chord of the First Symphony to the jubilant conclusion of the Ninth, it is hard to believe that such development lies within the sphere of human life. The only comparable growth among the great composers is Verdi's: How can the same man have written *Oberto* and *Falstaff*?

I think that the first piano piece by Beethoven that I played, as a child, was the Sonatina in G. Later, I learned many of the sonatas and the first two piano concerti. In Leó Weiner's class, I played a good deal of Beethoven's chamber music: at least three of the violin and piano sonatas, one or two of the trios, and the Wind Quintet.

Fidelio was performed at the Budapest Opera during my time as répétiteur; I heard Toscanini's rehearsals and performances of it at Salzburg, and it was the first opera I conducted after the war, in Stuttgart and in Munich. And by then the symphonies had begun to enter my repertoire.

I make no apologies for occasionally using technical language in the following pages, because I feel that it is important for seasoned musicians to share the results of their practical experience with younger musicians of today and the future. I hope that music lovers who are not professional musicians will also find interesting substance in these lines.

Even Beethoven's First Symphony is unmistakably different from any symphony written in Haydn's time or in the tradition of Haydn, who was one of Beethoven's teachers. Although the First Symphony has some of Haydn's lightness of touch, the Second is totally different and is the first real Beethoven symphony, with its exuberant first, third, and fourth movements and its intensely lyrical second movement.

The two opening chords of the Third ("Eroica") Symphony demonstrate beyond doubt that Beethoven had found his own language. In this first movement as in many other pieces, during the last few years I have been daring to take faster and faster tempi, and I now believe that Beethoven's metronome mark for the movement is more or less right. Beethoven took great interest in the clockwork metronome of Maelzel, whom he knew, and at the beginning of every page of every new movement of his works he gave an indication of tempo in the form of a metronome mark. For a long time, however, and even when I was a student in the 1920s, Beethoven's metronome markings were considered wrong; the "inaccuracy" was explained by saying that Maelzel's early metronome did not work properly. More and more, I think that this was a fairy tale and that Beethoven's marks give good approximations of the tempi he intended.

Although I observed the repeat of the exposition of the first movement when I recorded the Third Symphony, I do not do so in live performances, because I feel that it makes the movement too long and that it spoils the proportions of the symphony; I do, however, observe all the other repeats in the Beethoven symphonies. The metronome mark of 80 for an eighth note that Beethoven set down for the second movement of the "Eroica" is practically too fast for a funeral march, but it indicates that it must not be taken too slowly; at a mark of 50, as it is often played, the movement becomes endless and drags along. It is essential that one should feel that it could be conducted in two beats in the bar rather than in four. Giving the opening grace notes to the double basses was a daring stroke. The metronome mark of 116 for a bar in the third movement is fast but good, and the one of 152 for a quarter that he gives to the finale is right; I try to play the movement at that speed.

The Fourth Symphony is filled with difficulties. The introduction to the first movement must be mysterious but not too slow, and this is hard to achieve. The second movement seems straightforward, but if the conductor does not keep the structure clearly in mind the piece can easily sound choppy and disconnected. It must not proceed too slowly. There are no great technical (as opposed to purely musical) difficulties in the fourth movement of the symphony, provided you have a fine principal bassoon who can deal with the tricky solos. It is better to play the finale well at a slightly slow tempo than to spoil it by taking it too fast.

The leap from the Fourth Symphony to the Fifth is as remarkable as the leap from the Second to the Third. The opening bars of the Fifth are probably the most famous bars in musical literature. Where did they come from? How did Beethoven conceive of those stark unisons and octaves? Traditionally, everyone played the first five bars at a very slow tempo and then the sixth bar in tempo. But this did not feel right to me, and for more than forty years I did not know how to conduct the opening. Then I realized that if I thought of the first bar, with its three notes, as the last bar of a four-bar phrase, then the opening worked. And by asking for the first five bars to be played in the same tempo as the sixth bar and after, it was not difficult to explain to the orchestra what I wanted. Long experience has also taught me to keep a fairly strict tempo throughout the movement, with the exception of the oboe cadenza, of course, and perhaps also the last soft passage, before the final explosion.

(The Dutch conductor Willem Mengelberg once interrupted a rehearsal to give an oboist a long, profound lecture on the phrasing of that oboe cadenza. He said that he had learned the phrasing from a pupil of Liszt, who had in turn learned it from Schindler, Beethoven's friend, who had learned it from the Master himself. When Mengelberg had finished talking, the oboist asked him, "Dr. Mengelberg, should I play it forte or piano?" There could not be a better lesson for a conductor: Do not talk too much.)

The second movement of the Fifth, Andante con moto, must be fluid, not slow. The recurring ritardando that first appears near the opening of the third movement ought not to be either too much or too soon, and the basic tempo should be maintained in the trio as well; it is hard for the basses, but if they are good enough they will get it. Beethoven indicated that most of the finale is meant to sound powerful but not to be taken very fast, whereas the coda ought to be extremely fast. I am not afraid to follow these instructions.

The Sixth ("Pastoral") Symphony is the most difficult Beethoven symphony to get right, with the exception of the first movement of the Ninth. The structure seems straightforward and natural, but it is really a tone poem in symphonic form. It is the first program symphony; each movement is headed by a short written description—a technique later taken up by such composers as Berlioz, Liszt, Wagner, and Richard Strauss. The entire work is filled with difficulties for both the orchestra and the conductor. The opening phrase of the first movement can be taken slightly under tempo, but it can be played equally effectively in tempo. The metronome mark of 66 for a bar is too fast, but indicates that the tempo should be fluid rather than slow. A beautiful poetic tone should be maintained throughout, especially in the string section, in keeping with the movement's overall happy feeling, and the forte chords must always be sweet, never dramatic or powerful. The second movement has the same gentle tempo and should flow like a stream, which is the text description for the movement. The metronome marks for the third movement, the "Merry gathering of peasants," are fast, but not ridiculously so, even for the trio, which has a mark of 108. In the fourth movement there is an abrupt change as the storm comes, indicated at first by raindrops and then by lightning and thunder. The storm is not long, but it is violent. Because of the fifth movement's delicacy, it is very hard to find the right balance between tempo and dynamics, and to make everything sound in proportion. The last chords must be neither too abrupt nor too emphatic.

Throughout the Seventh Symphony, Beethoven's metronome marks are not ideal, but close to it. As always, one must be flexible, but the indications work well as guidelines. Many conductors have sinned against the Allegretto (second movement) by playing it as if it were an adagio or even a funeral march. The solution lies in the phrasing, which must have a mysterious quality even at a relatively quick tempo: The short notes must not be too short. I always tell orchestras to think of a mystical, nocturnal, torch-lit Buddhist march. The fugato section of the second movement is brilliant but also delicate, and it requires virtuoso playing, *sempre pianissimo* (always very soft). There should be no slowing down for the crescendo into the climax. A first-rate orchestra will give this movement both fluidity and nobility. The trio of the third movement must not be too much slower than the main part of the movement. The first four bars of the finale are often played at half tempo, but I do not see the point of this. It is important to establish the shock of the basic rhythm immediately.

The Eighth is the only Beethoven symphony that is fundamentally cheerful from beginning to end, and that begins by jumping into the main theme, with no preparation at all. It is as short and concise as a Haydn or Mozart symphony, but its playfulness reminds one more of Haydn than of Mozart. Its form is classical, but its substance is brilliantly original. The pianissimo staccato of the winds in the second movement is hard to bring off, and so is the entire trio section of the third movement, because the horns tend to rush their melody and make the cellos sound as if their accompanying figurations are dragging. The finale is difficult because it is a combination of virtuosic delicacy and brilliant humor as, for example, in the characteristic sharp dissonances.

Structurally, harmonically, and instrumentally, the Ninth Symphony explodes into new territory. The first movement is the hardest part of this enormously difficult work; in the first sixteen bars alone, there are many problems. The symphony starts with a series of perfect fifths and fourths on the violins, in which Beethoven introduces the skeleton of a melody, as if the melody was being formed far away in space. The metronome mark for this movement is very fast but not unreasonable. I cannot think of any other symphonic movement that makes so much use of unison and octave writing. The main theme is violent, and even the more lyrical second theme is interrupted by violent outbursts. I learned only recently that Beethoven wrote the word *Verzweiflung*, "despair," on one of the sketches for the first movement, and this may help to explain what he was trying to express through this violence. Typically, Beethoven builds a huge structure by using and reusing a few motifs and rhythmic patterns in various ways, and the task for the conductor in this movement is to create form out of these fragments and to establish a unity of tempo. Furtwängler's recorded performance of the Ninth that reopened the Bayreuth Festival in 1951 seems to me much too slow. His widow told me that while she was driving him home the morning after that concert, he asked her to stop the car so that he could take a breath of fresh air in order to get the previous night's "horrible performance" out of his head. The lesson of this story is that all serious artists are often dissatisfied with their work. The Ninth's first movement has a long coda, the theme of which seems to be the suffering of this world, and the last part of the coda ends, without hope, in a funeral march. There must be no slowing down at the end of the movement, which is abrupt, brusque, and violent.

A good orchestra has no difficulty in playing the marvelous scherzo, the second movement, at the metronome mark or even faster, but the indication of 116 for the trio part is impossibly slow: I play it at 164.

The third movement, like the second movement of the "Pastoral" Symphony, must flow. The metronome indication seems to me a little fast, but it points in the right direction. In the fourth movement, the finale, the recitative that follows the first, big orchestral outburst should be stormy. Only gradually does the tone lighten. Beethoven reintroduces each of the major themes of the first three movements, one after another, examining each before casting it aside as though it were not what he was looking for. He then produces the theme, the setting of Schiller's "Ode to Joy," and affirms, in the last segment of the recitative, that this is the one he wants to hear. I like to think that Beethoven chose to use voices in the finale because the third movement is an endless *cantabile*, in which instruments are used "vocally" to the limit of their capacities. It is as if the music itself "forced" Beethoven to turn to the human voice to express the fullness of the concept. The vocal writing is dangerous throughout, and certain passages invite disaster; Beethoven uses voices—soloists and chorus—as instruments. Schiller's poem is somewhat bombastic, and yet it inspired this amazing work. Here, for the first time, with the possible exception of Mozart's "Jupiter" Symphony, the weight of a symphony is shifted from the first movement to the last: The Ninth's finale lasts about as long as the entire Eighth Symphony.

I sense, rightly or wrongly, that the finale's Alla marcia section, with the tenor solo, is meant to communicate something of the revolutionary, liberating feeling of the *Marseillaise*. When I come to the purely instrumental section that follows the march, I feel that the tempo, which is marked at 84 for a half-bar, should be taken faster, up to 120 for a half-bar. Likewise, in the double fugue that follows the "*Seid umschlungen, Millionen*" section, the metronome mark is impossibly slow; that tempo simply does not work. But the fluid indication of 120 for a half-bar for the penultimate section, with the solo quartet, does work if one takes care with it. The Ninth is both a classic and a Romantic work; its roots, like Beethoven's, lie in the eighteenth century, but it points toward the end of the nineteenth century and even into the twentieth century—the dissonances in the piece are amazing.

When one looks at the Beethoven symphonies as a body, one is astonished to see how much they differ from each other in character. The symphonies are clearly the fruit of a single mind, yet not one of them bears any similarity, as an expressive entity, to any of the others.

AND WHAT OF Beethoven's successors? Schubert is for me the most tragic figure in the history of music. He produced so much magnificent work, but died young without having received any significant recognition. If he had written only his lieder, he would still be one of the greatest of composers, not just because of the vocal writing, but also because of the piano parts, and the blend of the two. I do not know any of his operas, nor have I conducted his first four symphonies, but the last four are part of my repertoire and I adore the "Unfinished" and the "Great" C Major.

I admire Berlioz enormously, but, to my shame, I have not conducted many of his works. He was the first major composer whose talent for orchestration was probably even greater than his purely musical talent. Whenever he invented a new musical color scheme, it was invariably revolutionary. I have performed the *Symphonie fantastique* many times and recorded it twice, and I have also performed and recorded *La Damnation de Faust,* which is a unique work that seems to have neither ancestors nor descendants. Excerpts from the *Roméo et Juliette* Symphony figure in my repertoire, but I ought to have taken the time to do the entire work. Berlioz's opera *Benvenuto Cellini* is one of the works that make me wish I had twenty more working years ahead of me.

Liszt is another composer I greatly admire. I used to play some of the piano pieces from *Années de pèlerinage,* but I have not played some of Liszt's most difficult pieces, such as "La campanella" from the Paganini Études, although late in my pianistic career I played the B Minor Sonata and the "Mephisto" Waltz. (The piano version of the "Mephisto" Waltz is perhaps better than the orchestral version.) I have never conducted the *Dante Symphony,* but I have often performed the *Faust Symphony,* which was dedicated to Berlioz, and I think that it is a neglected masterpiece. *Les Préludes* is another work that I have conducted many times. I am fascinated that Liszt, the most celebrated piano virtuoso of all time, was a complete master of orchestration. There is nothing pianistic about his orchestral writing.

I have not conducted vast amounts of Mendelssohn's music, but I have done both of the piano concerti, the Violin Concerto, the Overture and incidental music to *A Midsummer Night's Dream,* the *Hebrides* Overture, and the Third ("Scottish") and Fourth ("Italian") Symphonies. These two symphonies are among his most beautiful orchestral works. Their form is classical, and they are both transparent in orchestration and rich in melodic invention. I shall not comment on the Fifth ("Reformation") Symphony because I have never conducted it.

I believe that Robert Schumann's greatest works are his songs and his compositions for solo piano. As a student, I played many of the piano works and accompanied many of the lieder. Among lieder composers, only Hugo Wolf created such complex intertwinings of voice and piano as those of Schumann. But Schumann was also an outstanding composer of orchestral music. Many musicians have taken an interest in his orchestral works and have tried to better his instrumentation; even the great Mahler took the time to reorchestrate each of Schumann's four symphonies. I have conducted the Piano Concerto, the Cello Concerto, and all the symphonies, but I have never made changes in Schumann's orchestration or believed that there is any need to do so. Once, during the 1950s, I conducted a performance of the Third Symphony at the Hollywood Bowl. At the first rehearsal, the orchestra started to play something that I neither expected nor recognized. It was Mahler's reorchestration of the piece, which is interesting from a historical point of view, but completely wrong: It sounds like Mahler, not Schumann. I insisted that the orchestra return with the original score for the second rehearsal. There is, undeniably, a certain abstinence or lack of brilliance to Schumann's orchestration, but this is part of the music's character. I believe that conductors ought to play his music as written, even if it takes a special effort to make the balances work. The rewards are enormous, because these pieces are as good as any of the four Brahms symphonies.

Schumann's First Symphony is a beautiful work, but I have not conducted it often. The Second has figured much more frequently in my programs. In order to create the proper, flowing atmosphere in the introduction to the first movement, the rhythm must be precise. This may seem paradoxical, but if the rhythm is not exact one cannot distinguish one motif from another or feel the flow. An excellent string section is required for the second movement, not only because the music is fast, but also because it lies awkwardly for the players: The diminished seventh chord formations are more pianistic than violinistic. I think of the third movement as a song without words, and as such, it must not be played at a tempo so slow that it could not be sung in a natural way. Schumann's Third Symphony, the "Rhenish," was the last he composed, and it is probably the best written of all. (The Fourth Symphony was an earlier work that he revised after having completed the Third.) I have often been asked whether, when I study or conduct the "Rhenish," I sense that depression and madness were about to overtake the composer. The answer is no: The first three movements are full of joie de vivre. And the fourth movement is solemn rather than mournful. Tchaikovsky said that it was the most beautiful composition that any mind could imagine. The movement was inspired by Cologne Cathedral, and it reflects both the majesty of the new dome and the enthronement ceremony of the Cardinal Archbishop, which Schumann had witnessed in 1850. Early in 1854, Schumann attempted to kill himself by jumping into the Rhine; he survived, but was put into a madhouse, where he died two years later.

In one way, the Brahms symphonies are easier to perform than either Schumann's or Beethoven's. The fundamental differences between one Beethoven symphony and the next are gigantic; with Brahms, although each symphony has its own character, it is not wrong to think in terms of a "Brahms sound." There is a certain heaviness to Brahms's orchestral sound because it derives from his piano music, which tends to be heavy in texture. I found his piano music exceedingly difficult when I was a student, because he wrote enormous intervals and I have small hands, but I did play quite a bit of his chamber music. To me, his greatest piano compositions are the two concerti, and they must also be counted among the greatest concerti ever written. The blending of solo instrument and orchestra is so brilliantly achieved that the works could as properly be called symphonies with piano obbligato as concerti. I also love the Violin Concerto and the Double Concerto.

The ongoing battle that I hear in Brahms's piano music is also present in the symphonies, and nowhere more so than in the First. This is the most revolutionary piece he ever wrote, with its opening melody accompanied by timpani, the 6/8 time signature, the wildly fluctuating harmonies, and the themes that enter in keys distant from the tonic C minor. One must not begin the first movement too loudly; Brahms marked only a forte and saved the fortissimo for later in the introduction. Many questions remain open, no matter how many times one conducts this movement. Should the tempo of the introduction match the tempo of the coda? How much tempo fluctuation is desirable? Should the violas' motif be taken more slowly than the basic tempo? Should the winds' last chord end with or after the strings' pizzicato? (The same question presents itself at the end of the third movement.) Real flexibility is required in the second movement, especially in the sections in which tension and relaxation are in constant contrast. The unison passage of oboe, horn, and solo violin is hard to bring off: One usually hears only the horn and violin; if necessary, they should be scaled down so that the oboe is clearly audible. Conductors must remember not to make too big a climax in the chorale section of the finale's introduction; it should be forte, not fortissimo, otherwise the movement has too many climactic moments. A generation or two ago, Furtwängler and many other conductors would begin the main theme slowly and gradually speed up. This may once have sounded right, but it does not today. The *animato* indications must also be observed.

There could be no bigger contrast in character than between the turbulent First Symphony and the sunny Second; but the jump from the Second to the Third is also huge. The Third is problematic, and I have always suffered with it and felt that I was not doing it well; this is why I have avoided performing it for several years. Simply holding the first movement together is technically difficult for the conductor! He must beat two to the bar, because if he were to beat in six the tempo would be far too slow; in two, however, it is awkward to propel forward. Whereas in the Second Symphony the repetition of the first movement's exposition is optional, in the Third it is a necessity. The obvious reason for this is that the Third's exposition is relatively short. But I have another reason, which is purely practical: I always hope to conduct it better the second time around. The two middle movements are among the most beautiful Brahms ever wrote and present fewer technical problems for the conductor; the main point is to let them flow forward. The last movement begins easily enough for the conductor, but the coda, which is slower, is difficult to control.

The Fourth Symphony has been in my repertoire for fifty years and, along with Beethoven's Fifth and Seventh, I have conducted it more often than any other symphony. I used to begin the first movement slightly under tempo and gradually reach the basic tempo, but I now begin in tempo. In the third movement, I used to slow down a great deal for the *Poco meno presto* section, but I now feel that a slight relaxation of the tempo is what the composer wanted. The finale is one of the greatest of all of Brahms's creations: Out of a single, eight-note sequence he constructed an amazing series of variations. But I have decided to leave the Fourth alone for a while, to distance myself from it and to forget how I have been conducting it.

Despite all the proof to the contrary, many people still say that Brahms did not orchestrate well. I think that the Variations on a Theme of Haydn demonstrate conclusively that these critics are wrong. Brahms was not generally interested in virtuoso orchestration, but there is virtuosic writing in this piece—some of it difficult for the orchestra, some for the conductor. I love the work for its brilliance and because it lacks the heaviness that characterizes some of Brahms's writing. I also love the *German Requiem,* which I have conducted a few times. The *Academic Festival Overture* and the *Tragic Overture* are not among Brahms's most successful works, but the *Tragic* has great power if it is done well.

Among the North German composers who ended up in Vienna, Brahms, it seems to me, was the only one whose music remained entirely North German—notwithstanding such intentionally "Austro-Hungarian" pieces as the *Liebeslieder* and other waltzes and the Hungarian Dances.

If I had to make a list of my ten favorite composers—and I hope I never have to make the choice—Verdi would certainly be one of them. During my Budapest days, I knew only the most frequently performed Verdi operas: *Rigoletto, Il trovatore, La traviata, Un ballo in maschera, Aida,* and, occasionally, *Otello.* I heard *Falstaff* for the first time at Salzburg in 1936, with Toscanini conducting and Mariano Stabile in the title role. It was so wonderful I felt I was in a trance. The next winter, Annie Fischer and I often played through the score, so I knew it well before I went back to Salzburg in 1937. It was through Toscanini that I was awakened to the miracle of *Falstaff* and of Verdi's music as a whole.

I adore Verdi's modesty and his concern for his fellow human beings. His correspondence with Arrigo Boito, his last librettist, remains among the great documents in music history. Even though Verdi became much wealthier than Wagner, his exact contemporary, it is hard to imagine Wagner, under any conditions, building a hospital for local peasants, creating a rest home for old musicians, or taking a keen interest in the running of a farm.

From an artistic point of view, I am constantly amazed by Verdi's extraordinary development. There are wonderful moments in his early operas—especially the choral writing—but, as I have said, the leap from *Oberto* to *Falstaff* is astonishing. I love *Ballo,* which is as nearly perfect an opera as one is likely to find; I love *La forza del destino* and *Simon Boccanegra* and *Don Carlos;* I love the Requiem and his last work, the Four Sacred Pieces. I admire Verdi's economy

of composition: He can say in twenty minutes what other composers need an hour or more to say. This is especially true of the Te
Deum from the Sacred Pieces: It is only fifteen minutes long, but
how much profundity it contains. It is almost surrealistic—and
indeed, no one of Verdi's generation was more modern than he.
Verdi's orchestration is brilliantly adapted to the voices; no conductor with common sense has to worry about drowning out the
singers—although in *Otello* the brass can become a menace if one is
not careful. I sometimes think of Verdi as Mozart's pupil from the
south, and *Falstaff,* in particular, should be played as if Mozart had
written it. *Falstaff*'s orchestration presents a problem only because
it requires a brilliant woodwind section, which few opera orchestras have.

Verdi requires outstanding, *musical* singers who can give character
to their roles. We know from Verdi's letters that he considered convincing delivery more important than vocal beauty, and that he was
opposed to rhythmic self-indulgence. Singers need a degree of freedom, but they must not hold on to high notes forever, in order to
impress the less sophisticated members of the audience. To this day,
the appreciation of works such as *Boccanegra, Don Carlos,* and *Falstaff*
demands great musical sophistication.

Puccini is in a different category: He was an extremely sophisticated composer, but all his works have popular appeal. For thirty
years, he had one major success after another, and even the operas
that had at first a lukewarm reception caught on in a relatively short
time. Among his works, I have conducted *La Bohème, Tosca, Il
tabarro, Gianni Schicchi,* and *Turandot,* all with great pleasure. Puccini was a great composer, and his importance in the history of opera
is undeniable. Although I confess that I do not care for *Madama
Butterfly* or *La fanciulla del West*—the fault of the pastiche Japanese
or Wild West settings rather than of the music—I like most of the
others very much. Indeed, *Gianni Schicchi,* the most Mozartian of
Puccini's works, is one of my favorite operas.

And then there is Tchaikovsky. I have conducted all of his symphonies, *Eugene Onegin,* the First Piano Concerto, the Violin Concerto, suites from several of the ballets, and various other pieces, and
I am planning to perform *The Queen of Spades* in the near future.
Tchaikovsky was one of the greatest of all melodists and masters of

orchestration. The secret to revealing his greatness lies in the word "equilibrium": The performer must avoid excessive self-indulgence and excessive strictness. Tchaikovsky's works should be performed with at least a degree of classical restraint, and certainly not too sweetly.

I HAVE ALREADY discussed Wagner, Bruckner, Mahler, and Richard Strauss. Their musical heir Arnold Schoenberg has played a reasonably large role in my repertoire, which includes such major works as the operas *Erwartung* and *Moses and Aaron*. The Variations for Orchestra—probably his most difficult orchestral work—I conducted for the first time in Los Angeles in the 1950s, and suffered a great deal over that experience. In the 1970s, when I performed the Variations with the Chicago Symphony, which can play anything, it went much more easily. I consider the Variations more revolutionary than *Moses*. I have also conducted the frighteningly hard Violin Concerto and Piano Concerto, and I would like to do *A Survivor from Warsaw*.

I confess, however, that other "classic" twentieth-century composers appeal to me more directly than Schoenberg. At the Budapest Academy we were taught a great deal of Debussy's music, and I quickly developed a love for it. Playing Debussy was one of my great joys as a pianist, and I regret that I no longer play much. The best Debussy pianist was Walter Gieseking, a German. (So much for the national character of Debussy's music!) I have conducted many of Debussy's orchestral works: *La Mer*, the Three Nocturnes, *Ibéria* from *Images*, and the *Prelude to the Afternoon of a Faun*. Alas, I have not done *Pelléas et Mélisande*, and this is one of my last musical ambitions. At one time or another I have also conducted a number of Ravel's orchestral works, as well as the opera *L'Heure espagnole*, all of which I greatly admire.

I have spoken of the awe in which I held Bartók during my student days at the academy, but I want to say a few words about his music. I consider his *Mikrokosmos* no less important than Bach's *Well-Tempered Clavier*. Both instruct how to play keyboard instruments well, using excellent music as a vehicle; each piece teaches something new while reinforcing the old. I was never a good enough pianist to play the piano concerti: No. 1 is very difficult, No. 2 exceptionally difficult, and by the time the slightly easier Third Concerto was circulating I had given up my career as a pianist to concentrate on conducting. I have played the Sonata for Two Pianos and Percussion and the *Allegro barbaro*. I love Bartók's six string quartets, and I count the last two among the greatest works in their genre since the Beethoven quartets, and certainly the greatest since those of Brahms.

Among the orchestral works, I never conducted the early symphonic poem *Kossuth* or the *Wooden Prince* ballet, although the latter is on the list of works I would like to add to my repertoire. I have done the suite from *The Miraculous Mandarin;* the opera *Bluebeard's Castle;* all three piano concerti; the two violin concerti and the two violin rhapsodies; Two Portraits; the *Cantata profana;* the Dance Suite; the Divertimento; the Music for Strings, Percussion, and Celesta; and, of course, the Concerto for Orchestra; many of these works I have also recorded. I find *The Miraculous Mandarin* one of the most difficult, technically, of all the Bartók orchestral works: The texture is thick and the rhythms complicated. Another terror for the conductor is the First Piano Concerto, which presents endless problems of balance, rhythm, and changing tempi; if pianist and conductor do not feel the eighth-notes and quarter-notes in exactly the same way, the situation is hopeless.

Performers must follow Bartók's metronome marks. Those of us who are at home in the Hungarian musical idiom know that one cannot go wrong if one follows those indications. When I was to record the Concerto for Orchestra in Chicago, I decided to follow the metronome marks slavishly—which was fine, except in the movement called "*Giuoco delle coppie,*" which is very sluggish at 74 to the quarter-note. When I began to rehearse it at that tempo, the musicians looked at me as if I were crazy. "This is what Bartók wrote," I said, "and I want to do it his way at least once in my life."

"Maestro, I have 94 written in my part," said Gordon Peters, the principal percussionist. I could not believe my eyes when he showed it to me. I checked with the Library of Congress, which owns the original manuscript, and 94 was confirmed as correct; 74 was a printer's error that has been published and republished for over fifty years. Ninety-four is somewhat faster than the movement is usually performed, but it is a natural, fluent tempo—and that is how I did it.

As with the metronome marks, so with the dynamics: Bartók's indications are usually perfect and must be maintained.

I have already talked about Stravinsky, who remains one of my gods. I am sorry that I have conducted so few works by Prokofiev, his near-contemporary and compatriot: the Second and Third of his five piano concerti, the two violin concerti, the "Classical" Symphony, excerpts from *Romeo and Juliet*, and little else. I would like to learn the Fifth and Sixth symphonies, at least.

For many years I did not conduct much music by Shostakovich, because I was convinced that anyone who could have written such relatively progressive music in the Soviet Union must have been politically compromised with the regime. It was not until Solomon Volkov published his recollections of conversations with Shostakovich that I began to understand the tremendous pressure under which Shostakovich had worked. When I realized how wrong I had been, I began to conduct more of his music. I started with the two "happy" symphonies—Nos. 1 and 9—and proceeded with the Eighth, Tenth, Fifth, Thirteenth, and, most recently, Fifteenth. These works have given me great pleasure, and I would like to learn all eight remaining symphonies.

I would particularly like to conduct again the Thirteenth Symphony ("Babi-Yar"), which consists of settings to poems by the Russian poet Evgeny Yevtushenko that speak out against dictatorship and oppressive government. At the symphony's world premiere in Moscow in 1962, the select audience came by invitation only and a police cordon surrounded the theater because the authorities were afraid that the students would demonstrate in support of Yevtushenko. The next day, *Pravda* reported the event with a single sentence, merely stating that the first performance of Shostakovich's Thirteenth Symphony had taken place. What an eternal shame it is that this masterpiece's political significance was ignored at the time!

MORE THAN ANYTHING else, "Babi Yar" made me realize that a musician has a responsibility not to remain silent about political oppression. One cannot close one's eyes to what goes on in one's own country and around the world. Bartók was a shining example of a musician who made the great sacrifice of leaving his native country—

which he loved and which inspired his music—as a gesture against an oppressive regime. Likewise, Toscanini had the courage to defy Mussolini and fascism and then to leave the homeland he loved.

As a Jew who has lived under the Habsburg's Austro-Hungarian Empire and then through early Hungarian communism, fascism, the division of Europe during World War II, military government in postwar Germany, and on into the democratic regimes of Western Europe and the United States, and who has worked with colleagues of all nations, races, and creeds, I firmly believe that racial persecution and discrimination are evil forces that hamper the progress of the human race. The only way forward is for all citizens of the world to learn to respect and live alongside each other, embracing democratic principles such as freedom of speech and equal rights. Although I feel that the special qualities and identity of individual nations should not be lost, I am a committed European. Europe should surely become a united continent and wipe out, once and for all, the prejudices and religious and territorial disputes of the past that have so needlessly destroyed human lives throughout history.

I have had an enormously lucky life. I have said many times, and believe more every day, that I have a guardian angel who guides me and protects me. Looking back, there have been disappointments and unachieved ambitions, but all in all, I have had a wonderful time.

I have no intention of slowing down: pacing myself, yes, but slowing down, no. I am grateful that I am still able to work because I believe that I am continuing to develop as a musician, and that I still have much to give. During the past fifteen years I have totally changed my approach and have developed a new technique of learning, which I think has contributed a great deal to my musical development and interpretation. I used to study by taking a score, going through it, and marking in red pencil all the tempi, dynamics, and details I needed for the performance. I would then proceed to a second stage in which I followed the score at the same time as I listened to my own recording, if it existed, or one by the composer or a conductor whose performance I admired. Now, all this has changed. I no longer repeat works I have conducted many times within the previous ten years. I put them aside for several years and then, after an appropriate silence, I study them again, but I do not use my old scores with the markings in them. Instead I buy new scores and have them

enlarged so that I can see the notes without my glasses. With anticipation I sit at my desk, open the new clean score, and let the notes
lead me to the composer. The dialogue from then on is between the
two of us, the servant and the master. I feel that this musical understanding is greater than ever before.

The Liszt Academy gave me the tough discipline that has been
the infrastructure of my entire professional life. I still get up early in
the morning, make myself two cups of coffee (the only domestic task
I am able to perform), and then turn to my scores. It is a good start to
the day.

I cannot approach the end of this book without giving a message
to young musicians. My life is the clearest proof that if you have talent, determination, and luck, you will make it in the end. My motto
is "Never Give Up."

My life has now come full circle. Recently I returned to Hungary
for a week to make a recording of Bartók's *Cantata profana,* Kodály's
Psalmus hungaricus and Weiner's Serenade in F Minor, as a gesture of
gratitude to my teachers. One day, after the morning's recording session, my old friend Zsuzsi Dancs suggested that we make an excursion to the village of Balatonfökajár, where my father was born. I was
tired and the idea of the hour-long drive didn't appeal to me. But
Zsuzsi was determined, and so after lunch we set off from Budapest.
What I didn't know was that Zsuzsi had arranged a surprise party
for me. When we arrived I saw a large group of people standing in
the village square, and as I got out of the car, a group of children
started to play some Hungarian folk songs on recorders. Zsuzsi had
arranged for me to plant a tree in honor of my return to my ancestral
village. At the side of it was a stone and a small brass plaque recording the visit of Stern György, and now the conductor Georg Solti.
The young mayor made a speech, I planted the tree, and the children
sang and recited poems.

When the ceremony was over the mayor took us down a narrow
country lane to the old Jewish graveyard where I saw for the first
time the graves of my grandparents Solomon and Fanny Stern and
that of my uncle Lipot, my cousin Elisabet's father. It was a miracle
that the graveyard had survived, as it had been part of the front line
between the advancing Russian army and the retreating Germans at
the end of the war. After the war my cousin Elisabet had returned to

the village and had all the many gravestones, some of them ancient, reset, and it is thanks entirely to her initiative that they still exist amidst the tall grasses.

As I stood in the afternoon sunshine surrounded by the graves of my ancestors, and later, as I stood on a hill overlooking Lake Balaton, I felt for the first time in sixty years a sense of belonging. I realized that Hungary was becoming part of Europe again—the boundaries had disappeared. The stag had returned home; his antlers had been able to pass through the door, because during his absence the doorway had become taller and wider.

AFTERWORD

Our beloved Gyuri and Papa died, unexpectedly, in the South of France, on Friday, September 5, 1997.

Only hours before, he had completed the final corrections to this book. We hope it will give an insight into the most rare and wonderful of human beings, who enriched and blessed our lives beyond any words. No family could have had a more loving, generous, and wise husband and father.

Valerie, Gabrielle, and Claudia Solti

Acknowledgments

I HAD NEVER intended to write my memoirs, because, as a musician, I had always believed that only the life of a major composer is interesting or important enough to merit writing about. Two factors, however, made me change my mind. First, I realized quite recently that I am one of the last remaining musicians to have lived through two world wars, communism, fascism, the arrival of Stalin and Hitler, and the subsequent mass murder or displacement of many millions of innocent people of all races, throughout the world. The second reason is that one day, after I had turned down a request from yet another publisher to write about my life, Valerie, my wife, said, "If you don't write a book, someone else will, and you won't like it!"

I have tried to be honest, insofar as this is possible when writing about oneself and other living people. Eighty-five years is a long time to cover, and the task has been far more difficult than I ever anticipated. I have not had the luxury of sitting down in one place and working for a few concentrated hours each day over a period of several months. The book has had to fight for a place in my daily routine, and it has traveled with me from Chicago to Cleveland, New York, Salzburg, Paris, Antibes, Roccamare, Villars, and London.

I could never have completed the book without Harvey Sachs, who has been my shadow for the past two years, in person, over the telephone, and via fax. He has drawn memories from the back of my mind, done the research, and turned my Anglo-Magyar-Teutonic speech into understandable written English. Most important, we have enjoyed our time together.

My family has been very involved in this project. Valerie has been steadfast in her support, from early in the morning until late at night, jogging my memory and recollecting stories old friends or I had told her. Without her, this book of recollections would never have existed. Gabrielle and Claudia, my daughters, have made valuable comments. Gabrielle, in particular, has examined the text with her critical historian's eye, helped with the typing, and coped with the impossible technicalities of sending copy to Roger Cazalet via the "Heath Robinson" fax system we have in Roccamare.

I am grateful to my ninety-nine-year-old cousin Elisabet Pogány, who lives in Budapest and who gave me invaluable information about my father's family. My dear friend Zsusi Dancs and her husband, István, helped with the story of my Hungarian years. My right hand, Charles Kaye, has been a constant support, keeping the project going when I despaired of ever finishing, and so has Deborah Rogers, my extraordinarily patient literary agent.

I must thank my editors, Jonathan Burnham and Roger Cazalet at Chatto & Windus in London, and Jonathan Segal and Ida Giragossian at Alfred A. Knopf in New York. In particular, Roger's patience and good humor were remarkable during the long hours he devoted to making revisions with me. Thanks also go to Heather Gessino in Cleveland and Caroline Loeb in London, who typed much of the material for the text; to Ben Shaw, for his contribution to writing the legend of the seven stags; to Pat Hughes, for coordinating schedules; to my friend Adolf Wood, for his objectivity and comments at a critical moment; to David Monod, for sending me documents regarding my Munich years; and to the publicity department at the Decca Record Company for help with the illustrations.

Harvey Sachs's research was aided by James O'Connor of the Boston Symphony Orchestra; Brenda Nelson-Strauss and Frank Villella of the Chicago Symphony Orchestra; Christina Putnam of Colbert Artists Management, New York; Victor Marshall of the Dallas Symphony Orchestra; Didier de Cottignies, Chrissie Wild, and Emma Ansell of the Decca Record Company; Anthony C. Pollard of *The Gramophone;* Franco Fisch of the International Competition for Musical Performers, Geneva; Frances Cook of the London Philharmonic Orchestra; Jon Millington of the London Symphony Orchestra; Orrin Howard of the Los Angeles Philharmonic; Julie Griffin-Meadors of the Lyric Opera of Chicago; Barbara Haws of the New York Philharmonic; Nicholas Payne of the Royal Opera, Covent Garden; Claudia Mayr of the Salzburg Festival; Kathy

Brown of the San Francisco Symphony; Richard Warren of the Toronto Symphony Orchestra; and unnamed archivists at the Bavarian State Opera, Munich, and the Frankfurt Opera. Special thanks go to Maria Cristina Reinhart, who helped Harvey with his research, spent many hours assisting him at the computer, and gave much useful advice about the text.

I am grateful to several long-suffering friends—Paul and Françoise Findlay, Brian and Marge Eagles, Peter Grandell, Irene Pritzker, Michael Szell, and George and Felicity Tullis—all of whom have read the text and made valuable comments.

Finally, I would like to thank everyone who has helped and supported me throughout the past eighty-five years. Without them, there wouldn't have been a story to tell.

Sir Georg Solti
Roccamare, August 1997

Appendix

Listed below are the works Sir Georg Solti has conducted in live performances in his positions as music director. Some factual information was not retrievable, so what follows is meant as a general guide.

1. Operas conducted at the Munich Opera, 1946–1952

(Dates of first performances—month/day/year—are followed by composer, work; principal cast members; and director.)

4/9/46	Beethoven, *Fidelio;* Rennert
1/1/47	Bizet, *Carmen;* Braun, Kupper, Fehenberger, Hotter; Hamel
4/29/47	Wagner, *Die Walküre;* Schlüter, Schech, Barth, Völker, Hotter, Dalberg; Hofmüller
11/6/47	Wagner, *Tristan und Isolde;* Braun, Selder, Dalberg, Hager, Barth; Georg Hartmann
1/6/48	Verdi, *La forza del destino*
3/13/48	Hindemith, *Mathis der Maler;* Schech, Sommerschuh, Barth, Reinmar, Kusche, Kuen, Klarwein, Fehenberger, Dalberg; Hartmann
9/4/48	R. Strauss, *Salome;* Kupper, Barth, Fehenberger, Klarwein, Reinmar; Hartmann
10/21/48	Verdi, *Aida;* Cunitz, Barth, Fehenberger, Reinmar, Dalberg; Hartmann
2/26/49	Mozart, *Don Giovanni;* Kupper, Holm, Sommerschuh, Reinmar, Proebstl, Reich, Kusche, Peter; Hartmann
4/30/49	Gutermeister, *Raskolnikoff;* Lindermeier, Barth, Klarwein, Kusche; Hartmann
6/11/49	R. Strauss, *Der Rosenkavalier;* Braun, Cunitz, Sommerschuh, Hann; Hartmann
7/2/49	Purcell, *Dido and Aeneas*
10/28/49	Haas, *Tobias Wunderlich;* Peter, Kupper, Sabo, Schmidt; Hartmann
1/31/50	Mussorgsky, *Boris Godunov;* Sommerschuh, Lindermeier, Barth, Hopf, Kuen, Klarwein, Reinmar, Kusche, Hann; Hartmann
4/9/50	Verdi, *Rigoletto;* Reinmar, Hopf, Nentwig, Proebstl, Sabo; Schröder
5/29/50	Wagner, *Tannhäuser;* Söderström, Cunitz, Schech, Hann, Schmitt-Walter; Hartmann
10/22/50	Wagner, *Der fliegende Holländer;* Frantz, Braun, Proebstl, Holm; Hartmann

1/10/51   Orff, *Antigonae;* Goltz, Uhde, Haefliger, Schech, Barth, Kusche; Arnold

4/1/51   Mozart, *Così fan tutte;* Kupper, Cunitz, Schmitt-Walter, Holm, Nentwig, Kusche; Arnold

6/22/51   R. Strauss, *Ariadne auf Naxos;* Kupper, Fehenberger, Nentwig, Cunitz, Schmitt-Walter, Sommerschuh; Arnold

10/14/51   Verdi, *Don Carlos;* Hotter, Cunitz, Hopf, Schmitt-Walter, Höngen, Böhme; Arnold

1/15/52   R. Strauss, *Elektra;* Borkh, Kupper, Fischer, Klarwein, Frantz; Arnold

5/22/52   Wagner, *Das Rheingold*

2. Operas conducted at the Frankfurt Opera, 1952–1961

(Dates of first performance—month/day/year—are followed
by composer, work, principal cast members and, most often, director)

3/7/52   Bizet, *Carmen;* Zapf, Gonszar, Ludwig

9/25/52   Verdi, *Otello;* Aldenhoff, Gonszar

10/18/52   Mozart, *Don Giovanni;* Kupper, Eipperle

3/18/53   Hindemith, *Cardillac;* Wolff, Schlemm, Zapf, Dahmen; Rennert

5/29/53   R. Strauss, *Salome;* Borkh, Aldenhoff, Zapf, Gonszar; Arnold

6/24/53   Wagner, *Tristan und Isolde;* Braun, Ernest, von Rohr, Gonszar; Tietjen

9/2/53   Mozart, *Così fan tutte;* Lorand, Schmidt, Schlemm, Wolinski, Wolff, Adam; Berger

12/25/53   R. Strauss, *Arabella;* Richter, Schlemm, Gonszar; Gielen

4/7/54   Stravinsky, *Oedipus Rex, Mavra, Renard;* Rennert

6/15/54   Verdi, *Un ballo in maschera;* Roth

12/2/54   Liebermann, *Penelope;* Lorand, Schmidt, Ambrosius, Kozub; Roth

1/1/55   Mozart, *Die Zauberflöte;* Kozub, Lorand, Schlemm, Ambrosius; Rennert

4/20/55   R. Strauss, *Der Rosenkavalier;* Joesten, Zapf, Steffek, Böhme; Gielen

6/21/55   Offenbach, *Les Contes d'Hoffmann;* Zapf, Kozub, Wolff, Schlemm, Lorand; Hartmann

10/26/55   Gluck, *Orfeo ed Euridice;* Hartleb

1/27/56   Mozart, *Le nozze di Figaro;* Wolff, Lorand, Schlemm, Adam, Steffek; Lindtberg

6/20/56   Puccini, *Il tabarro, Gianni Schicchi;* Rennert

10/3/56   Verdi, *La forza del destino;* Gutstein, Fehenberger, Zapf, Kreppel; Hartleb

12/30/56   J. Strauss Jr., *Die Fledermaus;* Laubenthal, Lorand, Steffek, Stern, Zapf, Kozub; Mittler

4/28/57   Wagner, *Der fliegende Holländer;* Ericsdotter, Kozub, Hotter, Böhme; Hartleb

7/10/57   Tchaikovsky, *Eugene Onegin;* Watson, Gutstein, Sergi, Adam; Hartleb

10/9/57   Verdi, *Don Carlos;* Kreppel, Watson, Kozub, Gutstein; Hartleb

4/8/58   Einem, *Der Prozess;* Witte, Wolff, Schmidt; Rennert

3/27/59   Wagner, *Parsifal;* Gutstein, van Mill, Kozub, Stern, Ericsdotter; Hartleb

7/8/59   R. Strauss, *Elektra;* Borkh, Kuchta, Höngen, Sergi, Wolovsky; Hartmann

11/1/59   Beethoven, *Fidelio;* Goltz, Kozub, Wolovsky, Adam; Buckwitz

1/8/60   Berg, *Lulu;* Pilarczyk, Gutstein; Rennert

6/23/60   Mussorgsky, *Boris Godunov;* Mastilovic, McKee, Kozub, Wolovsky, Gutstein, Lagger; Herrlischka

10/23/60   Wagner, *Die Walküre;* Meyfarth, Goltz, Kozub, Wolovsky, Lagger; Witte

5/28/61   Verdi, *Falstaff;* Gutstein, Kouba; Witte

3. Operas conducted at the Royal Opera, Covent Garden, London, 1959–1996

(Dates of performances—month and year—are followed by composer, work, principal cast members, and director)

12/59   R. Strauss, *Der Rosenkavalier;* Schwarzkopf, Jurinac, Steffak, Böhme; Busch

2/61   Britten, *A Midsummer Night's Dream;* Carlyle, Oberlin, Evans; Gielgud

8/61   Gluck, *Iphigénie en Tauride;* Gorr, Turp, Massard; Gentele

9/61   Wagner, *Die Walküre;* Välkki, Watson, Gorr, Vickers, Hotter, Langdon; Hotter

2/62   Mozart, *Don Giovanni;* Gencer, Jurinac, Freni, Siepi, Evans; Zeffirelli

6/62   Schoenberg, *Erwartung;* Shuard; Ustinov

6/62   Puccini, *Gianni Schicchi;* Carlyle, Vaughan, Turp, Evans; Ustinov

6/62   Ravel, *L'Heure espagnole;* Costa, Lanigan, Young, Savoie, Shaw; Ustinov

6/62   Verdi, *Otello;* Kabaivanska, Del Monaco, Gobbi; Mirabella Vassallo

9/62   Wagner, *Siegfried;* Nilsson, Windgassen, Ward, Kraus; Hotter

9/62   Verdi, *La forza del destino;* Cavalli, Bergonzi, Shaw, Ghiaurov; Wanamaker

1/63   Verdi, *Falstaff;* Ligabue, Resnik, Evans; Zeffirelli

5/63   Mozart, *Le nozze di Figaro;* Ligabue, Freni, Berganza, Evans, Gobbi; Schuh

9/63   Wagner, *Götterdämmerung;* Nilsson, Collier, Windgassen, Stewart, Frick, Kraus; Hotter

1/64   Britten, *Billy Budd;* Lewis, Robinson, Kerns; Coleman

2/64   Verdi, *Rigoletto;* Moffo, Cossutta, Evans; Zeffirelli

9/64   Wagner, *Das Rheingold;* Andersson, Veasey, Ward, Lanigan, Collier; Hotter

12/64   Offenbach, *Les Contes d'Hoffmann;* Grist, Harper, Collier, Veasey, Lewis, Lanigan, Evans; Rennert

1/65   R. Strauss, *Arabella;* Della Casa, Carlyle, Fischer-Dieskau; Hartmann

6/65   Schoenberg, *Moses und Aaron;* Robinson, Lewis; Hall

1/66   Wagner, *Der fliegende Holländer;* Jones, Pribyl, Ward, Frick; Williams

7/66   Mozart, *Die Zauberflöte;* Carlyle, Geszty, Wakefield, Evans, Ward; Hall

2/67   Beethoven, *Fidelio;* Jones, Pribyl; Copley

6/67   R. Strauss, *Die Frau ohne Schatten;* Hillebrecht, Borkh, Resnik, King, McIntyre; Hartmann

7/68   Mozart, *Così fan tutte;* Lorengar, Veasey, Popp, Alva, Ganzarolli, Engen; Copley

1/69   Wagner, *Die Meistersinger;* Ruk-Focic, Veasey, Thomas, Shirley, Bailey, Evans, Ward; Hartmann

5/69   R. Strauss, *Elektra;* Nilsson, Collier, Resnik, McIntyre; Copley

6/69   Gluck, *Orfeo ed Euridice;* Minton, Lorengar, Robson; Copley

2/70   Verdi, *Don Carlos;* Jones, Veasey, Cossutta, Glossop, Ward; Visconti

6/70   R. Strauss, *Salome;* Bumbry, Veasey, Ulfung, Bailey, Glossop; Everding

2/71   Tchaikovsky, *Eugene Onegin;* Cotrubas, Minton, Tear, Braun; Hall

6/71   Wagner, *Tristan und Isolde;* Dvorakova, Veasey, Thomas, McIntyre; Hall

7/73   Bizet, *Carmen;* Verrett, Te Kanawa, Domingo, Van Dam; Geliot

4/79   Wagner, *Parsifal;* Minton, Hofmann, Mazura, Bailey, Moll; Hands

11/87 Mozart, *Die Entführung aus dem Serail;* Nielsen, Watson, van der Walt, Magnusson, Moll; Moshinsky

11/91 Verdi, *Simon Boccanegra;* Te Kanawa, Sylvester, Agache, Scandiuzzi; Moshinsky

11/94 Verdi, *La traviata;* Gheorghiu, Lopardo, Nucci; Eyre

4. Works conducted with the Chicago Symphony Orchestra, 1954–1996

Gilbert Amy
> *D'un espace déployé*

Carl Philipp Emanuel Bach
> Concerto for Cello in A Major

Johann Sebastian Bach
> "Brandenburg" Concerti Nos. 1–3
> Concerto for Oboe and Violin, BWV 1060
> Concerto for Two Violins in D Minor
> Concerto for Violin in D Minor, BWV 1052
> Mass in B Minor
> *St. Matthew Passion*
> Suite No. 3, BWV 1068

Samuel Barber
> Essay for Orchestra

Béla Bartók
> *Bluebeard's Castle*
> *Cantata profana*
> Concerto for Orchestra
> Concerti for Piano Nos. 1–3
> Concerto for Viola
> Concerti for Violin Nos. 1 and 2
> Dance Suite
> Divertimento
> Hungarian Sketches
> *The Miraculous Mandarin:* Suite

Music for Strings, Percussion, and Celesta
Rhapsodies for Violin Nos. 1 and 2
Two Portraits

Ludwig van Beethoven
"*Ah, perfido,*" concert aria
Concerti for Piano Nos. 1, 2, 4, and 5
Concerto for Piano, Violin, and Cello (Triple Concerto)
Concerto for Violin
Coriolan Overture
Egmont: Overture and Incidental Music
Fidelio
Leonore Overture No. 3
Missa Solemnis
Romance No. 1 for Violin, Op. 40
Symphonies Nos. 1–9

Alban Berg
Concerto for Violin

Hector Berlioz
Benvenuto Cellini Overture
Le Carnaval romain, overture
La Damnation de Faust
Les Francs-juges, overture
Les Nuits d'été
Roméo et Juliette: Excerpts
Symphonie fantastique

Easley Blackwood
Symphony No. 4

Ernest Bloch
Suite for Viola

Luigi Boccherini
Concerto for Cello, Op. 34

Alexander Borodin
Prince Igor Overture

Johannes Brahms
Academic Festival Overture
Concerti for Piano Nos. 1 and 2
Concerto for Violin
Concerto for Violin and Cello (Double Concerto)
Ein deutsches Requiem
Symphonies Nos. 1–4
Tragic Overture
Variations on a Theme of Haydn

Benjamin Britten
Sinfonia da Requiem
Variations on a Theme of Frank Bridge
The Young Person's Guide to the Orchestra

Max Bruch
        Concerto for Violin No. 1
Anton Bruckner
        Symphonies Nos. 0–9
Stephen Douglas Burton
        Sinfonia per grande orchestra
Elliott Carter
        Variations for Orchestra
Francis Chagrin
        Roumanian Fantasy for Harmonica
Frédéric Chopin
        Concerto for Piano No. 1
Aaron Copland
        Music for a Great City
        Quiet City
        Rodeo: "Buckaroo Holiday"
John Corigliano
        Concerto for Clarinet
        Tournaments Overture
Paul Creston
        Fantasy for Trombone
Claude Debussy
        Images: Ibéria
        La Mer
        Three Nocturnes
        Prelude to the Afternoon of a Faun
Frederick Delius
        Brigg Fair
David Del Tredici
        Final Alice
Ernst von Dohnányi
        Variations on a Nursery Song
Paul Dukas
        The Sorcerer's Apprentice
Henri Duparc
        Four Songs
Antonín Dvořák
        Concerto for Cello
        Concerto for Violin
        Symphony No. 9 ("From the New World")
Edward Elgar
        Concerto for Cello
        "Enigma" Variations
        Falstaff
        In the South, overture
        Pomp and Circumstance, March No. 4

   Sea Pictures
   Symphonies Nos. 1 and 2
George Gershwin
   Lullaby
Alexander Glazunov
   Concerto for Violin
Mikhail Glinka
   Ruslan and Ludmila: Overture
Morton Gould
   Concerto for Flute
George Frideric Handel
   Concerti grossi Op. 3, Nos. 1 and 2
   Concerto for Harp, Op. 4, No. 6
   Concerto for Organ in F Major, No. 16
   Messiah
Howard Hanson
   Serenade for Flute, Harp, and Strings
Franz Joseph Haydn
   Concerto for Organ No. 2, Hob. XVIII:8
   Concerto for Violin, Piano, and Strings in F Major
   The Creation
   The Seasons
   Sinfonia concertante for Violin, Cello, Oboe, and Bassoon
   Symphonies Nos. 22, 44, 83, 93, 95, 96, and 100–104
Hans Werner Henze
   Heliogabalus imperator
Paul Hindemith
   Symphonic Metamorphoses on Themes of Carl Maria von Weber
   Symphony in E-flat Major
Gustav Holst
   The Planets
Johann Nepomuk Hummel
   Concerto for Trumpet
Engelbert Humperdinck
   Hänsel und Gretel: Prelude and Dream Music
Karel Husa
   Concerto for Trumpet
Jacques Ibert
   Concertino da camera
Charles Ives
   Decoration Day
   Three Places in New England
   Tone Roads Nos. 1 and 3
   The Unanswered Question
   Variations on "America"
   Washington's Birthday

Zoltán Kodály
>   *Háry János:* Suite
>   *Psalmus hungaricus*
>   Variations on "The Peacock"

Marvin David Levy
>   Concerto for Piano No. 1

Franz Liszt
>   Concerti for Piano Nos. 1 and 2
>   *A Faust Symphony*
>   *Festklänge*
>   *From the Cradle to the Grave*
>   Hungarian Rhapsody No. 2
>   "Mephisto" Waltz No. 1
>   *Les Préludes*
>   *Totentanz*

Witold Lutosławski
>   Symphony No. 3

Gustav Mahler
>   *Lieder eines fahrenden Gesellen*
>   *Das Lied von der Erde*
>   Symphonies Nos. 1–9

Bohuslav Martinů
>   Concerto for Violin No. 1

John McCabe
>   Concerto for Orchestra

Felix Mendelssohn
>   Concerti for Piano Nos. 1 and 2
>   Concerto for Violin
>   *The Hebrides* (*Fingal's Cave*), overture
>   *A Midsummer Night's Dream:* Overture and Incidental Music
>   Symphonies Nos. 3 and 4

Gian Carlo Menotti
>   *The Consul:* Magda's aria

Wolfgang Amadeus Mozart
>   Adagio in E Major, K. 261
>   Adagio and Fugue in C Minor, K. 546
>   Concerto for Clarinet
>   Concerto for Flute No. 2
>   Concerto for Horn No. 4
>   Concerti for Piano Nos. 9, 12, 17, 20, 21, 23–25, 27
>   Concerti for Violin Nos. 3–5
>   *Don Giovanni* Overture
>   Mass in C Minor
>   Sinfonia concertante for Violin and Viola
>   Six Concert Arias

Symphonies Nos. 25, 35, 38–41
Die Zauberflöte Overture
Modest Mussorgsky
Khovanshchina Prelude
Pictures at an Exhibition (arr. Ravel)
Carl Nielsen
Symphonies Nos. 1 and 6
Niccolò Paganini
Concerto for Violin No. 1
Andrzej Panufnik
Sinfonia sacra
Sergei Prokofiev
Concerto for Piano No. 3
Concerto for Violin No. 1
Romeo and Juliet: Excerpts
Symphony No. 1, "Classical"
Sergei Rachmaninoff
Rhapsody on a Theme of Paganini
Maurice Ravel
Une Barque sur l'océan
Boléro
Concerto in G for Piano
Daphnis et Chloé: Second Suite
Shéhérazade
Le Tombeau de Couperin
La Valse
George Rochberg
Concerto for Violin
Imago mundi
Symphony No. 5
Gioacchino Rossini
Overtures:
L'assedio di Corinto
Il barbiere di Siviglia
La gazza ladra
L'italiana in Algeri
La scala di seta
Semiramide
Albert Roussel
Symphony No. 3
Miklós Rózsa
Concerto for Cello
Carl Ruggles
Men and Mountains

Camille Saint-Saëns
    Concerto for Cello
Arnold Schoenberg
    Concerto for Violin
    Erwartung
    Moses and Aaron
    Variations for Orchestra
Franz Schubert
    Symphonies Nos. 5, 6, 8, and 9
Gunther Schuller
    Concerto for Flute
    Recitative and Rondo for Violin
    Seven Studies on Themes of Paul Klee
Robert Schumann
    Concerto for Piano
    Konzertstück for Four Horns
    Symphonies Nos. 2–4
Roger Sessions
    When Lilacs Last in the Dooryard Bloom'd
Dmitri Shostakovich
    Concerto for Cello No. 1
    Symphonies Nos. 1, 5, 8–10, 13
Leo Sowerby
    Overture, *Comes Autumn Time*
Alan Stout
    George Lieder
    Symphony No. 4
Johann Strauss Jr.
    Die Fledermaus Overture
Richard Strauss
    Also sprach Zarathustra
    Concerti for Horn Nos. 1 and 2
    Concerto for Oboe
    Don Juan
    Four Last Songs
    Ein Heldenleben
    Macbeth
    Salome
    Salome: Dance of the Seven Veils
    Till Eulenspiegels lustige Streiche
    Tod und Verklärung
Igor Stravinsky
    Concerto for Violin
    The Firebird: Suite
    Jeu de cartes

Oedipus Rex
Orpheus
Petrushka
The Rite of Spring
Symphony in C
Symphony in Three Movements

Franz von Suppé
Pique Dame Overture

Piotr Ilich Tchaikovsky
Concerto for Piano No. 1
Concerto for Violin
1812 Overture
The Nutcracker: Suite
Romeo and Juliet
Swan Lake: Suite
Symphonies Nos. 4–6

Alexander Tcherepnin
Magna Mater

Sir Michael Tippett
Byzantium
Suite in D
Symphony No. 4

Ralph Vaughan Williams
Symphony No. 4

Giuseppe Verdi
Choruses
Falstaff
Four Sacred Pieces
La forza del destino Overture
Otello
Requiem
Simon Boccanegra: Prologue and Act I

Heitor Villa-Lobos
Ciranda das sete notas

Antonio Vivaldi
Concerti for Piccolo, P. 78 and 79
Concerto for Three Violins in F Major
Concerto for Two Violins in A Minor, Op. 3, No. 8

Richard Wagner
Der fliegende Holländer
Götterdämmerung: Act III
Die Meistersinger
Overtures:
Der fliegende Holländer
Tannhäuser (Paris version)

Preludes:
 Lohengrin: Act III
 Die Meistersinger
 Parsifal
 Tristan und Isolde (with *Liebestod*)
 Das Rheingold
 Siegfried: Act III
 Tannhäuser: "Dich, teure Halle"

William Walton
 Belshazzar's Feast
 Concerto for Viola
 Partita for Orchestra

Carl Maria von Weber
 Overtures:
  Euryanthe
  Der Freischütz
  Oberon

Leó Weiner
 Prince Csongor and the Goblins

Ellen Taaffe Zwilich
 Concerto for Trombone

Index

Illustration Credits

Insert following page 54

Béla Bartók; Zoltan Kodály: *Hulton Getty Picture Collection*
Richard Stauss (last two photographs): *Decca/London*
All other photographs: Courtesy of the family of Sir Georg Solti

Insert following page 150

Enid Blech: *Reg Wilson*
Lord Drogheda: *Donald Southern*
Old Metropolitan Opera House: *Decca/London / Louis Mélançon*
Die Walküre playback: *Decca/London / Elfriede Hanak-Broneder*
Rehearsals of *Otello*: *Decca/London / Jim Steere*
Sir Georg Solti: *Decca/London / Karsh*
Playing table tennis; Chicago Symphony at Orchestra Hall: *Decca/London*
Hedi and John Gielgud: *Hulton Picture Collection*
All other photographs: Courtesy of the family of Sir Georg Solti

A Note About the Author

Sir Georg Solti, one of the leading conductors of the century, served as music director with orchestras in Munich, Frankfurt, London, and Chicago, and performed all over the world. He made 250 records and CDs for Decca/London, including more than forty operas, and received thirty-one Grammy Awards. He was granted honorary degrees by Oxford, Yale, Harvard, and a score of other universities. He was knighted in 1972.

A Note on the Type

This book was set in a modern adaptation of a type designed by the first William Caslon (1692–1766). The Caslon face, an artistic, easily read type, has enjoyed over two centuries of popularity in our own country. It is of interest to note that the first copies of the Declaration of Independence and the first paper currency distributed to the citizens of the newborn nation were printed in this typeface.

Composed by North Market Street Graphics,
Lancaster, Pennsylvania
Printed and bound by Quebecor Printing,
Martinsburg, West Virginia
Designed by Anthea Lingeman